MUSLIM WOMEN SING

AFRICAN EXPRESSIVE CULTURES

Muslim Women Sing

Hausa Popular Song

BEVERLY B. MACK

Indiana University Press
Bloomington and Indianapolis

This book is a publication of

Indiana University Press
601 North Morton Street
Bloomington, IN 47404-3797 USA

http://iupress.indiana.edu

Telephone orders   800-842-6796
Fax orders   812-855-7931
Orders by e-mail   iuporder@indiana.edu

© 2004 by Beverly B. Mack

The paper used in this publication meets the minimum requirements
of American National Standard for Information Sciences—
Permanence of Paper for Printed Library Materials, ANSI Z39.48-
1984.

MANUFACTURED IN THE UNITED STATES OF AMERICA

Library of Congress Cataloging-in-Publication Data

Mack, Beverly B. (Beverly Blow), date
  Muslim women sing : Hausa popular song / Beverly B. Mack.
      p. cm. — (African expressive cultures)
  Includes bibliographical references and index.
  ISBN 0-253-34504-9 (cloth : alk. paper) — ISBN 0-253-21729-6
(pbk. : alk. paper)
  1. Popular music—Nigeria—History and criticism. 2. Hausa
(African people)—Music—History and criticism. 3. Hausa (African
people)—Poetry—History and criticism. 4. Women musicians—
Nigeria. I. Title. II. Series.
  ML3503.N6M32 2004
  782.42162'937'0082—dc22

                                                    2004008469

1 2 3 4 5 09 08 07 06 05 04

In Nigeria, to Hausa women poets, singers, and appreciative audiences.

In North America, to Bob, Tom, and Sarah.

CONTENTS

PREFACE

This book was first completed in 1981, but it has been a work in process since then. It includes poems recorded during a period of residence in Kano (1982–1983) and visits in March 1987 and September 2002. A CD at the back of this volume includes the Hausa performance of the works that appear in English translation in part 2. The poems that constitute the book's second half are my English translations. Where they read especially smoothly I credit Professor Neil Skinner's generous guidance over the years; I am grateful for his help and patience. When I was in Nigeria, I returned to the authors whenever possible to inquire about the sense of the poem's content. Thus, in what appears here as my own final form in English, I have tried most of all to preserve both the sense of the poem's content as well as the rhythm of the line, couplet, or pentastich, trying to preserve the poet's own style. The problem of translating poetry has long plagued those who wish to offer the works of one culture to the people of another culture. I agree with scholars who assert that true transformation of a single artistic piece from one tongue to another is impossible; the result is always at best a new poem, at worst a poor imitation. Whenever I have lectured publicly about these poets and their poems, I have not just relied on the English words but have also played a tape-recording of the passage performed in Hausa, simultaneously doing a read-over of it in English to allow a non-Hausa audience both an aesthetic and literal appreciation of the work. The English versions are here for the benefit of non-Hausa speakers, and I have tried to remain true to the spirit as well as the literal meaning of the words. I take full responsibility for the awkwardness and errors that may result from this approach.

The Hausa versions of the works are included only in excerpts within the text; the complete works are available on the accompanying CD. Note that the dates, when given, on Hauwa Gwaram's and Hajiya 'Yar Shehu's works are the dates of original composition. For the Hausa versions, spelling and transliteration presented unanticipated problems. For spellings in the written works, I adhered to the authors' own versions. Readers should note that Hausa has several glottalized consonants indicated in print by the hooked letters ɓ, ɗ, ƙ, and 'y; these are distinct from the English forms of b, d, k, and y. I regularized the Hausa throughout the poem wherever it vacillated between Hausa and Anglicized versions, as in Gwaram's "Waƙar Naira-Kwabo," in which she often used the alternative form *kobo*. In transcribing from recorded tapes of extemporaneous performances, I tried to transliterate in concord with the Latin Hausa orthographic form, according to Hausa publishing format. Most often, problems were not with ancient forms but with the English amalgams, over which I puzzled long and hard before returning to the authors for assistance. It was often the case that I had been looking for a Hausa term when an English one was staring me in the face: Hajiya 'Yar Shehu's *kabord* (in "Waƙar Zamani") is the English term "cowboy." When I asked Hauwa Gwaram about the line *walkom, siddom hiya* (in "Waƙar Naira Kwabo," v. 4), she upbraided me for failing to recognize my own language, in which it suddenly made sense as "welcome, sit down here"!

This last point, although it relates to a technical problem, emphasizes the timeliness of these poems. That the authors, who did not speak English, matter-of-factly incorporated English phrases in their works underlines the degree to which English borrowing pervades the Hausa language. Furthermore, they incorporated such phrases not to impress elite, educated patrons—for those were not their audiences—but to communicate with other women like themselves. Their poems function to tell other, usually secluded, women what is happening in the contemporary world—and what words are being used to describe it. These poems lift the whole idea of the veil, bringing the outside world into the privacy of women's quarters. The poems themselves testify that it is not the case that secluded Hausa women do not know about the world, only that the world knows too little about them.

ACKNOWLEDGMENTS

Many individuals have contributed to the inspiration for this book. In graduate school at the University of Wisconsin, Professor A. Neil Skinner introduced me to Hausa language and culture and suggested, in his characteristically quiet way, that "Hausa women praise singers might not have been studied yet." Professor M. G. Smith and his wife, Mary, helped prepare me for fieldwork and maintained interest in my work for years after. In the field and afterward, Professor Mervyn Hiskett was the kindest of critics. I am fortunate to have had these mentors and am grateful to them all.

In the course of fieldwork and residence in Kano, Nigeria, I was fortunate to have been welcomed into the palace community of His Highness Alhaji Ado Bayero, Emir of Kano, through an introduction to his wife, Hajiya Hafsatu Abba Bayero. The emir generously allowed me the freedom to visit the women of his harem almost daily and has always been supportive of my research. Hajiya Abba not only welcomed me almost daily but also fed me, loaned me her children, and corrected my Hausa language and manners. She introduced me to women in the palace and suggested ways to expand my research, most significantly by insisting that I visit Hauwa Gwaram and Hajiya 'Yar Shehu in addition to Maizargadi. She spoke frankly and has remained a dear friend.

Several institutions and individuals have facilitated the production of this book. A Fulbright Hays doctoral dissertation grant supported my initial fieldwork and a Woodrow Wilson fellowship helped in the creation of an early draft of this book. More recently (2001), a fellowship from the National Endowment for the Humanities funded a year of writing to complete the final version. Indiana Archives for Traditional Music has preserved my full collection of audio tapes since 1981 (81-100-f/b) and generously converted them to CD format for me. I thank Dan Reed and Marilyn Graf for their help. John Chernoff demystified the miracles of modern technology and encouraged me to create a full MP3 format CD to hold all the Hausa performances of works discussed in this book; at the University of Kansas, Jonathan Perkins of the Ermal Garinger Academic Resource Center facilitated my creation of that master CD. I am grateful to them both. Aminu Gusau checked several translations at the last minute; I appreciate his insights. At Indiana University Press, Kate Babbitt copyedited with careful attention to the complexities of Hausa poetics. My editor, Dee Mortensen, has been cheerful and supportive from the inception of this project; I am fortunate to have worked with her.

If not for the many tasks that consume Hausa women's days, there would be much more of their poetry and song in print and in the world. I am grateful to Hausa women—poets, singers, and nonspecialists—who gave so freely to me of their time, energy, hospitality, and friendship. I hope that this work will engender appreciation in those who read it and inspire further studies of Hausa women's creative performance.

If not for my children, this book would have been published years ago, resulting in a volume of undeveloped perspectives on the topic and the absence of the wonderful preoccupations inherent in family life. I am grateful to them for the long delay.

If not for my husband, the book would never have been written at all. He has been its biggest fan and my constant support.

Map of Nigeria

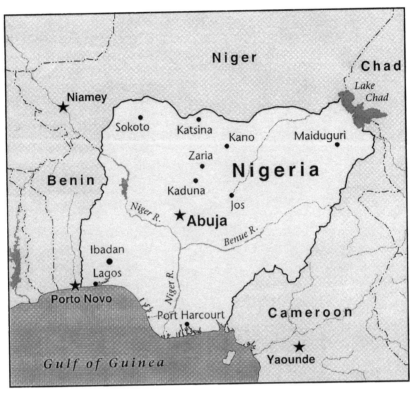

Part 1

THE SINGERS
AND THEIR WORLD

ONE

"Every Woman Sings"

POETRY IN KANO, NIGERIA

In 1979, when I arrived for fieldwork in Northern Nigeria, a Hausa man said to me, "Hausa women don't write poetry" while another told me "Every woman is a singer."[1] Finally I asked a woman, and the answer was completely different: some women write poetry and then sing it, and some just make it up as they go along. When I attended wedding and new baby celebrations I saw women in action, professionals entertaining other women with abandon that derived from delight in what they were doing—singing and dancing to entertain audiences of other women. Women do write poetry, and not every Hausa woman is a singer. But poetry and sung entertainment is common among Hausa women and important to the quality of their lives.

Hausa men's conflicting views about what women do reflect the degree to which men and women go their own ways in Hausa society. Part of this habit is founded on Islamic perceptions of men's and women's separate gender roles, but such separation also works to the benefit of both groups. Since the beginning of the nineteenth century, colonial perceptions about gender roles have permeated Hausa men's public pronouncements about women's roles, reinforced by Western scholarship, which has long focused on Hausa men's social arenas. Hausa Muslim women have been stereotyped as being illiterate, subservient to men's control of their activities, and lacking freedom of movement and agency in their own lives. Both Western and Hausa scholars report that Hausa women are subject to the will of their husbands, secluded (*kulle*) in the home, neither working nor moving about in public. There is a presumption that the practice of wife seclusion militates against a wife's autonomy. This is a poor reflection of the reality of women's lives in Northern Nigeria. Women writers and singers produce, perform, and market their craft and give shape to their own lives through their creative artistry. The reality of their lives as contemporary Muslim women includes active attention to their talents and enthusiastic participation in the performances of other women.[2]

Muslim Hausa women's poetry and song demonstrate that women's status in Northern Nigeria is neither subservient, static, nor stoic. Women are their own agents, their roles are flexible and negotiable, and they insist on lives that incorporate creative activity into the demands of their primary domestic roles. Muslim women not only sing, they dance and create fun in their lives, even in the context of their traditional patriarchal Muslim setting. At celebrations they shake their hips, joke with one another, and hold one another's babies so they can get up and dance, laughing through the afternoon with their friends. Hausa men do not know the details of women's entertainments because they are not invited to participate. These are closed parties, where women use the socially mandated separation of the sexes to advantage, enjoying the freedom to be at ease with one another. These are occasions for release from the daily obligations common to wives and mothers the world over. When there is a party, the cooking, child-tending, and housework are left behind for a while.

This is a book of poetry and songs produced by Hausa Muslim women in Northern Nigeria during a period of significant historical and political change (1966–1980) in that region of the country.[3] It contains the poems that men say women do not write, the songs men say women do not sing. In truth, many Hausa women performing artists compose for themselves and their audiences of other women. Women poets compose during precious moments of private time, which rarely are moments of silence or solitude, living in extended family settings as they do. The circumstances under which they write make the fact of their composition extraordinary, as they wax poetic about current events, political issues, and social concerns. Although women may sing while they process grain or do housework, not every woman is a singer in the professional sense because of the special role that such artists play in performing their works. Those who are professionals are "masters" of rowdy repartee and they often include enthusiastic hip-shaking in their deliveries; other women pay them handsomely for their entertainments.

Both poetry and song are known in the Hausa language as *waƙa* (pl. *waƙoƙi*).[4] Seeing women singers in action in Northern Nigeria clarifies this definition: *waƙa* means chanted poem. This exploration of women's *waƙoƙi* focuses on two points: the first is that Muslim Hausa women's autonomy is evident in their enjoyment of extemporaneous performance—whether as performers or audience members—which is a source of access to history, politics, and current events. The second point is that—for the writers of poetry—women's literary and extemporaneous composition has long been a means of spiritual and educational fulfillment for Muslim Hausa women; Islam has not restricted but in fact has fostered women's literary composition. Within an Islamic framework, women negotiate the latitude they need to pursue their artistic and scholarly activities using changes in their age-related social roles and educational status to cross gender lines.

Western scholarship long has ignored Hausa women at best, stereo-typed them at worst. When I went to Kano in 1979, the only book on Hausa women was Mary Smith's 1954 book *Baba of Karo*, based on con-versations with a colonial-era woman who was neither urban nor contem-porary. Nana Asma'u (1793–1864), the scholarly daughter of jihad leader Shehu Usman dan Fodiyo, was at the time a mere footnote in a few works about the caliphate (Hiskett 1973; Last 1967). I set out to collect praise songs performed by women affiliated with the Emir of Kano, Alhaji Ado Bayero, but it rapidly became clear that royal praise songs were related to nonroyal praise songs and that these were connected to other extempora-neous performances of material other than praise songs. As my scope of performers expanded, I came to know of literate women poets who were important to the society. Thus, my fieldwork soon involved collecting from a variety of women a wide range of oral and written materials, all of which existed in oral form.

Women's poetry and performances are long overdue as additions to the corpus of Hausa poetic works. Equally important is attention to what these materials and performances demonstrate about the roles of Hausa women as Muslims. Women's social status and degree of independence are nego-tiable, depending on many factors, including ethnicity, socioeconomic sta-tus, age, marital status, and educational level. Within their highly struc-tured Islamic culture, women poets and performers can maintain their sta-tus as respected Muslim women while writing poetry and declaiming praise song. They can enjoy freedom of movement not only beyond the confines of their homes but also between the separate settings of men and women as they cross lines of gender boundaries for performances (Pittin 1979, 1983, 1984, 1996). In some cases they can even reach secluded women without appearing in public by sending their poetry over radio airwaves that ignore spatial and temporal limitations.

This is not to imply that all these artists are equally respected as pillars of society, even though they are well distributed on the continuum be-tween the extremes. What is impressive is that such a range of women poets and singers thrives in a conservative Hausa Muslim context and that they reach such a wide audience of both men and women with material that educates, informs, and entertains.

GENDER ROLES AND WIFE SECLUSION

By providing a representative collection of written and spoken verse by Hausa Muslim women, this book examines the extent of women's ability to negotiate their social roles within the contexts of Hausa tradition and Islamic tenets, which stipulate that men provide for the family while women bear and raise children as Muslims and oversee the domestic domain. These separate gender mandates are widely perceived, while the idealistic goal for both is less often acknowledged: both women and men are expected to fulfill their talents to the best of their abilities. Most Muslim Hausa women in Northern Nigeria accept the Islamic obligation to fulfill their roles as wives, mothers, and homemakers; society, not Islam, dictates that they remain at home during the years in which they raise their children. Very often these expectations override concerns about education, resulting in Hausa women's literacy levels being lower than those of Hausa men. Since Nigerian independence (1960), statistics consistently have demonstrated that Hausa Muslim women's literacy levels are far lower than those of men, but these statistics are based on measures of Western educational programs without accounting for levels of Qur'anic education.

This condition is the constant lament of Hausa women who are educated, who insist that a woman must be literate "in order to know her rights" as outlined in the Qur'an. I heard this comment constantly from many women during my fieldwork years of 1979 to 1982 in Kano.

The degree to which the pursuit of an education is respected depends in large part upon parents' educational level and the open-mindedness that education can provide. More important for a woman's social role, however, is the fact that social status changes with maturity (Coles 1990; Cooper 1997). Since women marry early, at puberty, they fulfill a rite of passage early in their lives. Even if they do not conceive, marriage confers a new social status even when they divorce or are widowed.

The practice of wife seclusion used to depend upon a man having sufficient capital to provide domestic labor for tasks that required leaving the home. Thus, in rural areas where women were needed for carrying water and firewood or planting crops, wife seclusion was impossible for any but the wealthy who could afford servants. But now in urban Kano, piped water and electricity make wife seclusion possible for many, even those in lower income brackets, and the constraints of wife seclusion last only during a woman's active childbearing years. The pattern of serial divorce and changing relationships common in Kano means that Hausa women experience seclusion as a several-year portion of their lives, not a lifelong defining experience.

Furthermore, even those who are secluded find many opportunities to go out for naming and wedding celebrations, funeral condolences, and family visits. Cases of strict seclusion do exist, but these are examples of wife abuse and misogynistic misreadings of both Hausa tradition and Islamic intention. Perhaps the only legitimate reason for strict wife seclusion is royal status; the sheltered life of Hausa royal women is not so different in the constraints it imposes from that of royal women in other cultures. Yet even the emir's wives bring entertainments into the royal harem on

celebratory occasions. A new wave of fundamentalism means that :
cases of strict wife seclusion are self-imposed, as women choose to intei
the custom for themselves, but seclusion never prohibits entertainm
within the restricted arena of the harem, where only women and children
are privy to the show.

The practical, idealistic aim of wife seclusion is to free a woman of
childbearing age to focus on the family without obligating her to engage in
wage-earning activity. Nevertheless, the practice has come to hold symbolic status, indicating the wealth of a man and the privileged nature of his
household. A secluded woman's obligatory tasks are labor intensive, including food preparation, laundry, housekeeping, and child care. Wife seclusion is often reported by scholars to be restrictive and oppressive, but
anyone who has lived in Kano knows that it would be a privilege to be
freed from doing the marketing, standing in line to pay taxes or electric
bills, or negotiating traffic in a car or on foot.[5] Women are excused from
having to show up at the mosque for Friday prayers because it would be a
hardship to drop everything in the middle of the day; nevertheless, there is
a place for those who wish to attend.

Despite a focus on the household during their years of seclusion, many
women also continue to pursue their educations at this life stage, whether
during the day or in night classes in the adult education programs sponsored by the local governments. Furthermore, any income a woman derives from selling snacks or crafts is hers alone; in theory, the husband's
income provides for the family while the wife's becomes her own nest egg
(Schildkrout 1979, 1982). It is a misperception to think that seclusion constitutes men's imprisonment and control of women by preventing them
from acting in public, because it is not men and their public activities that
constitute the nexus of Hausa society (Pellow 2002; Pittin 1996; Schildkrout 1982). Rather, Muslim Hausa culture is focused inward, with the
family at its core and the wife and mother as overseer of this context. The
sanctity of the family and the woman's primacy in this context turn Western models of public-private dichotomies on their head. One has only to
consider descriptions of Arab architecture and aesthetics to recognize the
value placed on the interior of the home (with its central fountains and
courtyards), the "interiority" of Qur'anic passages hidden in intricate cal-
ligraphies, and the Ultimate Truth as it resides in the deepest Sufi para-
digms to grasp the inward-focused nature of Arab-Islamic cultural influence
on Hausa society.

WOMEN'S MUSICAL ACTIVITY

Seclusion means that musical activity in women's lives is not publicly
recognized because much of it is performed in private. In that private set-

ting there is room for other, nonprofessional accompaniment by aspiring singers. In his study of singers in West Africa, David Ames notes that "[a]mong non-professionals, women of all ages more often perform than men" (1973, 133). Hausa women, whether professionals or not, enjoy more freedom to choose their singing style than men. If men do sing professionally, they are identified as certain types of singers who perform for the public or as members of a group of royal musicians. They are less inclined than women to vary their performance specialties, while women can perform songs in a variety of styles and situations. Women professionals who perform in public milieus vary their performance style and song topics according to the venue.

For Western scholars, the public-private paradigm carries the expectation of power-powerlessness, with implications for women's roles as poets and entertainers in Hausa culture.[6] But the concept of powerlessness is not part of Hausa women's self-image. In the process of negotiating their way around social proscriptions, Hausa Muslim women make use of various tactics, most evident of which is the process of "ungendering" themselves. During fieldwork, as an American, I played a role as "honorary female" among Hausa women. At the same time, as a highly educated person, I played a role as "honorary male" and was free to move about in more public circles. This dual identity allowed me to visit women in the royal harem and the private women's quarters of homes, but it also allowed me to have audiences with the emir, travel to the university, and drive my own car around town. The social role I played was identical to the role played by the poets and singers described in this study, who also moved between women's and men's worlds and moved around in public at will. What we had in common was respectable behavior and attire in public, which gave us the freedom to go where we wished, and specific talents, which afforded us leeway in transgressing gendered social boundaries.

Some women performers would argue that all women have special talents that make them able to do whatever work they wish to do. In a public performance for a university audience in 1980, Binta Katsina inspired women to be self-directed, urging them to take charge of their lives:

8   Women of Nigeria,
9   Women of Nigeria,
10 You should try to understand,
11 You could do every kind of work.
13 Women of Nigeria, you will do every kind of work,
14 You should be given the chance to take charge.
15 You can do office work,
16 You can do administrative work,
17 You should be given the chance to take charge.
    ("Song for the Women of Nigeria")[7]

The secluded, less educated women of Binta Katsina's audience are the subject of her song, but she advocates that these women participate actively in the public domain. Some Hausa women do work in the public sphere as broadcasters, journalists, architects, and lawyers. Although Binta Katsina's message may appear to run counter to the stereotype of a Hausa Muslim woman, her popularity was testimony to both the appeal of her message and the complexity of contemporary women's roles in Northern Nigeria, where the gender equity described in the Qur'an has been compromised by traditional Hausa patriarchal interpretations of Islam. That Binta Katsina was illiterate herself indicates clearly that artistic ability depends on neither literacy nor gender.

SONG IN DAILY LIFE

As creative artists, Hausa women singers and poets are inspired as readily as artists anywhere else in the world. They are praise singers, popular songwriters, and authors of political, religious, instructive, romantic, and admonitory tracts. Performers who extemporize songs are anonymous beyond the immediacy of their social circles unless their works are recorded, and since more of women's performances occur in private settings, there is less likelihood that their work will be preserved in recordings than the work of male artists.[8] When performances do occur in public, the oral nature of the popular song makes it ephemeral. Because their works are not widely heard or distributed, both the artists and their work remain relatively unknown.

The legacy of poets also depends on gender roles. Women poets sometimes recite their works in public poetry circles, but they are less often published than the works of male poets. This has everything to do with a male-focused agenda in publishing houses and women's lack of access to agents to market their material for them. In addition, it has to do with attitudes toward the value of the printed word, which is not held in the same esteem in traditional Islamic contexts as it is in the West. Thus, it might appear that African women—especially secluded Muslim women—do not have a voice in the artistic or literary life of their cultures.

Although it is likely that Hausa women have performed extemporaneous poetry for much of Hausa history, literacy was the key to women's composition of poetic works that would win recognition in the public domain. Furthermore, although women's literacy was a main concern of nineteenth-century jihad perspectives, indigenous and colonial patriarchal interests interfered with this aim, resulting in low literacy rates for women. British policy theoretically supported the education of women in the region, but this was not actually put into effect until decades after the onset of the colonial era and the establishment of schools for boys. One of the first girls' schools in the north was established in Kano in 1930, twenty-one years after the first boys' school opened there (Mack 1988, 65).

In nineteenth-century Hausaland, the renowned scholar and poet Nana Asma'u, daughter of jihad leader Usman ɗan Fodiyo, wrote Islamic verse in three languages and was respected as a scholar and teacher. Still, many critics call her an exception, as they do twentieth-century Muslim women novelists such as Zaynab Alkali of Nigeria and Mariama Ba, Naissfatou Diallo, and Aminatou Sow Fall of Senegal. It is argued that because these women are educated, they cannot be representative of the average Muslim African woman.[9] This line of reasoning is based on the presumption that only published material constitutes creative composition and discounts the productivity of illiterate composers.[10]

The artists profiled here are women who, despite a cultural trend toward educating boys instead of girls, have nevertheless benefited from both orthodox Islamic and colonial legacies with regard to education policy. Because contemporary women in postindependence Nigeria composed it, the poetry collected here reflects both these Islamic and British social policies, 150 years after the jihad of Islamic revivalism and 65 years after the start of British colonialism. It represents the views of women who fulfill social roles as Muslims and as members of a culture with Western education policies.

My first encounters with Hausa women poets revealed the intricacy of the situation; I found poets of all ages who ran the gamut from illiterate to university educated. Some wrote out verses in careful rhyme and meter while others extemporized them. Some shared their verses tentatively and free of charge, intending them as instructional verse for a small group of women students. Others were hired for lively performances for mixed-gender public audiences. The most difficult group to explain among those with whom I worked was the group of artists who, chameleon-like, crossed social lines, performing both in the privacy of a home's secluded women's quarters and then for gatherings as open (and dangerous) as political rallies in town. These were the singers of extemporaneous poetry, who were usually less educated and less socially revered than any other creative artists. It is significant that their lower social status allowed them greater freedom to cross gender barriers, as is often the case.

Furthermore, such creative artistry is not restricted to recognized performers but is an integral part of individual expression in the culture. In casual conversations with me, a friend who was not formally a poet revealed her own creative spirit, relating stories about plays she and friends had written in secondary school and songs they had made up at play. She demonstrated the way to sing with the elongated gourd called a *shantu*, an instrument exclusive to women's gatherings because it is played on the inner thigh.[11] Indeed, her familiarity with music and performance became clearer as I grew to know her culture. Always as we talked, the rhythm of the day's work activities came to us over the walls from a nearby compound—women performed work songs to the task of preparing grain, making a musical instrument of the mortar and pestle, or singing as they rolled a grinding stone. Often the itinerant groups of children singing and dancing as they played in nearby courtyards enlivened the peaceful atmosphere of my friend's courtyard. Indeed, children's songs and stories are important to Hausa culture, and much has been written about them (Yahaya 1979).[12] As this description suggests, song is integral to Hausa culture and pervades daily life in many ways, between old and young, female and male, educated and illiterate.

Song play by both boys and girls occurs in annual religious festivals. On festival days, children sing songs from doorway to doorway, looking for holiday treats. At night in the courtyards of large households, groups of women musicians drum on the rounded side of bowl-shaped calabashes while others dance.[13] Outside the privacy of the women's quarters, among the (mostly male) court musicians, women play instruments and sing as official royal court musicians. And every morning as the emir walks to his reception room in the women's section of the palace, a stout, deep-throated woman strides before him as she has done for many years—one of his official praise singers, announcing the arrival of the king.[14] Thus, music, song, storytelling, and verse are integral parts of Hausa/Fulani culture; they are not reserved for special occasions or restricted to performance by individuals with higher educations. While not everyone shares a talent for creative artistry, it is readily recognized and appreciated where it does exist. And certainly women are as much a part of the culture's creative talent as men, regardless of whether they are seen publicly or not.

BEING MUSLIM, NOT MUTE

The majority of Hausa women are devoted to Islam, domestically oriented, and minimally educated. They dress modestly; they do not cover their faces in restrictive burqahs or chadors, but they do cover their hair and arms in brightly patterned cloth. Operating within the patriarchal social system, many Hausa women find ways to exercise their creative and entrepreneurial talents in spite of cultural barriers, circumventing the social limitations placed on them. Hausa Muslim women are not restricted by their social roles. There is flexibility in Hausa culture for mature women (i.e., those who have married at least once) to pursue an education or a career in creative performance or business and to live independently if they so choose. Descriptions of separate gendered social roles in Hausa society often fail to discuss Hausa women's autonomy, but arenas of literary and extemporaneous expression provide a forum for the examination of the range of Hausa Muslim women's social roles, the choices they make, and the ways in which they challenge the perception of restrictions in their pursuit of personal interests.

Hausa Muslim women performers inspire audiences in myriad ways, simultaneously proclaiming their religious obligations to domesticity and declaiming—reclaiming—their equal rights under that same Islamic law. These creative artists urge their sisters to fulfill their God-given talents and make their voices heard in Hausa culture. Hausa women's oral and written works constitute entertainments that are central to their daily lives in contemporary Northern Nigeria. Some women choose to pursue public careers while their children are young, while others wait until they are free from child-rearing obligations. Many finish an education that was interrupted by early marriage by attending evening adult education classes. Transition is common in a Hausa woman's life; what Binta Katsina's song advocates is not beyond the grasp of a woman who may be secluded at the time she hears such a song on the radio; that woman has many unsecluded years ahead of her.

LIFE IN A WALLED CITY

I went to Kano, Nigeria, in 1979–1980 to study and collect Hausa women's praise songs for the emir. I returned for postdoctoral work in 1982–1983. My ability to speak Hausa and my residence in the Old City, near the emir's palace, afforded me an experience in the heart of traditional urban Hausa life. The people of the neighborhood took it upon themselves to defend me against anyone who questioned my presence there, and the women of the palace exhibited infinite patience in feeding me choice morsels of Hausa culture, served up daily along with meals that I was never able to replicate.[15] The emir, Alhaji Ado Bayero, was generous in granting me permission to go nearly anywhere in the palace; I know now that through the reporting of his royal retainers he knew my every move and trusted my discretion to preserve the privacy of the family's life in the palace. The emir's third wife, Hajiya Abba Bayero, became a close friend and valued teacher of Hausa custom. Upon hearing that I wanted to learn about women praise singers, she enthusiastically suggested that I give equal consideration to authors of written poetry, perhaps because her own education (to the teacher-training certificate level) had instilled in her an appreciation of the written word. Until that time I knew nothing of women writing poetry in this cultural setting—no one had studied it—but Hajiya Abba clearly felt that women writers were important to her culture.

I learned quickly that regardless of one's preference for one form over another, praise songs cannot be studied in isolation from written poetry. Interest in them leads one to extemporaneous performers who praise ordinary citizens and then to poets of written verse. The works included here range from royal praise song to ordinary song to written poetry of praise, admonition, eulogy, and current events. This list does not represent a hierarchy but a continuum, along which one can find any type of poem or song, depending on the context being served by the performance.

Many Hausa women are singers and poets to some degree; some get paid for their creativity, most do not. Chanted verse pervades both men's and women's cultural experience, ranging from devotional expression of Qur'anic verses to the bawdiest of entertainment songs. The social order is a blend of Muslim orthodoxy and Hausa tradition, and the two cultural influences can hardly be distinguished from one another. Despite the variety of types of songs, common threads bind all types of women's *waƙoƙi*; they share a cultural inclination toward chanted verse and oral recitation mode as well as imagery that includes Islamic language embedded in Hausa tradition. Extemporaneous oral performances for live audiences are sometimes videotaped for television broadcast. Written poetry is produced more methodically: it is planned, written, and revised in privacy. When completed, written works are disseminated in written form on paper or orally, recited by the authors for live or radio audiences. Although the performance of song and poetry begin at the opposite extremes of public and private, they meet in the mode of oral recitation for a live audience, demonstrating that illiteracy is no impediment to creating or enjoying these entertainments.

The ancient northern Nigerian walled city of Kano, the setting for my work, has been a terminus for the trans-Saharan trade routes for the past 500 years. Located in the rolling savannah that is farmed outside the city center, Hausa culture has long maintained both traditional culture and the Arab-Islamic culture brought to the region by traders and travelers from across the desert (Hiskett 1984; Fika 1978). Its active trading culture has established a complex society that includes urban and rural, Muslim and non-Muslim, and a cosmopolitan mix of immigrants settling in Kano and pilgrims passing through, headed for Makka (Works 1976). The stratification of Hausa society is remarkable for its intricacy, affecting individuals at all levels of society, from the king at the top of the hierarchy to the beggar at the bottom (Smith 1959). Such stratification places oral singers/entertainers at the very bottom, regardless of their monetary success, demonstrating that more is at work in the establishment of social hierarchy than wealth alone.

Identification with Islam has been a major determinant of social status since the nineteenth-century jihad launched by Shehu Usman dan Fodiyo in 1803. This campaign sought the reformation of Islam in the region, resulting in a shift of ethnic alliances as Fulani emirs replaced Hausa kings throughout the north (Hiskett 1973; Last 1967). The jihad firmly established Islam as the measure of cultural values and was promoted by Fulani campaigners who spoke Fulfulde; nevertheless, Hausa remained the lingua franca of the masses. Another important historical influence was the period of British colonial rule (1903–1960) in Nigeria, which established principal infrastructures throughout the country and English as the common language. Colonialism led to an era of Western education, industry, and communication media such as newspapers, radio, and television. After independence, during the second half of the twentieth century, Nigeria sought to stabilize self-rule, establish a democratic polity, and maintain social services in an era of political and economic instability.

The deeply Islamic nature of Hausa culture constitutes the theological framework for both oral and written works. These works reflect issues of historical concern from Muslim women's perspectives. They are contemporary works, composed during the mid-twentieth century by women without postsecondary levels of education. As such, they represent the poems that a vast majority of Hausa women hear and to which they respond; they are written by women who share a deep devotion to Islam and who are typical in their levels of social, economic, or educational privilege. Unlike Western poems that sometimes serve only to evoke emotions, the works by these poets are never without informative purpose.

Earlier scholars of Hausa poetry distinguished only between the categories of popular and religious verse, stipulating that popular verse is song that is not normally written down; its subject matter is secular, not sacred. By that definition, many of the written verses in this study are actually popular verse. Yet they fulfill the more rigid stipulations of Mervyn Hiskett's definition of Islamic written "verse of the literate tradition, normally committed to writing at some point in its dissemination and which deals with matters essentially connected with the religion of Islam" (Hiskett 1975, xiv). More recently, Graham Furniss's comprehensive study (1996) of literary forms in Hausa includes attention to topical, narrative, and sociopolitical works in addition to modern religious poetry. The opening and closing doxologies of the written verses in this volume follow the pattern for the opening of any activity in this Muslim society, beginning with "Let us begin in the name of God . . ." ("*Bismillahi a Rahamani a Rahim . . .*"), and the content reflects Islamic philosophy on social issues. Yet the poems—whether extemporaneous or written—are solidly grounded in contemporary secular issues of social propriety, historical events, and politics. As popular verse in the context of an Islamic culture, it is not surprising that many of these women's poems constitute a synthesis of contemporary and religious issues in daily life and demonstrate women's inclination to offer social commentary. The poems themselves belie the assumption that Hausa Muslim women lack awareness of the outside world because of the practice of wife seclusion.

* * *

Reflecting the culture in which they are created, these women's *waƙoƙi* often describe traditional values and illuminate the ideals by which both women and men should live. But just as often they constitute news bulletins for secluded women, bringing the public world to them in their private domains. The subject matter of these pieces ranges widely, regardless of the gender of the author. Some of the topics reflect universal contemporary social concerns: the war on drugs, irresponsibility among teenagers, hygiene campaigns for young mothers. Other poems report local current events: the change from left- to right-hand driving, the change from British to Nigerian currency, the opening of the Bakolori Dam serving the north's electricity needs, and so forth. The poems mourn slain heads of state, lament over losses in Biafra, prepare people to cooperate with census-takers, urge women to vote, and praise the government's education policy. More daring performers sing publicly about prostitutes' "alternative" careers, shake suggestively when praising their own craft, and state blatantly that their own entertainment-derived wealth belies their low social position as entertainer. Their success is their rationale for overstepping the bounds of a woman's proper comportment.

Poetic inspiration serves many purposes in Hausaland; in addition to its own intrinsic value, the poetry produced by Hausa women explains, instructs, and entertains in both private and public settings. The works discussed here reflect the interests and attitudes of women in a culture that is an amalgam of traditional and Western influences. The works produced by Hausa women in the politically turbulent years 1966–1980 reflect the society in which they were created. The women performers who are the principal artists of this study range from educated to illiterate, from devout to just nominally Muslim. All of them live in the northern Hausa/Fulani region of Nigeria; they perform for private or public occasions, sometimes for both. Performing in the Hausa language, they are well known among their peers, and some have been taped for video cameos on local television stations. Some are popular figures on local radio shows. Nevertheless, these women remain unrecognized beyond, and often within, their own culture as equal counterparts to the male performing artists of Hausa/Fulani society due to the pervasive notion of Muslim women as silent members of society, restricted to the privacy of the home. Hausa women have their own way of being performing artists and scholars; this book seeks to celebrate Hausa women poets and singers in their own right. Judging by the response I got to inquiries about studies on women singers and poets during my visit to Sokoto and Kano in 2002, there are many more studies on the topics forthcoming; this is just the first of a great number of further studies of Hausa women's artistry which will be written by Hausa women scholars themselves.

Hauwa Gwaram, 1979

Profile One: Hauwa Gwaram, Hausa Poet

Hauwa Gwaram was born in 1940 in the village of Gwaram, outside Kano. She died in Kano in 1998. Hauwa Gwaram attended primary school to level four (age ten or eleven) in Gwaram and received her Qur'anic training there, where her father was an imam. She taught in the Ministry of Education's adult education courses in Kano in the 1970s and attended a training course at the Kano children's hospital. After that she worked for the Local Government Self-Help organization in Kano. Divorced twice, Hauwa Gwaram lived most of her adult life in Kano. She had one daughter, from her first marriage.

Hauwa Gwaram's skill in writing poetry was influenced by her Qur'anic education at an early age, which shaped her composition style. Her technique evolved through the compositions she wrote for adult education courses for the Kano State government in the 1960s. For women's education classes on literacy, crafts, hygiene, and maternity care, Hauwa Gwaram wrote long poems in couplets and quintains, using the poems as mnemonic teaching aids. Her skill as a poet was further honed during her membership in the Kano poetry circle known as the Wisdom Club (Hikima Kulob), which was established by renowned poet and political figure Mudi Sipikin in 1964, just four years after Nigeria's independence from British colonial rule. The Wisdom Club was one of many such organizations in Kano at the time. Its access to Radio Kano meant that many of the poems created for the club were also broadcast to a wider audience (Furniss 1996, 54, 238, 250).

Hauwa Gwaram was eager to affirm that she was not a praise singer, saying, "I wrote this poem, but I am not a *zabiya.*"[1] Members of the Kano Wisdom Club were adamant about refusing payment for their compositions in order to disassociate themselves from praise singers, who are paid by their patrons (Furniss 1977, 42–64). Though some of the better-known male members of the club have published their works, the main purpose of the club was to provide an opportunity for sharing and evaluating one another's poems, not to make money.

In interviews, I asked Hauwa Gwaram how she had learned to write poetry, what inspired her, and whether she was passing her skills on to someone in the next generation. She regretted that no one was taking up the craft:[2]

> HG: People with modern knowledge are too proud [to compose]. They think that if they do songs [write poems] they are failures. You see how it is in Arabia—all [those] who can arrange songs are important people. But people here nowadays don't want to waste their time writing songs. Take for example a student nowadays. If you write him a long letter, he reads the first and second pages, then he starts hissing and hitting his head in exasperation [trying to figure out the rest]. He doesn't want to waste his time. All the teachers in the old days could experience something and write it down and keep it for their ancestors. But now it is not like that. They're preoccupied with politics.

Initially, Western education in Nigeria had no place for Hausa poetic composition. Although it was unusual for girls to attend primary schools during the 1940s, Hauwa Gwaram did. Hauwa Gwaram's experience in being sent to primary school reflects historic conflict during the colonial era. When the British instituted secular education in the north, they ran into a great deal of resistance. People feared that their children would be corrupted by such a Western education experience. Although girls normally were left at home during the early days of public education, the British tried to encourage village heads to send all their children to the new schools to set an example for others, although many cases are documented of village heads sending substitute "sons" instead; such was the resistance to Western education during the colonial period. Little Hauwa's identity as a child of one of Gwaram's leaders overrode her identity as a girl, and she was sent to primary school along with her brothers:

HG: When I went to school, girls didn't normally go to school; only the sons of emirs, of rich men, the judge's son. . . . As for us children of the head of Gwaram, we were forcibly brought to school. [At that time]—you know the grain storage bins that one can open to pour millet into?—well, they'd put children in these. Mothers would put their children in big pots and cover them. That is, they'd hide them from those who wanted to put them in school. In my song on the war on ignorance didn't you hear me say that in times of illiteracy they were reluctant to say they were sick, lest someone take them to the hospital and make fun of them? That was in the times of ignorance, around 1942 or 1944.

As Hauwa Gwaram grew toward a teaching profession in adulthood, she began to use the poetic mode to instruct secluded women. This practice dates back to at least the nineteenth century, when Nana Asma'u established the 'Yan Taru women extension teachers program in the region and used poetry as the format for lesson plans. Hauwa Gwaram seemed unaware of any enduring tradition of women teaching women or of using poetry as a curricular device to aid in teaching. Hauwa Gwaram's work as an instructor in adult education classes was the framework for her first didactic compositions:

HG: Well, we did a play about health care work. Then the teacher said, "Let's do a song on health care work." There was no one to do it, so I made an effort. I wrote "*A hayye tsabta, a tsabta wata ta fi wata a tsabta ko ni na fi* . . . (Hey! cleanliness, when it comes to cleanliness, some are better than others, and perhaps I'm better than most at cleanliness . . .)" I prepared this one. Well, because of that since they heard that one I did every other song that we needed, and I did it well. There was another year when we did a play at Kofar ta Kudu. I did this song on cleanliness and played the part of Malam Tanko, who married one clean woman and one dirty woman. Even the Emir of Kano, Alhaji Ado, [saw it and] gave me a watch for this play that we did. I sang that song on cleanliness there at the play. Thereafter for every play that we did, I composed a song. Whether a play on farming or any event in Kano . . .

In her work with the Association for Women of the North, Hausa Gwaram used her poetry to instruct women on topics such as child care, health care, and the importance of literacy. Decades after they were composed, these versified lessons are still popular and are often aired over local radio stations.

POETIC STYLE AND COMPOSITION

The mode of composition that Hauwa Gwaram used consists of a combination of traditional rhyme and meter schemas familiar to them through their Islamic educational training and the influence of poets who were their contemporaries. In the Wisdom Club (which consisted of mostly men, but a few women as well), poets would draw upon versification skills assimilated through years of Qur'anic education. In the adult education courses, Islamic values and local history were emphasized in the curriculum and were popular poetry topics.

> HG: [W]hen we were working on the course [for adult education], if I saw that someone had done something interesting or surprising in Kano, when we were in school, I saw that I should preserve history and that's why I sing. . . . When I started writing songs there was a superintendent of ours—God's mercy upon him—whose name was Shetima. With him we did the course [on adult education] at the Friday mosque at Gidan Dogon Lamba. He said, "Look here, we are doing a job; is there among you one who can make an effort to write a song on this work that we are doing?" I raised my hand and he said "How will you do it?" I said, "I know how. I will do it at night." There were about four of us women who said we would write songs. Well, when I got home I was thinking. I said, "As for me, if God agrees, let me try to compose this song." I took up the Ma'aza Hadeja book and looked at it; there was among his songs one on hypocrisy. I said to myself, "Okay, let me write on the war on ignorance," and since he began with the end rhyme "ca," I decided to use it as my rhyme too. This is how I began writing the song for the war on ignorance in this way. And every song I did thereafter, I never looked in a book. I just thought about a subject and made my own effort to write. But at first I had to refer to a book. When Shetima came and we gathered and met with Sarkin Dawaki—God's mercy upon him—I handed them the song in the morning and they looked at it. When I handed it to them they said, "You have to sing it—it's better if we hear it from the composer." When I sang it they said, "Ah, she's really a good artist." I said, "I am not a scholar, I only tried my hand at writing." All the rest of the women who performed their songs giggled through them.

Hauwa Gwaram's grounding in Qur'anic study formed the basis for her poetic capability. Copying the Qur'an can be understood as a devotional act, and artists of lesser works also take care in approaching the poem with respect for the degree to which it can reflect God's creation. Rumi's Sufi perspective is that "God is the calligrapher who writes with the pen of the human heart" (Renard 1996, 127). Ultimately artistic creativity is felt to be a gift from God, as is every other good thing:

HG: So you see, no one taught me how to compose. God taught us. It's not that I'm a knowledgeable person.

TWO

"The Song Is Poetry's Domain"

TRADITION AND ISLAM

Sing in every poem you compose. That song is poetry's domain.
—Hasan Ibn Thaabit (d. 674)

HAUSA POETIC SONG: INDIGENOUS AND ISLAMIC INFLUENCE

No matter where you are in the world, you can be sure that the person whose bag or shirt sports the Hausa heraldic symbol, the knot of the north (*dagi; durƙusan taguwa*), will respond to the greeting "*Sannu.*"[1] The design's four-sided diamond shape overlaid with two ellipses in interlaced loops appears on clothing, accessories, and architecture in an ancient symbol of unknown origin that represents Hausa culture. Its inherent duality reflects the duality of traditional Hausa culture, which has coexisted with

Arab-Islamic culture for centuries in Northern Nigeria,[2] and Hausa literary art forms, especially the oral and written verses known collectively as *waƙoƙi*. Just as Hausa artistic tradition includes Arab-Islamic influence along with pre-Islamic forms, so too Hausa *waƙoƙi* artistry includes both written poetry and declamation, incorporating features from both classical Arabic verse forms and indigenous styles.

The angel Gabriel's first words to the Prophet Muhammad were "Proclaim! Read! . . . Proclaim! And thy Lord is most bountiful He who taught (The use of the Pen), Taught Man what he knew not" (Chapter 96:1, 3–4). The central metaphor concerning the Qur'anic message itself is that the worldly Qur'an is but a fragment of the ultimate Word of God, whose complete version is housed in the heavens. All aesthetic influence in Islamic art is founded on this focus on the spoken Word of God; that the Sacred Word was "revealed as a book, rather than as a human being as is the case in Christianity, [means that] the sacred art concerns the manifestation of letters and sounds of the Holy Book rather than the iconography of a man who is himself the Logos" (Nasr 1976, 15). Islamic calligraphy offers beautiful artistic expressions of the sacred.

But despite a focus on the Word of God, literacy is not necessary for creative composition in Hausa culture; not everyone who is literate writes poetry, and not everyone who creates poetry is literate. This situation has to do with separate approaches to education: Islamic schools have long been active in the region, while Western schools are a vestige of colonialism. Children's schooldays are usually divided in half, between the Islamic and secular. Each school involves instruction in literacy, but the Islamic school includes Arabic script and grammar and attention to Qur'anic study, while the *boko* ("book") Western classes are conducted in the Hausa language, which is written in Latin script, and concern literacy, numeracy, and current events.[3] Some of the extemporaneous singers profiled here are illiterate, but they certainly are familiar with Islamic versification and likely have memorized significant portions of the Qur'an, even without being able to read or write it.

As for the poets who become literate through the public education process, none of them learns poetic technique through the schools' curricula. Instead, developing an intuitive sense of poetic technique depends equally on studying the Qur'an with traditional teachers and having a well of personal creativity from which to draw.[4] Memorizing Qur'anic verse—something nearly everyone in Hausa culture does to some degree—is the best means of acquiring a sense of poetic rhythm. The popular music that is pervasive in Hausa media and public performance also influences an individual's poetic style. It is common for little boys who are Qur'anic students to get food for themselves and their teachers by chanting Qur'anic verses and popular songs door to door each day. Little girls hear both Qur'anic verse and popular songs on the radio and enjoy the entertainments of women musicians who perform for women's parties. Thus, Hausa children are exposed to songs in their daily lives from an early age and devote formal attention to Qur'anic verse daily at school; it is not surprising that many Hausa children feel comfortable composing their own works later in life.[5] Hausa performing artists commonly compose by imitating what they hear without knowing the formal Arabic names for the metric arrangements they choose (Muhammad 1977, 128). With the tools for composition in place from an early age, the inspiration to compose is believed to come from God, while the poem's structure comes from internalized patterns of meter and rhyme arrangements. Some written poems are modeled on exposure to the works of other poets, delivered orally in public declamation in poetry circles or radio broadcasts.[6]

The women who compose written poems model their style—both the content and form of their works—on earlier poems written by both men and women. Women poets use *waka* as an instructive art form, a means of teaching proper behavior, a vehicle for explanation of new social trends and descriptions of far-reaching news events. They regard composition with a reverence instilled by their Islamic training and the high regard for the written word that is inherent in Islamic attitudes toward education. Yet their commentaries are neither dry nor dour. These written poems express their respect for education and morally acceptable behavior in both form and content, and the organization of their works is highly structured by rhyme and meter. Nevertheless, they often amuse, holding the audience in rapt attention as they send their message through examples such as the exploits of bumblers who fail by lacking the literacy skills necessary to function successfully in life.

Hausa women's *wakoki* also reflect the impact of Westernization on a Hausa Islamic culture. Many of the written poems discussed in this study incorporate references to risqué trends in Western fashion, drug abuse, modes of transportation, and nontraditional attitudes among Nigerian youth. The poems measure these social influences against conservative Islamic moral codes. Perhaps the most striking and complex aspect of Hausa culture is its flexibility in the mingling of traditional and modern, Hausa and non-Hausa characteristics, all of which are evident in Hausa poetry.

ARABIC/ISLAMIC LITERARY INFLUENCES ON WOMEN'S ROLES AS POETS

Contemporary Muslim Hausa women regularly cite the Islamic rights of women emphasized by Muslim reformist Shehu Usman ɗan Fodiyo and actualized in the life of his renowned daughter.[7] Nana Asma'u (1793–1865), daughter of Shehu, was encouraged in education by her father, who believed in the importance of literacy and knowledge (for both men and women) for the greater glory of God (Boyd 1989). Asma'u was well educated, as were most members of her Fulani Fodiyo clan; the surname Fodiyo means "learned," indicating the family's status as Islamic clerics. Nana Asma'u's written poetry distinguished her as an internationally respected scholar; a letter to her from a Mauritanian scholar indicates that her work was considered to be of consummate skill (Boyd and Mack 1997, 282–284). Evidence of Asma'u's classical education in a particular canon is also evident in one of her poems, "Sufi Women," which is clearly modeled on a poem by her brother Bello ("Kitab al Nasiha"), which was in turn modeled on a poem of the same name by twelfth-century poet Ibn al-Jawzi.[8] What marks this as Asma'u's distinctive work is her integration of the names of her nineteenth-century peers in the latter portions of the poem. The order in which twelfth-century Sufi women are named is the same in each work, but Asma'u's verses are her own, and her addition of contemporary women by implication elevates their status to that of renowned Sufi women saints. The practical nature of Asma'u's works relied on traditional chanted verse as a vehicle to disseminate current material.

In addition to her erudite writings in Arabic and Fulfulde, Asma'u used literacy to practical ends. At home, her lifelong efforts to educate refugees and children resulted in her establishment of a corps of itinerant women teachers (*jajis*) of secluded women. Asma'u trained these women, who were beyond their childbearing years and therefore were under no obligation to be secluded in the home, in a wide range of topics. In a labor-intensive economy, few women had the luxury of devoting themselves to study. Therefore, the poems that the teachers taught to newly Muslim women in their homes dealt with practicalities as often as theology. Using her poems as lesson plans, the women teachers memorized the poems, recited them for their students, and taught through exegesis. The works explained how to dress and pray appropriately, informed women of their rights and obligations in Islam, and described recent history in Islamic context, comparing the recent jihad with the battles fought by the Prophet Muhammad centuries earlier.

In the same way, twentieth-century women composers in Kano used the poetic mode as a teaching tool to describe current events, women's rights and obligations, political concerns, and relevant history. These contemporary women poets relied on Nana Asma'u as a role model, whose poems were familiar to them through oral transmission. When I asked Hauwa Gwaram whether she needed her husband's permission to write poetry, she replied indignantly, "If Nana did not need permission to write, why should I?" The magnitude of Asma'u's legendary status is evident in this, since her collected works were not published until 1999.[9] Thus, her role as a scholar-poet in history was sufficient to inspire women in subsequent generations to compose. The fact that their twentieth-century compositions are so similar to Asma'u's in both form and content attests to the strength of an enduring Islamic educational canon and the influence of Qur'anic literary style to which Muslim women have had access in direct relation to their level of education.

COMPOSITION AND EDUCATION

At the Northern Nigerian Publishing Company, as throughout society, it is assumed that Hausa women do not write poetry. To some extent, the men who believe this have been right; few women had time to write. What woman had time for education leading to literacy—much less time for writing poetry—when sent to her marriage home at puberty? What woman could spend twelve hours each day on domestic labor and still have energy to spare for leisure creativity? Underlying these were other implicit questions regarding women's literary capabilities: What woman could possibly have an opinion to express, even if she could write? And what woman could possess the talent to compose poetry on a par with a man? But women who were inspired to write did find time for these pursuits, and they had plenty to say about history, religion, and political events, as is demonstrated here.

Two major waves of cultural influence have affected women's education over the past two centuries and are in large part responsible for these assumptions: the nineteenth-century Sokoto jihad and the twentieth-century British colonial occupation. Both the jihad's Islamic reform movement and the colonial cultural influence created support for universal education systems, one religious and the other secular. Yet both also instituted social schemes that overtly relegated women to the domestic scene, on the one hand to fulfill a religious and cultural mandate and on the other to reinforce Victorian attitudes. Although the nineteenth-century jihad strengthened restrictions on women's access to the public—positing that proper devout Muslim women should remain secluded in the home—it also implicitly validated the benefit of education for all. Jihad women were encouraged to leave their homes to attend school. In the Sokoto caliphate, literacy and learning were integral parts of what was recommended for a devout Muslim, and the Shehu's support of his daughter's scholarship is testimony to his approval of such pursuits. The Shehu believed in educating women, warning:

> One of the root causes of the misfortunes of this country is the attitude taken by *Malams* [teachers] who neglect the welfare of their womenfolk, leaving them abandoned like animals, not having taught them what Almighty Allah has said they must

be taught, for example the prayers they must know in their hearts, how to perform the ablutions, prayer and the fast. Moreover they are not taught what they ought to know about trading transactions; this is quite wrong. . . . How can these *Malams* allow their wives, daughters and slave women to remain lost and in ignorance while at the same time they are teaching their pupils twice daily? . . . It is obligatory to teach wives, daughters and female slaves: the teaching of pupils is optional and what is obligatory has priority over what is optional. . . . Muslim women, do not listen to them when they mislead you, telling you to obey your husbands but omitting to tell you to obey Allah and his Prophet. They say that a woman's place in Paradise depends on whether or not she has been obedient to her husband. Of course they only tell you that in order to make you do what Almighty Allah and His Prophet have not made obligatory, cooking, washing clothes and so on, while at the same time they do not require you to do things which Allah had said you must do. (*Nur al-albab*, quoted in Boyd 1986, 128–129)

Practicing what he preached, the Shehu educated the women in his family; four of his daughters wrote poetry and prose.

His daughter Nana Asma'u's was an especially talented intellect; her language skills in Arabic, Hausa, Fulfulde, and Tamshek (Berber) allowed her to communicate with the major ethnic groups of her region, and during the first quarter of the nineteenth century she was renowned well beyond Northern Nigeria—as far away as Mauritania—as a teacher and scholar. She was known for the classes she conducted for both men and women and is revered to this day as an accomplished scholar in her own right. Yet she remains acknowledged only as an exception to the tradition that Hausa/Fulani women are neither literary artists nor scholars. Countering criticism by citing Nana Asma'u as an example, some Muslim Hausa women of Northern Nigeria have continued to educate their peers through the written and spoken word over the past two centuries. Occasionally men—primarily a few farsighted politico/religious leaders—have fostered such activities over the years. Just as the Shehu encouraged his daughter in her work, so too men like the late Alhaji Aminu Kano have become known for their active support of women's involvement in educational activities. Perhaps the most pervasive reason for such support is the symbiotic bond of religious obligation and the obligation to educate under the tenets of Islam. Enlightenment is a form of prayer; educating an individual necessarily involves instruction in Muslim law. Therefore, teaching can be a means of fulfilling one's obligation to spread the word of God.

A century after the jihad, when Nigeria was under British control, boys' schools were established for the Western education of future leaders while girls were ignored. The story of how girls' schools were established varies between official and informal accounts. The official line is that the British provided women teachers for separate girls' schools with the support of influential Hausa men and women at the level of the royal courts; in this version, the establishment of girls' schools depended largely on the foresight of several northern emirs and their wives and sisters (Hull 1968; Mack 1988; Perham 1956–1960, 1983). Such inclusiveness, however, was not the case in practice.[10]

The authority figures in colonial Hausaland, both Hausa men and English men, maintained the prevalent attitude of the time and occupying culture: that regardless of their education, women should be relegated to domestic functions while men could operate in public. For women, the compromise in practice was to send girls to primary school only until they were given in marriage (before or at adolescence), after which they were expected to focus on their domestic roles. Colonial rule complicated women's access to public activity and public education, offering opportunities only in social realms separate from men. Such separation extended to expression through the performing arts as well.

Public policy in the 1960s allowed for somewhat more widespread teaching of and among Kano women. Some were trained as itinerant home-education workers who visited secluded women to teach them, but this process was never well organized.[11] The politics of Nigeria's First Republic brought new social institutions that further promoted women's education. In the 1970s, two major policy changes occurred that had direct impact on women's educational opportunities. The first was the establishment of the universal primary education (UPE) policy, which took effect on January 1, 1976. From this time on, all primary-school-aged children theoretically were required to attend classes during the day, yet the program was ineffective because it was launched without financial support at the federal level; as a consequence, it lacked teachers, buildings, and equipment.[12] Hauwa Gwaram and Hajiya 'Yar Shehu describe the program in their written poetic works. Although the program failed in its attempt to educate a generation broadly, women poets who understood its potential to change their positions in society praised its intention.

Shortly after the establishment of UPE, Kano State established the Agency for Mass Education, whose innovative approach to adult literacy was recognized by the United Nations in 1978. Initially the agency's Women's Education Program involved only the Kano City Center for Women's Education, but it quickly grew to include approximately a dozen rural centers throughout Kano State, where both daytime and evening classes were offered to married women eager to complete educations—usually still at the primary level—that had been interrupted by marriage. In addition to the practical skills that had been offered by the extension classes of the 1960s, the Women's Education Program included instruction in Islamic religious knowledge, Hausa and English literacy, and numeracy. Literacy classes in both languages commonly relied on chapbooks of verse popular in the Muslim north. Since its publication in 1983, the first of such books by women—*A Pen in the Hands of Women (Alƙalami a Hannun Mata)*—has been used in women's adult education classes.

HISTORY OF WRITTEN HAUSA POETRY

Until the nineteenth century, poetic verse was more religious than topical and nearly always in Arabic; *qasida* (praise poem) works focusing on the Prophet Muhammad's life and religious praise poetry set a pattern that was eventually used as the format for discussion of current events and transmission of local histories.[13] As Hausa scholars gradually began to write in their own language, they maintained both Arabic script—known as *ajami*—and Arabic verse form, with its opening and closing doxologies and deliberate rhyme schemes. In the nineteenth century, the prolific output of the Fodiyo clan—women as well as men—focused on works expressing the tenets of a Sunni way of life for Muslims in the region.[14]

The arrival of Europeans in sub-Saharan Africa in the late nineteenth century signaled a turn toward secular concerns in Hausa poetry. Western education and colonialism had profound effects on Hausa poetic style, and eventually a distinctly Hausa form of popular verse focused on secular concerns began to emerge. Faced with a strong cultural identity among the Hausa, the British shrewdly investigated northern traditions, learning the language and collecting tales and traditions in the original Hausa. To further this approach, they established a Literacy Bureau in Kano in 1929, later moving it 100 miles south to Zaria. The bureau aimed to represent the north through publications that could compete with missionary publications that were rapidly gaining the attention of the masses throughout the rest of the country. Therefore, its publications were in the Hausa language and initially were histories from the Middle East rather than tales, since the former could best be appreciated by Muslims, whose respect for the study of history is well established in their Islamic tradition (Skinner 1980).[15] C. E. Whitting, later the author of a collection of Hausa and Fulani proverbs, headed the Translation Bureau from 1930 to 1932. Dr. R. M. East replaced him then and ran the bureau for the years of its early growth. It became the Literature Bureau in 1935, and its new name implied a new purpose. East explained in 1936 that part of the reason for the change rested with an earlier (1933) decision of Nigeria's director of education to engender interest in literacy through interest in fiction among the Hausa. However, fiction was not available for publication: the Bureau had the problem of needing to find authors. The cultural obstacles in such an endeavor were many, as Rupert East explained in 1936:

The first difficulty was to persuade these *Malams* that the thing was worth doing. The influence of Islam produces an extremely serious-minded type of person. The art of writing, moreover, being intimately connected in his mind with his religion, is not to be treated lightly. Since the religious revival at the beginning of the last century, nearly all the original work produced by the Northern Nigerian authors has been either purely religious or written with a strong religious motive. Most of it is written in Arabic, which, like Latin in Medieval Europe, was considered a more worthy medium for any work of importance than the mother tongue. Whether any literary works of a less serious nature were written before this time is unknown, since the leaders of the Jihad destroyed the writings of their predecessors in order to purge the land of all memories of a more heathen age. (East 1936, 351–352)[16]

Eventually they found authors and published several stories.

As the war machinery started up in Europe in 1939, the British felt compelled to combat German and Italian propaganda in their West African colonies. With this aim in mind, they established a Hausa newspaper with the expectation that the strength of oral communications in the region would guarantee an even wider exposure than sales indicated. Indeed, public readings of the newspapers spread their news in much the same format used for traditional narrative expression. The Hausa newspaper *Gaskiya Ta Fi Kwabo* ("Truth is worth more than a penny"—the newspaper's cost) was published twice a month in 1941; it continues to be popular into the twenty-first century, although it certainly costs more now. After World War II, the Literature Bureau and the Gaskiya Corporation were incorporated, moving toward textbook publication and eventually to fiction writing. The Northern Regional Literature Agency was established in 1950 to promote adult literacy, and publications reflected the agency's needs for the next decade. At Nigeria's independence in 1960, the Gaskiya Corporation became a full-fledged commercial venture and in 1965 was taken over by Macmillan Publishers, who established the Northern Nigerian Publishing Company. After that, its mandate changed with market needs, but this major Hausa press published hundreds of volumes, a large portion of which are religious and topical Hausa verse—the popular song. Nevertheless, throughout its long evolution over sixty years, only a single volume of Hausa women's written verse has appeared. *Alkalami a Hannun Mata (A Pen in the Hands of Women)*, by Hauwa Gwaram and Hajiya 'Yar Shehu, was published in 1983, and then only because it was promoted by an outside advocate who had access to a publisher.[17] No one spent much energy looking for women's manuscripts; perhaps they assumed there were none. Whether there are to be more publications like it depends on the complex situation of Hausa/Fulani women's lives; it will take the intervention of highly educated (and thus credible) advocates of women writers for this to come about. Women writers are not always the ones who are best situated to promote the publication of their own works.

HAUSA *WAKOKI*: ORAL AND WRITTEN POEMS

Contemporary Hausa *waƙoƙi* are as varied in style and theme as the circumstances in which they are performed, and their content is suited to the performance venue. Singers entertain at naming ceremonies and wedding celebrations and in praise of important people; their songs serve as commentary on social behavior, as announcements of changes in social practices, as work songs, and as mnemonic teaching aids. That the songs are appropriate for such a wide range of social situations is testimony to the genre's pervasive role in Hausa culture. The works discussed here are popular pieces by contemporary Hausa women who use *waƙoƙi* as entertainment that is alternately didactic, informative, ritual-oriented, celebratory, and paced to domestic tasks.

Hausa scholars distinguish between written and oral *waƙoƙi*; the works studied here represent both types. *Waƙar baka,* literally "poetry of the mouth," and *rubutacciyar waƙa,* written poems, are terms that some among the Hausa use to differentiate between these forms (Furniss 1996, 131; see also Muhammad 1979; Umar 1984; Smith 1957; Besmer 1971; and Ames and King 1971). Orally composed songs include praise songs and ritual music for the spirit-possession cult (*bori*) and naming and wedding celebrations.[18] They are not written; they are delivered only extemporaneously. But these pieces are not completely ephemeral. They follow established patterns of the genre that may be studied as readily as one of the written poems. Repeated performances of extemporaneous orally composed songs on the same topic indicate that a poet's repertoire consists of many interchangeable patterns. There is an established form for oral songs just as there is for written ones, along with a great deal of leeway for variants. Like the extemporaneous works, written poems are delivered orally too, though they also may be printed in local newspapers or published in books. They are more often transmitted over the radio and performed live.

Just as poetic form can vary from oral to written, performance situations range widely as well, from public to private, from royal to nonroyal. Female artists are not restricted to performing for specific occasions but commonly adapt their songs to the entertainment context. For example, a woman who performs for a private audience of women during a naming ceremony might also perform in public for a mixed university audience. Her repertoire would vary depending on the situation. One who performs in the palace might also perform in the privacy of the women's quarters (*cikin gida*; Ar.: *harem*) of a home in town. Oral poets perform by invitation only, unlike itinerant beggars who shout praises in public, hoping to collect money. A woman who is normally accompanied by an all-male chorus must sing without male accompaniment when she performs in the privacy of a home's *cikin gida,* because this area is off limits to men who are not part of the household. The author of metered, rhymed written verses is more likely to perform for didactic purposes—at a school or for a radio broadcast—than for a venue where active entertainment is expected.

Many of the recordings on which this book is based were taped in a harem setting with an audience restricted to the women of the household and their female friends, relatives, and guests; they were performed at wedding and naming celebrations and during other events when music and song were purely for entertainment. Other recordings cited here—especially those of professional women singers—were dubbed from local radio, television, and ministry tapes.[19] These recordings were broadcast on local media and were regularly enjoyed by the public, especially by women in seclusion who modeled their own songs on them.[20]

Wakoki produced by both men and women share many structural characteristics. Opening and closing doxologies, complete and partial repetitions (including both rhyme and assonance), end rhyme, and metaphor are common to both kinds. Among orally composed *wakoki* by a particular artist, those on similar topics are often close variants of an artist's basic composition patterns. The formulaic technique evident in this style of composition is comparable in function to the repetition and rhyme patterns of written works (Lord 1960; Kunene 1971). Written *wakoki* delivered orally and oral extemporaneously composed *wakoki* share many stylistic techniques in common while remaining distinct from each other in theme and function.

Wakoki are sometimes distinguished by their social function: there are praise songs (*wakokin yabo*), work songs (*wakokin sana'a*), royal praise songs (*wakokin sarauta*), and songs of co-wife jealousy (*wakokin kishiya*). Of the ten types of orally composed songs cited in Habibu Ahmed Daba's study, all types except the men's songs are performed by Hausa women, with or without musical accompaniment (1981). Daba's categories include praise (*yabo*), satire (*zambo*), limericks (*ban dariya*), work songs (*aiki*), men's songs (*maza*), occupational songs (*sana'a*), *bori* music, childcare music (*reno*), girls' songs (*gada*), and children's songs (*yara*). In fact, women perform work songs, childcare songs, girls' songs, and children's songs far more than men do, if not exclusively. Both men and women perform in the spirit-possession cult activities unless the session is held in the privacy of the women's quarters of a home. Another Hausa critic distinguishes between male and female performers, saying that only men chant admonitory verse (*gargadi*) while women chant only praise (*yabo*) and both perform historical accounts (*tarihi*).[21] As will be evident in the material collected here, this clear division by gender is not the case. Women perform nearly all the types of *wakoki* that men perform—including admonitory verse—as well as some types that men never perform.

The two closely related types of *waƙoƙi*—*waƙar baki* (oral) and *waƙar rubutu* (written)—are quite similar. Sometimes they are indistinguishable, except by being categorized as *waƙa* I and *waƙa* II (Muhammad 1977, 9–14). Dalhatu Muhammad discusses the differences between these two classes of *waƙoƙi* by men. He considers three elements—sound organization, language, and theme—essential to the evaluation of poetic quality in *waƙoƙi,* in that order, while the order is reversed in written works (Muhammad 1977, 12). Thus, he determines that it is not dissimilar components but different emphases among them that determine the genre's subdivisions. However, for women's *waƙoƙi* the differences do not apply in the same way. In women's oral songs, theme is often predominant, while sound organization and language can be of primary interest in written works.

In another study of men's poetic works, Mervyn Hiskett distinguishes between orally composed and written *waƙoƙi* according to their Islamic content, finding the written works replete with Islamic allusions, unlike orally composed works, which he describes as popular, often bawdy songs. These distinctions cannot be made about women's oral and written compositions. Although it is true that women's contemporary written poetry is influenced by familiarity with Qur'anic verse form, its content can focus on contemporary politics and social reform. While these poems may be written, they are likely to be disseminated in oral performance and often are broadcast on radio programs. The poet recites the poem without musical accompaniment, relying only on the rhythm of the verse for its musicality. Thus, an audience need not be literate to be familiar with the written word, and a poem's existence is never limited to its appearance in print. At the same time, many of the orally composed extemporaneous works in this study are replete with religious allusions, echoing the formulaic style of the Qur'anic verse. Members of any Hausa audience would be intuitively familiar with this delivery style, which echoes Qur'anic versification integral to their lives, whether in spoken or written form.

Within the ambit of women's works, the theoretical dichotomy between written and oral *waƙoƙi* seems not to apply. Women educated to the secondary level usually include oral composition techniques absorbed at an early age as part of their own writing styles, just as they are likely to mix traditional and Western-oriented concerns in their works. They draw the line, however, at the profession of praise singing and participation in spirit-possession activities, which carry a social stigma.[22] Less literate women are more likely to perform praise songs or extemporaneous entertainment songs. Women's perspectives are inevitably contained in the *waƙoƙi* they compose, and each piece, whether it is entirely original or a revised version of an older work, reflects a lifelong familiarity with orally composed *waƙoƙi* to which the singer or composer has been exposed while growing up in traditional Hausa culture. Since women are more likely than men to be singing and composing during their daily domestic activities, perhaps their *waƙoƙi* are more representative of the attitudes and artistic styles common to daily activities in Hausa culture than are men's compositions. Integrating poetry into their daily lives may also account for women's tendency to overlap styles and themes in both oral and written works.

All *waƙoƙi*, unlike much Western poetry, are performed more with the intention of entertaining an audience—of a few or many—than as expressions of personal introspection. This function is evident in the performance venues described here. The multiplicity of contexts for oral song performance determines the kinds of material and artists appropriate to the circumstance. Hausa poetic performance is an art form for the masses: it is the audience that enjoys and supports the performer, however significant the patronage received from the musicians' famous patrons (Ames 1973, 138).

Testimony to the social function of Hausa poetic expression is the fact that song rarely exists as music without words. Even when humming a tune without lyrics, an individual will sing a nonsense rhyme instead of just humming. Sometimes these nonsense rhymes are the names for specific metric patterns, such as *"Ahaiye iyenana iyaye yi yurai yurai"* in Hajiya 'Yar Shehu's "Song on the Census of the People of Nigeria" (v. 47), or *"Hayye iye nanaye ayyururuy yuruy"* in her "Song of Warning" (v. 10). Such a practice is evident in the instrumental music as well, where tones blown on a horn—especially on the long *kakaki* horn blown exclusively for an emir—intentionally imitate tone patterns in words. The Hausa interpret instrumental music, translating the "words" produced by the musical tone patterns. The *kakaki* echoes praise epithets for the emir, imitating the tone pattern of those epithets. For example, "Ga Sarki" ("Here's the King") is scanned low-low-high. The *kakaki* repeats this two-tone pattern. In 1980, the horn on the emir's Mercedes was outfitted to imitate the *kakaki*, announcing his arrival traditionally, even when he traveled by car.

The best-known extemporaneous forms of *waƙoƙi* are praise songs, especially those connected with the courtly tradition. For nearly 1,000 years—long before the establishment of trans-Saharan trade routes—royal praise poets have performed laudatory epithets for kings in the region. Hiskett suggests that Al-Bakri's eleventh-century comment on talking drums implies the use of praise poetry in the nearby sub-Saharan court of Gao, while Ibn Battuta has mentioned praise song in conjunction with such drumming in the fourteenth-century Mali court (Hiskett 1975, 2). Two oral accounts of Hausa origins—the "Kano Chronicle" king list and the "Song of Bagauda" ("Waƙar Bagauda")—attest in both form and content to praise singing as an ancient performing art among the Hausa (Last 1983; Smith

1983). The tradition thrives in contemporary times; anyone visiting Kano may still witness the virtuosity of royal praise singers and royal court musicians as they embellish an emir's public appearances. A cacophony of voices, drums, and horns elevates the occasion of an emir's presence to a (literally) noteworthy experience quite out of the ordinary.

Oral praise song (*wakar yabo*) is comprised of short praise epithets (*kirari*) that are strung together according to the praise singer's ingenuity and skill. An orator aims to flatter a patron by recounting laudatory actions, nicknames, and attributes unique to that individual. Most studies of Hausa praise song have identified patrons as chiefs, war heroes, and office holders. Certainly these are the types of patrons remembered in king lists and tales of origin (Hiskett 1975, 2; Smith 1959). History records very few praise songs extolling women, although the Inna of Gobir has praise songs, as does the Inna of Tsibiri.[23] Hausaland's Daura has preserved in its history legends of queens (Smith 1978, 56), and sixteenth-century Zaria is said to have had a woman warrior and queen (Palmer 1928, 109), yet they are not remembered in the praise songs that have been preserved. A rare exception to this is fifteenth-century Hauwa, who is said to have influenced her grandson in his position as Emir of Kano. The "Kano Chronicle" records accolades to her:

> Mother! Kano is your country.
> Mother! Kano is your town.
> Old lady with the swaggering gait,
> Old lady of royal blood, guarded by men-at-arms. (Palmer 1928, 113)

Praise song supports the status quo, validating the culture's social and political elite; since at least the seventeenth century, such holders of power have been men. Since that time certain women affiliated with the elite have maintained sufficient authority to influence men in power, and some have exercised overt power directly, like the *innas* of Gobir, who waged war in the nineteenth century.[24] Several queens and women warriors are cited in Hausa history around the fifteenth century, but these remain legendary figures, and evidence of more recent women in such roles is not known (Mack 1991).

Thus, with some exceptions, in the public discourse passed from one generation of praise singers to another it was the decision-makers who were praised—men, not women. In the privacy of the royal women's quarters, however, female praise singers declaim for the emir in an official capacity. These same performers are also on hand for women's celebrations in the heart of the palace, shouting laudatory epithets for royal wives, concubines, and their esteemed guests. Since such praise song is common to the private women's celebrations for feast days and wedding and naming ceremonies during contemporary times, there is every reason to believe that the praising of women by women praise singers was a common feature of historical times as well. But such praises of women rarely have been recorded, in part because of their ephemeral nature but most emphatically because of the fact that they would have been performed in private settings exclusive to women.[25]

* * *

The many types of Hausa *wakoki*—oral, written, praise song, royal material, and nonroyal material—are distinct but not completely different from one another. Their forms overlap, as do their functions in Hausa culture. The Hausa *waka* genre has undergone many changes over the past few centuries, evolving through continually changing foci. The spread of Islam, the influence of Western culture, changes in public education policy and attitudes toward those changes, and incipient revisions in men's and women's social roles are all reflected in popular *wakoki,* both oral and written. Change in language usually follows in the wake of major cultural influences, and the Hausa language has been enriched with terms and structures particular to each period of change and external influence. As a means of social expression, Hausa poetry communicates what is culturally significant, simultaneously expressing the complex network of historical influence on Hausa culture.

In Northern Nigeria, the range of poetic expression is extensive, covering oral extemporaneous performance in addition to written, published works of strictly rhymed metric verse. Between these extremes, women performing artists combine methods of creative expression and performance in a multitude of ways. But no matter what the woman's educational level, her experience as a Muslim informs her use of the spoken, rhymed word, and it inevitably reflects what she has internalized as a practicing Muslim.

Hajiya 'Yar Shehu, 1979

Profile Two: Hajiya 'Yar Shehu, Hausa Poet

Hajiya 'Yar Shehu was born in 1937 in the village of Dambatta, on the
outskirts of Kano.[1] Like Hauwa Gwaram, Hajiya 'Yar Shehu attended
primary school and received extensive Qur'anic training in her youth. Her
father was an imam. She worked in a hospital for a year before marrying,
had one child, and then divorced. For a while after her divorce she worked
as a teacher and then joined the ground crew of Nigerian Airways at Kano
International Airport, where she worked her way up to supervisory head,
an unusually important position for a Muslim woman in the public sector.
In this capacity she made regular trips—about two dozen—to Makka, us-

ing her Arabic skills as a translator for Hausa pilgrims on hajj. Upon retirement from Nigerian Airways in 1981, she established a concrete-block business, employing several men to make and deliver concrete blocks in Kano. Like Hauwa Gwaram, Hajiya 'Yar Shehu was also a member of Mudi Sipikin's Wisdom Club in Kano in the 1960s, and many of her poems date to that era. Although she said that she had little time or interest in writing poetry after the period of club activities, each time I visited her in Kano (1979–1982) she had several more poems to recite for me, admitting she "had to write this one because [she] was inspired" by something. Like Hauwa Gwaram, Hajiya 'Yar Shehu also lamented that she saw no young women who were interested in learning to write poetry:[2]

> 'YS: Children nowadays are not even prepared to go to the school they are sent to. What they have in mind is just watching the video. This sort of habit can destroy their studies, or it will affect their studies and it is just by luck that someone will get through. You get more songs from children who go to school than from those who spend their time watching television. The song comes out better when it is written and it is more commonly accomplished in a place where they study [instead of where they waste their time].

Initially, Western education in Nigeria had no place for Hausa poetic composition. Although it was unusual for girls to attend primary schools during the 1940s, both 'Yar Shehu and Hauwa Gwaram did. Their creative composition occurred in spite of education; 'Yar Shehu's teacher tried to discourage her "writing habit" from the start, fearful that it would only disrupt her studies:

> 'YS: My father was an Arabic scholar. He didn't teach us himself—he taught adults— but he got us a teacher. I finished the Qur'an when I was nine. [This refers to the memorization of the entire Qur'an (114 chapters), an accomplishment which only the very brightest and diligent of students achieves.] I began [memorizing it] when I was three—that's when we normally began studies in my family. I began writing songs when I was nine. At that time, I was collecting verses. I would sing them if I saw that they rhymed. But since I wasn't aware of the use of preserving them, I just tore them up. I can remember the first song I did while I was in Arabic school. There was a song I made and our teacher demanded that I explain it to him and tell him who had taught it to me. I told him I just felt like making up a song. During the time I was singing that song the other children would answer [as in the call-and-response pattern of a song]. I can tell you a few lines from that song. I started by saying "Alifun kabla lamaini." I asked the children to say "La illah ha illalah." [Then] "Alifun aula lal isni," and they would answer "La illah ha illalah." "Waha in gayatun rasni," and they'd answer "La illah ha illalah." Now I've told you three lines of the song and the choral response. This was the first song I wrote but it was a very lengthy one. I did it myself and I had the children answer me and then the teacher forced me

to tell him the meaning of the words, to translate it for him. So I translated it for him. And from then on I was doing little songs that concerned my schoolwork. He told my parents that if they didn't forbid me to do such songs I wouldn't do any schoolwork. From then on I was prevented from doing songs.

'Yar Shehu's experience reveals typical aspects of childhood in Muslim Northern Nigeria and emphasizes the importance of Qur'anic education in shaping thought and mode of expression. Memorization is the first step in internalizing the Qur'an, and as the children progress in age they learn writing skills as they practice writing the verses. This practice has many purposes in the Islamic education process. As a spiritual endeavor it allows the internalization of the word of God, and as an intellectual exercise it places all of the Qur'an at an individual's fingertips. Qur'anic language is used in a practical mode, expressing guidance necessary to an individual's daily life. It is not surprising that Hausa poetry should reflect similar worldviews and functions. Like Hauwa Gwaram, 'Yar Shehu had first-hand experience in Qur'anic study. It was literally the ideal to be followed. And like Hauwa Gwaram, Hajiya 'Yar Shehu became a primary school teacher.

Although she was forbidden to compose verse while she was a student, 'Yar Shehu began writing in earnest as an adult. Her works are chronicles of historic events in Northern Nigeria:

> 'YS: [A]fter I grew up I started writing songs, some of which I destroyed, some I preserved. The songs I preserved were the songs I did on the first political regime, even though I'm not a politician and I'm not interested in politics. But if an important man has done something important, especially something in the development of the country, I should write a song for him, even if I had to do it without a chorus. Because of its importance to me, I would keep it, since there's nothing more important to me than the progress of my country. . . . During the first political regime [1960s], I did political songs. I did a song for Ahmadu Bello—peace be upon him— the premier of Northern Nigeria . . . [then] the government was overthrown and another came in. Before General Yakubu Gowon, the former head of state, asked people to make songs for the soldiers, I did a song concerning everything that happened then from the day they started the war to the time Enugu was captured.

Here 'Yar Shehu refers to the era of the civil war in Nigeria.[3] Her account of that war is over 100 verses long.

The Qur'anic background of Hajiya 'Yar Shehu is the foundation for the composition style and didactic nature of her material, but it also instilled in her a sense of responsibility for the quality of the works she produced. Islamic philosophy concerning artistic harmony involves the attitude that a reciprocal relationship exists between artistry and morality; the "harmony of the art can in subtle ways instill moral discipline in the viewer" (Renard 1996, 126).

THREE

Performing Artists

POETS AND SINGERS

WOMEN PERFORMERS IN KANO, NIGERIA

In Hausa culture, poets include both performers who recite their own verse and those who sing alone or accompanied; words delivered in these specific stylistic contexts constitute the art form called poetry. But artists and audience members alike are eager to distinguish between poets and singers. Seven women performers are profiled here. Of these, only the first two are literate poets; the rest are singers. Hauwa Gwaram and Hajiya 'Yar Shehu write poems, while Hajiya Ajuji Maizargadi, Hajiya Faji, Hajiya Binta Katsina, Hajiya Maimuna Barmani Choge,[1] and Hajiya Hauwa Mai Duala perform extemporaneously. Poets Hauwa Gwaram and Hajiya 'Yar Shehu spent most of their adult lives in or near Kano,[2] while performers Binta Katsina and Maimuna Choge traveled around Northern Nigeria, performing at public and private celebrations. The others remained in their own towns for most of their performances. When I visited Kano and Sokoto in September of 2002, I found that women singers continued to be popular. Hajiya 'Yar Kaɗa[3] and her group of seven accompanists performed for a television broadcast in Sokoto, for which she also gave an interview. Other women singers not covered in this book also have been popular: Fati 'Yar Issa, 'Yar Kana, Hauwa Mukkunu, and Uwaliya ma Amada.[4] Hausa scholars are working with women singers and poets, collecting and analyzing their works, which are an important part of Hausa popular culture.

SINGERS, MUSICIANS, AND POETS

Until now studies of poetry and song in Hausa culture have focused on poets who write, male praise singers, popular singers, and musicians (Ames and King 1971; Daba 1981; Furniss 1996; Muhammad 1977; Smith 1957), but none has profiled just women singers.[5] Praise singers have been described as praise shouters, or "masters of begging" (pl. *maroka*), as often as they are called "masters of song" (pl. *mawaka*) because they rely on the patronage of their subjects for their income. The praise singer's low social status has been the subject of studies that emphasize the singers' high income and powerful capacity for social influence, even in the face of their low social standing. They are often considered to be nonprofessionals. However, the social status of a poet is higher than that of singers and musicians, perhaps because literacy and the pursuit of knowledge are so highly esteemed in an Islamic culture. Despite the existence of a rich variety of popular song that defines contemporary Hausa culture, most scholarly works have focused narrowly on the extremes of the continuum: they describe praise song as ephemeral entertainment and poetry as permanent, written work. In fact, the complex array of Hausa singers and songs belies this simple description. A portrait of chaos is more accurate; each form of musical artistry overlaps with many others and each singer influences and is influenced by others in his or her performance.

The singer is less likely than the poet to see his or her performance in print unless someone records and transcribes those works, as is the case here. But contemporary music is popular throughout the culture, and its form depends upon its function. Singers mix words and music, performing with or without accompaniment, touring the region for performances, and sometimes cutting records or recording songs for radio and television broadcast. Hausa musicians never perform on the streets or without invitation but always for specific events to which they have been invited as paid performers. Among the women in this category, some have female choruses or bands with whom they can perform for both public mixed audiences or in private, exclusively female settings. In a royal setting, the emir has his own royal musicians, men whose job it is to perform only for him, for special occasions throughout the year (Besmer 1971).[6]

Performers in the category of praise singer function as public relations people promoting specific patrons, which they accomplish by shouting praise epithets without musical accompaniment. A praise singer's status depends on the patron served and the material produced, both of which affect audience perception of the role. The only female praise singers widely known in Kano perform only in the royal setting; it would be unseemly for an adult woman to be wandering around the city, soliciting money on the streets. Royal settings provide the most richly compensated venue for the delivery of praise epithets. Since the royal praise singer is attached to the royal house, it is rare that he or she will perform for other patrons, although exceptions sometimes are made, as in Maizargadi's case, discussed below.

Other public praise singers for wealthy patrons act as freelance artists, performing for various individuals on special occasions. Their purpose is to confirm the high status of the patron, and the quality of their praise determines the compensation the patron gives them.[7] Beggar singers (m., *maroka*; f. *marokiya*) imitate the form, hanging about the streets, shouting praise epithets for whomever they see whose attire and/or entourage indicates ability to pay. These shouters of praise epithets are poorly regarded in society and are seen as having little skill, perhaps by virtue of their not having honed their craft sufficiently to have acquired a high-status patron. It is only men who shout praises for strangers in the streets.

Distinct from a *mawakiya*, a *zabiya* (pl. *zabiyoyi*) performs for the emir and lives near the palace so that she may be summoned whenever she is needed. Because she is supported by her patron, her status is higher than that of a *mawakiya*. The term *zabiya* has been said to come from the word for guinea fowl because the woman's ululations are said to sound like the bird's shrill cry.[8] But the royal *zabiya* does not ululate, as the *marokiya* who accompanies her sometimes does. Women residents of the palace distinguish adamantly between those who shout praises and those who ululate, explaining that the work of the *marokiya* is different from that of the *zabiya* and less complicated. The *marokiya* women merely "speak praise epithets when the emir passes by, they say 'Tread softly (*Takawa a hankali*)'" and ululate. Conversely, the *zabiya* proves herself to be a professional singer by the skill of her performance. Women in the harem recognized Maizargadi's work as that of an accomplished artist because of her ability to sustain running narrative replete with both epithets and historical allusions.[9] The royal *zabiya* may also receive a royal title, thus raising her status above that of the *marokiya*.[10] Thus, the *zabiya* holds a higher social status.[11]

PERFORMANCE STYLE

Performance style varies among women, depending on the type of *waka* they deliver. Hauwa Gwaram and Hajiya 'Yar Shehu are the only two of the artists in this book who set their poems down in writing. As is indicated in their profiles, their literacy and love of the poetic mode derives from the influence of their fathers, imams who encouraged their daughters to study, memorize, and write the Qur'an. Hauwa Gwaram and Hajiya 'Yar Shehu read their poems for me to record, just as they had read them for the radio stations that recorded them. Whenever their poems are broadcast on public radio, these women continue to perform in public through the proxy of their own voices on tape without violating their commitment to a discretely private, if not secluded, life. In the process of reading, they would often pause to repeat a line correctly, using the same process followed by scholars whose reading is a confirmation of the correct form of another poet's work, like that of Nana Asma'u.[12] Their readings were not exciting to watch, nor were they intended to be; body movement does not play a role in the recitation of written poems, as it does in performance of oral *wakoki*. The poems written by poets like these are created for the express purpose of teaching; the poems are didactic and function to educate whoever hears them. The status of the poets is not tied to the works they produce, nor are they necessarily compensated for written poems, contrary to the situation of performers of oral extemporaneous songs.

Poets who read their works sit quietly, while singers entertain public audiences actively. They incorporate extensive gesture and body movement into their performances, like the sixth-century Arab poet-singer al-Khansa, who is said to have "rocked and swayed, and looked down at herself in a trance . . . [demonstrating] in orality . . . a 'meeting in action' of voice, body, word and gesture" (Adonis 1990, 16). Hausa women singers speak to their audiences, reading the reactions they invoke and modifying their presentation to maintain the interest and delight of the people watching. Those who perform praise declamation (*yabo*) for emirs follow a performance pattern more rigid than that of the nonroyal performers. Their repertoire is less freely arranged, geared to an accounting of historical facts and praise epithets for their patrons. Nevertheless, they use gestures to emphasize certain points. Maizargadi did not play an instrument as part of her regular repertoire, nor was she accompanied.[13] Instead she sang solo, either seated or in procession, preceding the emir. Her gestures were limited to the use of her arms; she jabbed at the sky with her index finger as she punctuated certain specific epithets with her voice. Such technique was especially a part of her late arrival at the palace inner compound, when the emir was already seated in his reception room. On these occasions, she entered the harem courtyard from the back gate, pausing at the entryway and then every few steps. Her hesitant pace was due to her lameness, but Maizargadi used the circumstances to her advantage. With every pause in her progress, she proclaimed another praise epithet, pointing to the sky for emphasis and shouting epithets modeled on those found in traditional Hausa king lists. In this way, Maizargadi transformed her late arrival and slow progress into a celebratory procession in praise of the monarch.

The performance styles of other solo women musicians vary. Some, as did Hajiya Faji, accompany themselves on an instrument while they sing; she plays the one-stringed lute (*kukuma*) and sings. Others played instruments and were accompanied by the voices and instruments of other women or men accompanying them on the *ƙore* (calabash) or *garaya* (guitar-like instrument made from a gourd) and as a chorus. Occasionally a praise singer's own husband was among the accompanists.[14] Binta Katsina often would beat her fingertips on an upturned calabash (*ƙwarya*) and sing without accompanists. Sometimes other musicians accompanied her, sometimes she sang alone. Her accompanists varied, depending on the situation. In public performances three men assisted her, playing *garayu* (pl.) and *ƙore* (pl). For performance in more private circumstances, she delivered songs solo or was accompanied by a group of women singing and drumming on calabashes (*kidan kwarya*). Maimuna Choge's public performances are lively. She does not play an instrument, but she dances evocatively to get the audience's attention, shaking her hips to accentuate her lyrics. Ames points out that the appeal of successful performers "lies in their ability to titillate" (Ames 1973, 147), but his emphasis is on the power of lyrics to evoke an emotional response in an audience. The public performances of *zabiyoyis* often rely on body movement and gesture to highlight images or to express them metaphorically.

Within any harem, however, whether in a palace or just a large house-hold, the music and dance are of a different nature than that exhibited in public settings. While it remains unrestrained, it is divested of its bawdi-ness. Due to the size and nature of their instruments, calabash drummers (*masu kidan kwarya*) in the Kano royal harem do not move around during performance. A group of six to ten women (though their number can vary greatly) sit on the ground in the courtyard with their overturned calabashes placed before them. Occasionally two women share one large calabash, each playing a different rhythm stroke, while the other musicians beat their own calabashes, using a fist, palm, or stick. Sometimes overturned cala-bashes are floated inside larger, water-filled calabashes and beaten with sticks to produce a different sound. This is called drumming on water (*kidan ruwa*). The hollow sound produced by beating calabashes overturned on water is distinct from that produced by beating calabashes overturned on the ground. Further sound variation is achieved according to the range of the calabash's size. As these women play music and sing, some audience members dance to the music, while other observers pay musicians, placing money on the singers' foreheads or directly in the laps of the musicians, with whom the dancers ultimately share all donations.

Other musical performances in the Kano palace involve women danc-ing in groups. When there is percussion with broken calabash pieces (*kidan mara*; *kidan sakaina*), the clattering effect of tapping calabash pieces to-gether creates the musical milieu for a dance in the round, in which younger women participate. Two lines of women wend their way into the center and then back out again to the circle's perimeter, clapping calabash pieces in time and singing.

The women who dance (*rawan kidan sakaina*) are often younger than the *kidan kwarya* musicians, and they usually have young children. They spend time with their children, telling stories that often include songs, playing word games, and reciting riddles and tongue twisters. Such mother-child interactions occur whenever there is leisure time together and when the children are not away from home playing with friends or marketing goods. The songs these women share with their children are largely didac-tic; they teach counting and verbal skills and instill codes for socialization.

Some young women play the long narrow *shantu* during the evening hours after dinner to entertain the children and other young women of the household. Because this music requires exposing the leg, *shantu* music is not performed in public, only in the privacy of the harem, among other women. It is often felt that the songs that complement *shantu* music are songs of co-wife jealousy (*kishiya*) (Yahaya 1973), but in fact they are songs that involve teasing or praise. Performed at dusk, *shantu* music is the appropriate platform for the expression of the ambiguous reference to the unmentionable: implications of young brides' evening activities, allusions to the *kunduru* (short girl) or to someone's having "done *tusa*" (passed gas) elicit gales of laughter and provide lively entertainment for the household. They are not at all scathing critiques of other women but light entertainment for the end of the day.[15]

While older women play *kidan kwarya* music and younger women perform work songs, children's songs, or celebratory songs on special occasions, groups of young girls also perform together, singing game songs or narrating to their friends and siblings the stories they hear from their mothers. On festive occasions, especially on the last four days of the month of Ramadan, during which Muslims fast, young girls wander around the community singing together like itinerant *maroka* (professional beggars) to collect gifts. This particular type of activity (*tashen salla*) is not real begging, despite the small contribution that is invariably offered to and accepted by them. Their performances signal the imminence of the lavish celebration that is to come during the festivities (*hawan salla*). Young girls' musical activity is in this way an important part of setting the community mood for the occasion that will follow.

In all musical performance, women are at greater liberty than men to entertain their audiences, and women may be more demonstrative than men. Ames observes that

> [m]en are not very demonstrative either in words or gestures. The size of the audience and the gifts given to a musician best indicate opinion. The donor quietly gives a gift to a professional praise shouter[,] who announces it to the crowd and transmits it to the musician. (Ames 1973, 146)

This process occurs when women perform as well, but the donor and the performer are both far more flamboyant. Affluent audience members flash large bank notes, dropping them in musicians' laps or at their feet, eliciting from the audience excited shouts of approval.

Female performers' deliveries also are often considerably more animated than men's. Whether during a naming ceremony performance restricted to women or for a mixed audience at a public gathering, a woman musician feels free to shake her head and toss her hips to illustrate her lyrics. With their gestures, women evoke enthusiastic audience response that is difficult for the "bearded ones" (*masu gemu*), that is, mature men, to elicit. Proper Hausa men are reserved, and restraint is expected of them at all times.[16] It is women who convey a true festive spirit in performance, inspiring the audience response that is the mark of a good performer. Their traditionally private social position affords women entertainers the freedom to play at their musical artistry, whether they are considered to be professionals or not.

INHERITING SINGING:
SOURCES OF ARTISTIC CREATIVITY

Among the Hausa, craft professions are inherited patrilineally within a family, so a musician's son or daughter will learn from his or her father how to play an instrument. A son traditionally assumes his father's ethnic identity and profession, along with the social standing attached to the profession.[17] "One of the most distinctive features of Hausa society is the place of the father, through whom descent and ethnic origin are rigidly derived" (Adamu 1978, 5; Ames 1973, 129). In homes where secular verse and music are part of daily life, mastery of these forms is a talent of which to be proud.

While the Hausa woman's primary role is a domestic one, it is sometimes the case that a man without sons will teach his daughter to sing and play the instrument he plays professionally. This process of taking on a man's role further underlines the process of "ungendering" by which women singers achieve a greater freedom of movement than most women in Hausa society. This is the circumstance that accounts for the rare case of a woman playing a wind instrument, which is felt to be an instrument that can damage a woman's reproductive capabilities. A woman might marry into the profession too, becoming a singer in her husband's band. But as is often the case with artists, Hausa women's musical and poetic talents are their own, not imposed by a tradition of inheritance. As a woman scholar in Sokoto noted, there are many singers, but they are inspired, not trained.[18] Maizargadi is a prime example of this; although she learned from her musician father, it was not until she visited Kano and stood before the palace that she was inspired to sing praises for the emir (see profile). A musician's inheritance of the father's craft and ascribed status seems not to apply as broadly to women singers (Ames 1973, 152); women performers are less likely to have inherited their professions than men and are less often fixed with a lowered social status as a musician than men.

The daughters of contemporary female artists have expressed little interest in learning their mothers' professions, choosing instead to continue their education or assume a domestic role. The consensus among Kano women was that fewer and fewer girls were interested in such a career at all. Hajiya Maizargadi echoed the sentiment. Neither her daughter nor her granddaughter was interested in taking her place as praise singer for the emir. A woman in the Kano palace complained on a wedding celebration day that only two or three groups of young girls had come around to entertain the women in seclusion: "They don't do what they are supposed to do anymore, they just sit around instead."[19] Perhaps the diversions that preoccupy young girls who are expected to sing songs in the private women's quarters are the same as those that preoccupy other young women who turn to Western entertainment instead of traditional forms and Western education or domestic roles as paths toward greater economic security and social status.[20]

Although traditionally the Hausa poet's craft is passed through a family, the lure of modern times seems to threaten the continued existence of Hausa poetry; fewer, it seems, are learning the craft, and fewer still are teaching it. The lament familiar in the West is also heard among creative artists in Kano: they complained that the younger generation was apathetic, focused only on modern life and material success, lacking—or ignoring—inspiration for poetic composition.[21]

TRAINING EXTEMPORANEOUS SINGERS

Some women performers inherit their interest in, if not talent for, singing, as is the case with Maizargadi, but many successful singers are self-taught (Ames 1973, 157). Women artists often teach themselves by observing others or paying a teacher to help them master an instrument, as Hajiya Faji did. When a woman is interested in learning to sing or play an instrument, she can ask a local musician for lessons. After agreeing on payment—usually a set amount per session and additional material gifts—a time is set for each lesson. The student is expected to practice between these sessions. The training technique involves an imitative approach, in which the student watches and imitates the instructor's manner. Such "conscious instruction" (Ames 1973, 152) is patterned on the Qur'anic education system of rote learning at the lower levels, in which each lesson is written, chanted, and repeated until it is committed to memory. This procedure depends heavily upon the practical application of effort rather than the analytic evaluation of technique.

Just as Hausa musicians teach by demonstrating their own styles, they also observe the styles of other musicians, borrowing tunes and imitating one another regularly. Such sharing is common among Hausa performers (Ames 1973, 152), and although each piece is ultimately an original composition, familiar rhyme schemes and metric patterns are often used as frames for new compositions. "The audience expects . . . a Hausa oral poet

. . . to compose his own original works" (Daba 1981, 209), yet sharing is also a significant feature of written poetry, dating back to traditions of pre-Islamic Arabic poetic style and involving the techniques of reworking a poem through the addition of lines, as in *takhmis*.

Women are well acquainted with songs broadcast on radio and television, and they often can cite the original piece on which the author has modeled the work.[22] It is not unusual to see someone acting out the part of the singer, imitating the voice and, if watching television, repeating the gestures that are an integral part of the performance. Thus they demonstrate familiarity with both an established canon of works and the contemporary performance of revitalized versions of the originals.

SINGERS' SOCIAL RANKING
AND COMPENSATION

Hausa culture has a long and rich history of oral traditions, but it also reveres the written word that is conveyed through a long history of Islamic cultural influence. As in many cultures, the acquisition of education and literacy is a measure of one's social status, and the ranking of musicians is lower than that of poets and scholars. Women singers who perform extemporaneous oral poetry often break the cultural rule of inheritance of professions. Professional male performers often have been trained by their fathers, demonstrate technical competence, and derive economic security from this specialization (Ames 1973, 130–131). In addition, male musicians often are formally attached to the emir or a professional music group.

In contrast, women performers are unlikely to have been instructed in their craft by a parent; they more often draw on their own inspiration and creativity in developing a musical style and act as free agents in setting their own performance agenda rather than being tied to a particular patron.[23] They acquire professional status by virtue of their skill and the compensation they receive for performance, even without formal training, and seem to be engaged in the profession simply because they enjoy it. Many male musicians have indicated that they would not play for their own pleasure if they shifted to another primary occupation (Ames 1973, 152).

Once they have achieved sufficient notoriety, musicians begin to earn money for their performances, both from the family that hires them and in cash gifts given by audience members during the performance. Singers may earn two to five thousand naira when they are hired and another fifteen to fifty naira in tips from the audience. The songs they perform that praise high-status guests bring in the most money, in turn enhancing the singer's own status.[24] Because economic status is a means to achieving social status, those who can earn a great deal of money in performance ignore the cultural social stigma attached to singing; as they pursue their vocation, they raise their social status in another way, through their incomes (Smith 1959, 3; see also Ames 1973; Besmer 1971).

Poets, on the other hand, rarely earn any money at all, but their profession is well respected because of their literacy and the association of poetry with Qur'anic style. Because poetry does not provide income, there are fewer poets than singers. A woman doctoral student at the University of Sokoto who is writing about women novelists in Northern Nigeria explained the dearth of poets: "Well you know money is an unspoken issue; you don't sell as many volumes·of poetry as novels."[25] We agreed that poets—like most artists who rely on their craft—are poor the world over.

Western scholars attest to the low social status of Hausa musicians, but a low social rank often belies the functional importance of musicians in society. The social functions and meaning of Hausa song are intricately related; often the status of the performer corresponds to the degree of seriousness of the message (Smith 1957). The alleged inverse relationship between a performer's social status and that performer's wealth indicates an important feature of the freedom a singer enjoys. The low social status assigned to praise singers (who nevertheless may amass a great deal of wealth from their patrons) allows them to say what those of higher social status cannot say; they may ridicule or defame as easily as praise, albeit keeping within the parameters of what is allowable. Everyone loves praise singers, but as a woman in the Kano palace said to me about male praise singers, "You would not want your daughter to marry one."[26] The women who compose and perform oral poetry choose to do so, accepting greater economic and performance limitations than men do because they are freelance performers, an indication of their sincere interest in their artistry. Perhaps because income is not the pressing concern for women that it is for men, women singers are free to enter the profession solely on the basis of its artistic appeal to them.

Zabiyoyi are paid on an entirely different basis than women poets. An emir may support any number of *zabiyoyi*,[27] but they are not paid as the male royal musicians are; instead they are kept on salary. This ensures that they will perform exclusively for him. *Zabiyoyi* also receive gifts of housing, clothing, and food, sometimes even a horse. Some of the women in this study earned money by recording for radio and television stations.[28] But few performers are successful enough to rely on their craft alone for income. Someone like Maizargadi, a widow with no extended family to assist her, needs to seek income through their work as a man would, but other women singers had financial support from their husbands, indicating that their dedication to their craft is motivated by the desire to create, rather than by financial need.[29] That some women continue to perform extemporaneously in public in a society that ostensibly demands their seclusion is testimony to their genuine interest in their work. American musicologist Alan Merriam argues that musicians' standing as professionals should be founded on a consensus about their dedication and craftsmanship rather than on the amount of wealth derived from performing: "[P]ublic recognition of musicians as a distinctive class of specialists is basic to identifying them as professional regardless of the amount of economic support received from that activity" (Merriam 1964, 125). This surely is the case among Hausa women singers, whose dedication to their craft persists despite social expectations that the profession is a man's.

MUSICAL INSTRUMENTS

Women's musical practice in the privacy of the harem underlines the pervasiveness of singing even among nonprofessional women. Song cannot be separated from musical instruments in Hausa culture; they rely on each other and often flow organically from daily work routines. Women whose songs are part of other activities than professional performances are busy doing tasks for which their music is designed, whether grinding millet, playing games with children, or inducing trance in a spirit-possession cult. Hausa women play a variety of instruments, but they are most commonly associated with calabash drumming (s. *kidan kwarya*; pl. *kore*). The calabash is the tool that is most commonly used both in domestic activities and as a musical instrument. The larger calabashes are round gourds cut in half for use as mixing bowls or as containers for large quantities of grains, fruits, or vegetables. Smaller gourd bowls are used as cups, spoons, and dishes. The calabash may be used in a variety of ways as a musical instrument, too. Its most popular use is as a percussion instrument; a round gourd, cut in half, creates two bowls. The bottom of the bowl is beaten like a drum, with a stick, fist, or the palm of the hand. But calabashes are used for other instruments as well, serving as the resonator bowls for stringed instruments, like one-stringed lutes (*kukuma* and *goge*). For these, the open sides of small calabash halves are covered with animal skins to create a resonator. A long piece of wood inserted in a hole drilled in the side of the bowl serves as the neck of the instrument. Gut or horsehair serves as the lute's string and bowstring. Broken calabash pieces (*mara; sakaina*) are useful as bowl scrapers in cooking, but they also are used as clappers in line and circle dances.

The *shantu*, a long narrow gourd, is an instrument even more closely associated with women than the *kwarya* because of its use in the application of henna, a cosmetic stain that Hausa women apply to hands and forearms. Long narrow gourds cut in half at their midpoints function as protective coverings; women apply the henna and insert their arms in the gourds for several hours, until the stain takes effect. Traditional *shantu* musical instruments are made of this kind of gourd, approximately two feet long, four to six inches in diameter, cut open at each end and decorated with intricate wood-burned designs on the outside. Coating the inside with groundnut oil is said to improve the *shantu*'s tone. The *shantu* is played by a seated woman with one leg folded under her. The player holds the long open tube in her left hand and alternately pops the large open end against her bare inner thigh and slaps the smaller open end with her right hand. The popping noises in sequence create a code of musical communication. The musician's finger rings or a buzzing device like a fixed rattle attached to the outside can produce additional clatter. When she does not have a real *shantu*, a woman may use her body as her instrument, producing *shantu*-like music by slapping her arms and her torso.[30]

A *shantu* may also be blown like a horn, though no woman is likely to play it in this manner, since wind instruments usually are played only by men. Hausa people say that women "lack the strength [i.e., lung capacity] to play wind instruments"[31] and that blowing a wind instrument might damage a woman's reproductive organs. But in the case of the double-reed shawm (*algaita*), which sounds like a bagpipe, not all players are men. An *algaita* player without sons might teach his daughter to play the instrument. The mortar (*turmi*), which is used for pounding grains, is also used as a woman's musical instrument. Pounding the *turmi* in rotation with another woman is called *lugude*. The *turmi* may also be beaten, inside and out, with an animal femur or a stick while women sing in accompaniment for the occasion, in much the same way they do when they pound grain as part of their regular domestic routine.[32]

It is women, not men, who shriek the high-pitched ululations (*kururuwa*; *guda*) ("you-you-you-you") that mark moments of excitement during any celebratory activity. Ululations are common throughout West and North Africa; they mark women's comments on significant public moments, such as during *salla* parades at the close of the month of Ramadan, *bori* activities, and naming and wedding ceremonies. One who uses her voice as a musical instrument in this way is known as *magudiya*.

Aside from using the voice as an instrument for ululations, the instruments described above, although commonly associated with women, are not necessarily restricted to women's use. Musical activity, like many other cultural practices, is not without flexibility, and one often finds exceptions to the norm. Men may play the women's *shantu*, and women may play men's stringed and wind instruments, especially during spirit-possession sessions in which the abnormal is indeed promoted. Perhaps the only rigid rules are those governing the extremes of the gender-oriented scale of musical activities. Women may not play the large drum (*tambari*) used for royalty on only the most special occasions or the long metal horn (*kakaki*) that announces the emir's presence. Similarly, men do not play the *shantu* in the same manner as women, nor do they often use their own work tools and bodies as musical instruments.[33] That women rely on household implements for their music is testimony to the pervasive role of music in women's lives.

* * *

Although both performers and audiences would like to differentiate neatly between singers and poets, the fact is that their areas of interest overlap in style and content. Both types are influenced by the spoken word and the use of musical rhythm. Both types of performers comment on social conditions and individual concerns. And both types must demonstrate sufficient talent to hold audience interest and win audience praise. In each case, the singer or poet uses words and music to convey a message infused with meaning about her social order.[34]

Media such as television and radio have a paramount role to play in the changing situation of Hausa poets, for they make available to all people all types of performances. Through these media, men and women can experience each other's musical performances in a way that was not previously possible without crossing social boundaries. The effect of such access is interesting, for not only are performers influenced by one another's styles but more women may be inspired to write verse in their homes after hearing what other women are composing.

While they encourage new artistic creativity in this way, however, the media may also undermine traditional performance styles by providing wider exposure for fewer performers. Recently interest in *zabiyoyi* and male musicians is more often satisfied by watching televised broadcasts than by supporting live performance in the home. When live performances are appropriate, as for naming and wedding celebrations, they are less and less often considered essential to the festivities. Twenty years ago, the annual celebratory parades around the city (*hawan salla*), perhaps the best cultural example of dramatic and musical ritual, were in danger of being eliminated because of elected politicians' fears of the procession's excessive demonstrations of loyalty to the traditional leader, the emir.[35] Now it seems to be threatened by a preference for televised entertainment.

The media's criteria for taping *waƙoƙi* are also important in determining the viability of the art. Kano and Kaduna radio stations have in their archives many hours' worth of *waƙoƙi* performance by *zabiyoyi*, but the television stations' policies depend on the judgments of men who control programming. While a forty-year-old woman's written material was rejected for taping on the grounds that she was "not old enough to know history,"[36] a woman of comparable age was invited on numerous occasions to tape her extemporaneous works that involved lively body movement illustrating entertaining, often bawdy lyrics. Decisions about what portion of this changing art form is preserved are now being made by men and political leaders rather than by public audiences at large.

Many factors determine a performer's success: age, ethnicity, occupation, wealth, educational level, and mobility. For Hausa women, these factors are ordered differently than for men. While one's age and ethnic background command respect in a similar manner for both men and women, the factors of occupation, wealth, education, and mobility figure differently in the earlier parts of their lives. The early years of a woman's marriage and motherhood impose traditional expectations of restriction in seclusion that are deterrents to mobility and educational and occupational opportunities. For women, access to and license in the public sphere comes with age and maturity, the context in which Hausa women approach equality with men in terms of freedom in public activity. Customarily, only wealthy men could afford to keep their wives secluded, and these women were free to express themselves only by performing music for other women or by writing long poems in verse. Women who appear in public as singers rarely travel as widely within the country as their male counterparts do; I have never heard of a woman traveling abroad to perform as male singers do. Performers make money in live performance, and because men travel more widely and perform more for live audiences, they earn more money as singers than women do. Women performers have worked at a disadvantage in relation to the situation male performers enjoy because of the constraints imposed by gender-related social expectations.

But women's roles at all levels are changing. Not only are more women completing educations that lead to professional opportunities outside the home but women performers are benefiting from technology that levels the playing field somewhat between male and female performers. Women singers can become well known with a minimal amount of travel if they are heard on the radio or seen on television. Several of the women whose poetry I recorded had had their performances recorded by local radio stations. While the payment they had received for radio-taping sessions was long spent, their songs were popular and continued to be broadcast often. In the same way, videotaping sessions with the local television station brought income only once, but the sessions were shown over and over again on evening programs and enjoyed by a large audience. Income cannot be the sole determinant in assessing the extent of an artist's influence; professionalism increasingly is determined by public recognition of talent. Whenever women's songs are given public exposure they are respected and appreciated, a sentiment corroborated by both men and women during my fieldwork in Kano, Nigeria, in January 1979 through June 1980. In follow-up discussions with people in Sokoto and Kano in September 2002, this perspective was confirmed. Despite restrictions on a woman's opportunity to earn a living by her craft, women singers are professional performing artists in Hausa society and will continue to play this role.

Maizargadi and Mai Duala, 1979

Profile Three: Maizargadi, Praise Singer in the Royal Court of Kano

In Kano, the position of royal praise singer (*zabiya*) was held by just one woman, Hajiya Ajuji Maizargadi, the official female praise singer for the Emir of Kano, Alhaji Ado Bayero. Maizargadi was a widow in her sixties when this study was undertaken circa 1980; she died in 1992 in Kano. Maizargadi said that she came to Kano from Ningi as a young woman and was so inspired by the magnificence of the palace entrance gates that she stood transfixed and then began to declaim praises. This is how she came to the emir's attention and became the royal *zabiya.* Maizargadi's father was a drummer (of the *ganga,* the double-membrane drum), and this is the reason cited by others for her skill. Since the talent was in her family and her father taught her how to create extemporaneous songs, she felt free to compose and confident about her ability.

Maizargadi did not write her compositions but delivered them extemporaneously and without accompaniment, which meant that she needed to appear in person, in public. In her younger years she also enjoyed a greater freedom of movement in public than some secluded Hausa women, presumably because she was from the rural town of Ningi, where seclusion was not as rigidly integrated into the social order as in urban Kano. For over twenty years she was a widow; this status, together with her age, allowed her to live independently in Kano and freedom to go where she needed to for praise singing. She regularly declaimed laudatory epithets for the emir at public gatherings and celebrations. In an ordinary week, the Emir of Kano receives greetings from female guests and women of the palace community each Friday morning in the inner courtyard of the palace. Maizargadi and several women shouting epithets strode before the emir to announce his entrance into and departure from his reception room in the harem. The other women are known as *maroka* (f. *marokiya*; m. *maroki*), a term that translates as "professional beggar." These women ululate but they do not proclaim, as the *zabiya* does. The *maroka* may announce the emir's arrival or shout the name of an honored guest, but it is the *zabiya* who strings together images of praise intended to enhance the emir's status both in the privacy of the palace, and in public. Women in the harem recognized Maizargadi's work as that of an accomplished artist because of her ability to sustain running narrative replete with both epithets and historical allusions and confirmed that her status as *zabiya* was unquestionably higher than that of the *maroka*. Although the royal *zabiya* is not honored in a turbanning ceremony, as are many royal male musicians, she may receive a royal title, thus raising her status above that of the *marokiya*.

The daily processional in the palace was not only important for alerting women who happened to be in the vicinity, it was also a means of letting the royal wives know of the emir's arrival in the royal harem. The royal wives are secluded in their suites surrounding the harem's central courtyard, and although they enjoy spacious gardens and open spaces, they do not have windows onto the central courtyard itself. Maizargadi's vocal cues also would signal to court musicians and visiting dignitaries that the emir was ready to receive their greetings. Each Friday morning it was also Maizargadi's habit and obligation to pay her respects to the queen mother (*Mai Babban Daki*), the emir's mother, who lives in her own home just outside the palace. During this visit she would declaim praises for the queen mother as well as for the emir.

Special occasions also called for Maizargadi's presence and performance. For each of the last ten days of Ramadan fasting, the emir receives guests after the final prayer period of the evening. Though most of his guests between ten and twelve o'clock at night are men, Maizargadi would precede him in procession to the outer reception room, announcing his arrival with her song. Maizargadi also participated in the annual *sallah* celebrations that follow the month of Ramadan fasting, which involves a massive parade of dignitaries on horseback from the surrounding rural emirates, and the Id al-Kabir, when rams are slaughtered to commemorate Abraham's obedience to God. At the end of the parade, Maizargadi would lead the emir and his entourage of court musicians as they moved into the harem courtyard. The wives and concubines could watch this last part of the parade through windows onto the courtyard while remaining secluded in their apartments. This is the only occasion when male musicians enter the harem, a tradition begun by the emir's father during his reign in order to let the secluded women of the harem see the parade they would otherwise miss. On these and other occasions, such as palace weddings and naming celebrations or the emir's return from a trip, Maizargadi would sing praises for the emir and his family whenever she could, her age and leg infirmities notwithstanding.

Since she lived just beyond the palace's south gate, Maizargadi could be summoned at any time to perform for the emir, but living outside the palace provided her access to the public arena too. Unlike traditional royal *zabiyoyi*, Maizargadi was permitted to supplement her income by performing on celebratory occasions outside the palace and for individuals who were not members of the royal family. These engagements usually were arranged during the emir's extended absences, as when he traveled outside Nigeria. Maizargadi's first obligation was to him, her primary patron. Such freedom carried no exemption from propriety—because she represented the emir, she was obligated to perform with discretion and always to broadcast praise for him, whatever and wherever the occasion. Maizargadi's age and lameness contributed to her periodic absences from the palace, but performances for other occasions were never a reason for her absence from the palace, where her first loyalty lay. In discussing the continuation of her role, Maizargadi lamented that neither her daughter nor her granddaughter was interested in taking her place as praise singer for the emir.

FOUR

Metaphor

> Metaphor is a bridge to Ultimate Reality.
> —Arab proverb

METAPHORIC LANGUAGE

Hausa women performers say poetic artistry "comes out like water."[1] Both water and good *waka* are crucial to Hausa culture; each is fluid, each is life-giving.[2] Water and poetry are disparate images whose comparison creates an effective metaphor. Water is central to life in Kano, on the edge of the Sahara. Not only is it crucial in sustaining physical life, it is also central to the life of the spirit, as water is important for ablutions five times a day in preparation for prayers. Water purifies, prepares one for prayer, and thus aids in sustaining one's soul as well as one's body. Fine poetry is held in great esteem among the Hausa. Its comparison to water indicates that its value is equally precious. Like good jazz in the West and pure water, good Hausa poetry flows.

While rhyme holds a poetic work together in an established structure, the form alone is empty without original and effective figurative speech to flesh out the image. Metaphor has been recognized since the time of Aristotle as a supreme form of figurative speech. It is the most effective means of imbuing a poem with meaning. Terminology for the elements of a metaphor distinguishes between the bearer of the image, or "vehicle," and the implied image, the "tenor" (Richards 1976). The vehicle is the set of words that creates an image, while the tenor is its implied meaning. In the example cited above, water and poetry are the vehicles, while the tenor is the fluidity and inherent life-giving cultural value that each carries. The images are not compared in their totalities; portions of the images are identified with other parts. Each retains its individual nature while suggesting some aspect of the other.

Among the Hausa, poetic creative capability depends on facility with metaphor, the juxtaposition of disparate images to establish an effect unanticipated by either of those images alone. The more complex a metaphor, the more effective it is. Any network of interrelated visions inspires an emotional response that is difficult to describe but is more effective than an intellectual image; less is more, as linguistic spareness fosters a fecundity of aesthetic appreciation.

Metaphor's necessary combination of images creates far more than the sum of the parts. Not only does a good metaphor require a plethora of related images, but those images should be distinct, even weirdly unrelated. Indeed, the more disparate the images compared, "the stranger the image appears and the more delight it arouses in the soul" (Adonis 1990, 46). The resulting magic conjured by metaphoric language gives poetry a multiplicity of meanings in a simple form. Good metaphor depends on distance from cliché and readily understood simile. A comparison of strangely juxtaposed images challenges and pleases the listener, whose imaginative appreciation of the contrast is at odds with her intellectual understanding. Determining the quality of good poetry is an imprecise science: "[M]eaning in poetry . . . is like the pearl in a shell. . . . Not every thought will lead to the discovery of what it contains, nor every idea be permitted to reach it; not everyone will succeed in splitting open the shell, thereby becoming one of the people of knowledge" (al-Jurjani in Adonis 1990, 47–48). The effort to understand is what underlines the process of appreciation; as Hausa poet Hajiya Mai Duala said, "Crack the shell if you would know the color of the nut" ("Song for the Emir of Ningi," l. 7). Knowing what is at its essence requires effort.[3]

The complexity required of effective metaphor is intensified when dealing with material from another culture; literal meaning can be quantified and translated, but figurative meaning must be intuited and almost never is translatable. Puns and jokes work by the same technique, which is why one cannot laugh at jokes unless one is sufficiently literate in the "cultural language" which facilitates understanding common ground between the disparate images. It is the synthesis of differences that elicits the emotional response in the listener; the "extreme convergence in extreme divergence."[4] Indeed, metaphoric expression defines an audience, unifying them in a mutual understanding of the performer's symbolic allusions and creating a community of the informed. The Hausa poets who rely on metaphoric language in their works appeal to their audiences to interpret what is implied by the metaphorical language they use. The use of metaphor involves "the capacity to form or acknowledge a (progressively more select) community, and thereby to establish an intimacy between the teller and the hearer" (Cohen 1980, 7). The mutual acknowledgment of a metaphor signals a bond between audience and performer. Whether alluding to the unspeakable or the sacred, the poem's multiple meanings are clear to a community of individuals who share a common culture. Thus, the cross-cultural poetic analysis that characterizes studies like this one is a means of examining Hausa culture at its deepest levels.

ISLAM AND METAPHOR

Northern Nigerian Hausa/Fulani women are Muslim, a fact that determines their values, ambitions, and opportunities in ways distinct from the contexts of non-Muslim women. The measure of Islamic influence is little understood in Western cultures; at this point in history, Western scholars are conditioned to expect that Muslim women's lives are restricted by religious tenets that constrain them and limit their chance to express or enjoy themselves. The Hausa Muslim women of this study work through their social system to achieve what they want, just as women anywhere else negotiate demands on their social roles. The Muslim women among whom I lived and whose literary works I recorded for three years in Northern Nigeria are typical of middle-class, moderately educated women in the region. They and their artistry are not exceptions to the social order; they are representative of women in their culture.

Hausa Muslim women's daily life is affected by the importance of the sacred word. From the moment that a child's name and a Muslim prayer of welcome are whispered in a child's ear just after birth, the word of God is meant to have profound meaning for every individual. Children begin the practice of formal prayer five times a day as early as age three or four, even if only in imitation of adults. The ritual of praying five times a day is arguably the most important of a Muslim's five obligations, and through these daily prayers, an individual's attitude toward her relationship to God is shaped. The Prophet Muhammad understood that belief could not be legislated, but habits could be instilled; through the habit of prayer five times a day, a Muslim lives in continued remembrance of God.[5]

The formal prayer performed five times each day familiarizes the average Muslim with the rhyme, meter, and metaphor of the Qur'an. It has been suggested that the Qur'an encourages "poetic" thought over the value of "scientific" thought because its words require metaphorical understanding: "It warns [Muslims] against imagining that the significance of phenomena is limited to their form and appearance, or to their relationship with other phenomena" (Murata 1992, 24). A *hadith* indicates that all creation is full of signs of God: God declared, "I was a hidden treasure, and so I created the world that I might be known."[6] For those who can understand, the word of God is expressed in metaphorical verse, which Muslims appreciate from a very early age as the vehicle for spiritual guidance. Poetic form and the concept of metaphor are familiar to Muslims, even those who are not educated, because daily oral recitation of the Qur'an makes recited poetry an integral part of a Muslim's spiritual life. Poetry—and therefore metaphor—is a familiar part of Islamic life for the uneducated as well as the scholarly (Schimmel 1994, 129). In Muslim culture, poetry is not a literary form separate from the rest of one's life; it is central to the core of one's religious identity, regardless of one's level of literacy.

Muslims believe that the Qur'an is the supreme poetic composition that provides humankind guidance in understanding the meaning of existence on earth and the promise of redemption or punishment after death. The poetry of the Qur'an is not only sacred language but also a message of equity among all, male and female. Barbara Stowasser's study of portrayals of women in the Qur'an argues that the Qur'an is understood as historical information conveyed in several modes: historical stories (Ar. *tarikh*), exegesis (Ar. *tafsir*), and tales of the prophets (Ar. *qisas al-anbiya*). She notes that "the exegetic search for social applicability of the tenets enshrined in the Qur'an's historical tales has . . . been persistent, especially in relation to Qur'anic women figures" (1994, 17). The roles of women are embedded in the written and spoken verse that forms the bedrock of Islamic culture; this poetic mode is neither exclusive to nor of men.

The essence of the message is evident in the ways Qur'anic accounts deviate from Old Testament stories in ways in relation to women's roles. For instance, in the Qur'anic account of the Garden of Eden, Adam's wife (who is not named) was created as an equal partner and complement to Adam (which means only "of the soil"), not as a subordinate creature.[7] Furthermore, the pair was not cast out of paradise for their sins but sent to the world so they might learn to live in a manner that would earn them the reward of paradise (Chapter 20: 123). Nor is Adam's female companion responsible for the imposition of original sin on every human being, because Islam does not recognize original sin. Rather, each child is born without sin and can bring sin upon him or herself only through wrong behavior (Chapter 8:53; 13: 11).[8] The Qur'an is equitable both in what it demands of men and women and in how those demands are expressed to each group. Both men and women believers are enjoined to exhibit right behavior, and the rights and obligations of each ideally are fair and complementary (Wadud 1992).

The equity of gender roles is embedded in the language of the Qur'an, where terms in Arabic masculine and feminine express implicit equity.[9] The fact that the word "moon" is masculine and the word "sun" is feminine do not affect the strength or weakness of the concepts associated with these planets; they are seen as equally strong regardless of the gender attached to the nouns in Qur'anic language. Other studies address the significance of Ibn Arabi's (d. 1240 C.E.) explanation of Ultimate Reality as linked to the feminine gender in grammatical usage as well as in the world. The unusual dominant use of the Arabic feminine gender in the Prophet's discussion of Ultimate Reality is understood to be intentional, indicating the connection of the feminine life force directly to God.[10] Extrapolating further on the implications of Qur'anic language for gender relations, al-Ghazali (d. 1111 C.E.) wrote extensively on the positive nature of the feminine in Islamic language and culture. The Qur'an, the predominant guide in Islamic life, places both poetic form and gender equity at the heart of one's most personal experience, patriarchal influences in many Muslim cultures notwithstanding.

The Qur'an is the primary poetic influence in Hausa culture. Internalizing God's word in its poetic expression is a part of becoming Hausa. Its metaphoric language is replete with imagery that cannot go unnoticed from the very beginning of an individual's Qur'anic education, usually at the age of five. To study the Qur'an involves the assimilation of figurative language and an understanding of simile and metonymy from the very beginning. By the age of four or five, every Hausa child has memorized its opening prayer, the *fatiha* (Ar.; lit., "the opening"):

> In the name of God, Most Gracious, Most Merciful,
> Praise be to God,
> The Cherisher and Sustainer of the Worlds,
> Most Gracious, Most Merciful;
> Master of the Day of Judgment.
> Thee do we worship,
> And Thine aid we seek.
> Show us the straight way,
> The way of those on whom
> Those hast bestowed Thy Grace,
> Those whose (portion)
> Is not wrath,
> And who go not astray. (Sura 1:1–7)

Although it has been compared to the Christian Lord's Prayer in length and intent, the *fatiha* is used far more often than the Lord's Prayer; it is recited in preparation for religious ceremonies and meetings and opens each of the five obligatory daily prayers (Schimmel 1994, 143). The aim of the *fatiha* is to prepare the individual to receive God's guidance, to "open" her to divine communication. Thus, it is not praise but an appeal to God in all His attributes to show the individual the right way to live. To understand its meaning, one must understand the use of epithets for the attributes of God, the metonymic "straight way," and the metaphor of "those who go not astray."

The straight way is right-minded behavior and worship that leads to salvation and unity with God. Indeed, the straight and the crooked are metaphoric expressions of good and evil that are not confined to Islam; they are evident in all Abrahamic religious expression. Those who go astray leave the straight path and lose the means to finding God. Even the youngest child understands this basic metaphor in which spiritual progress is described in terms of physical movement. Thus, one's introduction to literacy, theology, and poetic language happen simultaneously.

Islam and Qur'anic study provide the context in which literacy and morality are learned as integral to one another; the word is the means by which the Islamic value is expressed. The Qur'an presents a worldview in which certain obligations are incumbent upon the person who aspires to right living, and these underline the five obligations, the pillars of Islam by which one lives: the importance of faith, prayer, and charity are self-evident and are readily accomplished without imposing hardship. The observation that there is no compulsion in Islam[11] indicates that what is expected is also made easy for the average person to accomplish; God intended for Islam to be a mercy, not a burden. The spirit of the first three pillars is most readily discussed in the context of Hauwa Gwaram's and 'Yar Shehu's works. These attributes are not described in the abstract but are set in entertaining contexts in which the average Hausa/Fulani woman can understand a means of participating in the active, productive Muslim life of her society. The other two pillars, fasting and pilgrimage, serve to carry one's spiritual commitment to a higher level. Fasting is obligatory; pilgrimage is not. But these are both harder and are treated less often by contemporary women writers.

Being a supportive member of the community (*umma*) is a prime obligation of Muslims. In general, fulfilling one's obligatory role in society is incumbent upon each Muslim. For women, this involves bearing and raising children as Muslims and overseeing the domestic sphere. Men are obligated to provide for their families in every way—not just financially, but also socially, psychologically, emotionally, morally. A man must be a good husband and father, a role model for his family. In addition, specific obligations are described in the Qur'an as obligatory for all Muslims, such as caring for orphans and widows.[12]

A frequent criticism of Islam is that its gender-role obligations restrict people's freedoms, but in addition to the gender roles as described above, it is also incumbent upon each individual to fulfill one's God-given talents to the best of one's abilities. A *hadith* reports that Muhammad indicated any Muslim should be free to travel as far as China in pursuit of knowledge.[13] To seventh-century Makkans, China was the end of the earth, and this is the point. Pursuit of knowledge is a way of seeking God, and every individual has an obligation to follow the path toward Divine Truth. All of these guides for living one's life are discussed in some of the poetic works written by Hauwa Gwaram and 'Yar Shehu. The subject matter of their more pious poetry comes not from other poets but directly from the Qur'an, reflecting basic tenets as set forth in the recitation of God's word. "Qur'an" itself means "recitation of the word of God." Imitating the goal of that sacred recitation, these works serve to inform and guide. In writing them, these women are exercising their God-given talents to promote a greater good.

The *sura* and the *aya* are chapter and verse, respectively. The *aya* "properly signifies any apparent thing inseparable from a thing not equally apparent, so that when one perceives the former, he knows that he perceives the other, which he cannot perceive by itself. . . . God is invisible by definition. Yet, traces and intimations of His awesome reality can be gleaned from all things, if only we meditate on them" (Lane 1984, 135, quoted in Murata 1992, 24). Thus, metaphoric meaning is integral to the concept of *ayat*. Hausa Muslims know metaphor to be the language by which God's intentions are conveyed. At the same time that the Qur'an explains the natural world as the canvas on which God has painted, Qur'anic language discourages "scientific" language in favor of "poetic" language, reasoning that since God is unknowable, all that can be perceived is a sign of His essence. In Islamic cosmology, it is the qualities of things that bear meaning, not the things themselves: "[T]hings are pointers and not of any ultimate significance in themselves" (Murata 1992, 25). In Islam, one never expects to know all of any message, only a part. The metaphorical nature of the Qur'an was recognized as early as the ninth century, when several scholars discussed the centrality of figurative devices in the Qur'an,[14] which include metaphor, metonymy, simile, and allegory and the shifting of voice from second to third person. Scholarly works that examine these devices also emphasize the musical nature of the Qur'an, end rhyme, and meter. Just as each aspect of its language is only a part of the total meaning, the Qur'an's message depends on understanding that each thing in creation is merely a fragmentary sign of God's nature.

Hausa written verse exhibits evidence of Qur'anic language; both Hausa poetry and the word of God are as important to those who are illiterate as they are to those who can read them. Both are transmitted orally, their rhyme and tone cadences functioning as important mnemonic devices for the memorization of the piece. In orally composed Hausa poetry, metaphoric expression is a means of achieving broader imagery through greater verbal efficiency. Its nature is often irreverent, allowing the unspeakably obscene or otherwise forbidden to be implied without being baldly stated.[15] In both written and oral Hausa poetry, metaphor is common to aesthetic communication in Hausa culture and is integral to the Islamic experience. The integration of local with Islamic forms of expression is common: "Muslims throughout the world have continued to use indigenous literary forms in writing Islamic poetry and to indigenize Islam through those forms" (Renard 1996, 125). Although Hausa poetry does not recreate Arabic poetic patterns, the two traditions share a common influence—the inclination toward metaphoric language that is the essence of the internalization of the word of God.

HAUSA PROVERB

The Hausa definition of proverb is itself a metaphor for the phenomenon: it is *karin magana,* literally "folded speech." In his study of ellipses in *karin magana,* Clifford Hill (1972) explains the many metaphoric explanations the Hausa give for the term. They remark that its "foldedness" signals efficiency, like a neatly folded piece of yardage that is easier to carry in its compact state. They point out that the folded cloth conceals the material's true appearance, just as the ambiguous proverb conceals its true meaning. While ambiguity is central to proverbial expression, it is a feature central to other aspects of Hausa communication as well. Many studies address the issue of ambiguity in Hausa praise singing, emphasizing the right of the performer to engage in derogatory epithet, provided the patron is not blatantly—but only subtly—criticized (Hofstad 1971; Smith 1957). As with folded yardage, however, what is hidden in epithet or proverbial expression is concealed within a context familiar to the audience. A proverb compares at least two images. It functions by demanding of the listener an understanding of one or several of the relationships between those images and often requires the subsequent application of that quality to a third image or circumstance. The extrapolation is the proverb's message, just as it is in the riddle, long a means of spiritual teaching in Islam.[16]

A proverb resembles a metaphor in its inherent symbolism and a tendency to suggest parallels between seemingly disparate images. But in his work on ellipses in Hausa proverb, Hill points out that the *karin magana* differs from what is known as Western proverbs in its greater complexity: "[T]he structure of a *karin magana* may contain statement and response . . . [even] many pairs of statement and response, the whole maintaining its unity by sustaining a common set of figures" (Hill 1972, 24). A *karin magana* is commonly created by the juxtaposition of a grammatical segment which lacks a verb and its explicator, leaving the *karin magana* in its most succinct form (Hill 1972, 32). Here is an example from Hill: "Speech is a thatching straw; if it comes out, it can't be put back" (*Maganar zarar bunu; in ta fita, ba a mai da ita*). It is often repeated in its abbreviated form: "Speech is thatching straw" (*Maganar zarar bunu*). In this shorter form, the *karin magana* is a metaphor; the listener must infer diverse and common fields of meaning implied by the co-occurrence of the terms *magana* and *zarar bunu*.

The oral songs examined in this study contain standard *karin magana* more frequently than do the written ones, perhaps because established *karin magana* are easy to recall and include in spontaneous creation. Hauwa Mai Duala includes several *karin magana* in her "Song for the Emir of Kano and the Emir of Ningi," leaving them as isolated comments which may be interpreted according to the listener's preference. Early in her song (l. 5), after praising individuals from Ningi, she remarks: "Whoever despises anything small / Has not stepped on a scorpion" (*kowa ya rena gajere, / bai taka kunama ba ne*; ll. 5–6).[17] Ningi is a small emirate. Hauwa Mai Duala defends the respectability of her town with allusion to it through a proverb that emphasizes that power is not necessarily dependent on size.[18] Immediately following this remark is another that reinforces the sentiment of the first. Mai Duala warns against being misled by appearances: "Crack the shell if you would know the color of the nut" (*Sai an fasa, a kan san bidi*; "Song for the Emir of Kano and the Emir of Ningi," l. 7). In the same work, Hauwa Mai Duala also praises the women of the Kano palace, so her *karin magana* may refer to their ostensibly privileged position in the palace: palace women do enjoy high status, but since they are not allowed access to the larger urban community, such privilege is a dubious one.

Allusions to proverbs—rather than the rote repetition of standard *karin magana*—occur in both songs and poems. In her "Praise Song for the Hausa Conference," Maimuna Choge says the following line to express her appreciation for adequate recompense, "It's during stormy weather that one drinks from the pot" (*Da lokacin hadari ne, ka sha ruwan kwarya*; l. 45; i.e., "Be thankful for what you have got"). While this is not a standard *karin magana,* it bears significant resemblance to a quotidian one: "A storm is not the rain, only its sign" (*Hadari ba ruwa ba ne, alama ce*; i.e., "Don't count your chickens before they hatch"). The expression is the sort of apparent non sequitur that recurs in Hausa songs; it bears implicit meaning that must be interpreted to be understood. It is set between an invocation to God and a declaration of the era in which one lives, and the phrase may be understood to compare stormy weather with modern times. At the same time, she may be expressing gratitude for her material success:

44　For God's sake, let me pray attentively
45　It's during stormy weather that you drink water from the pot;
46　We are now in modern times.

Don Allah in sallata raino,
Da lokacin hadari ne ka sha ruwan kwarya
A zamanin mu na yanzu

In Choge's profession, money is a gift, just as water collected in rain pots is a gift. In each case, however, the gift is not entirely freely acquired; one must make some effort to receive it. One must prepare for it by performing, or at least by setting out pots. She will take what the times provide and be grateful for it.

Written poems are platforms for the authors' creativity in the *karin magana*. Proverbial expressions in written *waƙoƙi* are modeled on common proverbs, reflecting the authors' familiarity with established figures of speech and their desire to hone those expressions to suit their own purposes. Like the overwhelmingly didactic nature of the works' messages, these "created proverbs" are altruistic expressions of support for the political and religious status quo of Kano in the mid-twentieth century and that period's emphasis on development.

In Hauwa Gwaram's "Song for Audu Bako's Zoo," she remarks, "You see, whatever you plant / That's what grows in your garden" (*Ka ga abin da ka shuka, / Shi zai fito gonarka*; v. 22). This resembles closely in structure and import two common Hausa *karin magana*: "The seed that is sown is the one that sprouts" (*Irin da ka shuka, shi ya kan tsiro*; i.e., "As you sow, so shall you reap") and "Whoever sows deceit will find it sprouting on his farm" (*Kowa ya shuka zamba ta tsira a gona tasa*; i.e., "Honesty is the best policy"). Hauwa Gwaram's observation directly follows her praise of former Kano governor Audu Bako and directly precedes the stanza admonishing women to be upright. Such positioning in the poem indicates the proverb's moralistic intent, with Audu Bako as an exemplary figure.

Hajiya 'Yar Shehu repeats the phrase in her "Song of Explanation" on the Biafran civil war: "Everything a person plants / Will sprout without a doubt" (v. 14). This stanza's intention is clear; it is placed between verses of accusations against the Ibos for their transgressions during the war. Hajiya 'Yar Shehu implies that whatever misfortune has befallen the Ibo is retribution for their own actions.

Following in this moralistic vein is Hauwa Gwaram's proverbial advice in both versions of her "Song of Warning to Those Who Take Drugs II": "Seeing [something] in another makes us fear it [in ourselves]" (*Gane ga wane fa ta isa wani na ban tsoro* and *Gani ga wani ya sanya wani ya razana*; vv. 38, 42). Such admonitions, while not standard *karin magana,* are reflective of the genre's structure. The common *karin magana* structure they suggest is represented by this: "Seeing is believing" (*Gani ya kori ji*). This abbreviated form is common in the *karin magana* genre.

In "Poems of Condolence and Praise," Hauwa Gwaram alludes to another *karin magana* with the phrase "They dug us a pit and we fell in headfirst" (*To, sun haka mana rijiya mun wantsila*). This suggests the *karin magana* "If his hysterics are real, let him fall into the well" (*In bori gaskiya ne, a bar shi ya fada rijiya*; i.e., "Foolish behavior leads to disaster"). Hauwa Gwaram's poem observes that a trap was set for the people of the north during the Biafran civil war. Their loss was as significant—albeit on a larger scale—as that of one who through his own foolishness has fallen into a pit.

Following this image immediately, Hauwa Gwaram observes, "We lost trap and bird" (v. 10), suggesting the *karin magana*: "No trap, no bird" (*Babu tarko, babu tsuntsu*; i.e., "He's lost everything, both trap and bird"). The assassination of political leaders Tafawa Balewa and Ahmadu Bello in 1966 represented a significant loss of leadership for northerners, and Hauwa Gwaram's allusions—both that of falling into the pit and the loss of trap and bird—convey the magnitude of the sacrifice.

Hajiya 'Yar Shehu includes "No trap, no bird" in her "Song on the Census of the People of Nigeria." The phrase conveys the sense of waste that results from inaccurate accounting of or by the citizens of Nigeria:

20   . . . leaving one out is not wise;
       It is expelling him from among the people of Nigeria.
21   He's lost trap and bird, too.
       And is left with vain regret here in Nigeria.
22   God save us from doing this, brothers!
       The remedy for it is to tell the truth.

Inaccuracy in census-taking constitutes a dual loss: wasted effort on the part of the counters and the guarantee of disproportionate allocations of federal funds and thus unfair treatment of the nation's citizens. The vehicles of meaning in this *karin magana*—lost trap and lost bird—are negative entities. They emphasize that inherent sense of absence that becomes the tenor, the underlying import of the metaphor. The tenor is consequently applied to other images in the poem itself. The *karin magana*, which functions as a non sequitur until interpreted, is foregrounded by its aberrance in the context. Once interpreted, the meaning conveyed by its tenor can be applied to the larger images in the poem. At this point, it coheres in the work as a whole.

In the same poem, Hajiya 'Yar Shehu repeats her warning against the wastefulness of badly executed work, citing another standard proverb: "No use crying over spilt milk" (*Da na sani' ƙyeya a baya take tukur, / In an fade ta, ku tabbata an sha wuya*; i.e., "'Had I but known' is a past regret / If you hear it, you know someone has suffered"; v. 52). Hill cites several versions of this *karin magana* commonly found in Hausa speech:

"If I had known" is always behind regret.
("No use crying over spilt milk")
(*Da na sani' ƙyeya a baya take tukur.*)
May God curse the horse of "if I had known."
("If I had known" is always behind regret. / "No use crying over spilt milk")
(*Allah wadan dokin ɗa na sani'.*)

The horse "if I had known" is a cripple.

("If I had known" is always behind regret. / "No use crying over spilt milk")

Dokin ɗa na sani' gurgu ne.

Whoever mounts the horse "had I but known" will be thrown.

("If I had known" is always behind regret. / "No use crying over spilt milk")

Wanda ya hau dokin ɗa na sani' zai ka da shi. (1972, 140, 188)

That the Hausa version of the West's "Woulda, coulda, shoulda . . ." expression of regret is so often couched in terms of horseback riding reflects a common feature of traditional Hausa culture, the horse. Hajiya 'Yar Shehu has adapted the standard *karin magana* to fit her own structure. Her version represents a compromise between the straightforward repetition of common *karin magana* and the creative adoption of a *karin magana* to suit particular poetic meter and rhyme patterns.

Devices common to other literary forms among the Hausa also occur in *karin magana* forms. Gizo the spider is the Hausa trickster whose foul talk and irresponsible manners make him the catalyst in many dilemma tales. The danger of reckless chatter, one of Gizo's many bad habits, is expressed in a proverbial expression in Hajiya 'Yar Shehu's poem on the census, in which she says: "[Let's not] fall into the bad ways of loose-mouthed Gizo, / Who, when he couldn't bear something, just shouted louder" (*kada mu faɗa ayyukan shibcin Gizo, / Da ya kasa ɗauka sai ya ƙaro ƙugiya*; v. 8). Her comment suggests many *karin magana* that resemble this: "From a fool's mouth one hears talk" (*A bakin wawa a kan ji magana*; "A wise man holds his tongue"). The stanza that precedes Hajiya 'Yar Shehu's comparison of men with Gizo clarifies her point: "Oh God, the Wise, Your wisdom suffices, / Make us understand so that we may explain the truth, / Lest we fall into the bad ways of the loose-mouthed Gizo, / Who, when he couldn't bear something, just shouted louder" (*Allah hakimu hikimarka da ta isa, / ka sa mu gane don mu baiyana gaskiya, / Don kada mu faɗa ayyukan shibcin Gizo, / Da ya kasa ɗauka sai ya ƙaro ƙugiya*; vv. 7–8). Hajiya 'Yar Shehu continually stresses the need for an accurate count to know the true number of citizens in Nigeria. Failure to achieve this goal renders census-takers no better that lazy Gizo, the embodiment of irresponsibility.

The value of progressiveness in Kano is demonstrated in many of Hauwa Gwaram's poems. In a work that explains new laws of the road during the change from left-hand to right-hand driving, she summarizes her catalogued admonitions by saying: "The drummer changes the beat, so the dancer changes her step" (*Makaɗi ya juya ganga, mai rawa kuma sai ta juya*; v. 16). Inherent in this proverbial expression is the belief that one must not resist progress but must change with changing times. Once again, Hauwa Gwaram has created what sounds like a standard proverb, with two parallel and related phrases, which, by their juxtaposition, suggest a coherent relationship to each other. They are foregrounded in the work because they deviate from the subject of the poem until they are interpreted metaphorically.

Another proverbial expression modeled on *karin magana* is foregrounded in Hajiya 'Yar Shehu's poem for Ahmadu Bello. In the midst of stanzas about Ahmadu Bello, Hajiya 'Yar Shehu remarks, "Lost donkeys don't ask the way; / They are the ones who find fault with you, Shehu the Premier" (*Jakan da sunka ɓace fa ba sa tambya / To, su suke zargen ka Shehu firimiya*; v. 26). Implicit in this image is criticism of opponents of the former premier of the north, Ahmadu Bello. The lack of sense displayed by lost donkeys wandering aimlessly is extended to Ahmadu Bello's enemies, who were responsible for his assassination. They had no interest in learning the way to a better life; their only goal was to destroy what represented the status quo. Such phrasing allows Hajiya 'Yar Shehu to denounce Bello's opponents obliquely, neither accusing them directly nor allowing herself to be criticized for such an evaluation.

HAUSA PRAISE EPITHET

In Hausa, praise epithets are called *kirari,* and many of them together constitute a praise song (*waƙar yabo*). The metaphoric complexity of praise epithets, which make up the major portion of any orally composed praise song, constitutes the overall design of the song. The plan of Hausa praise song is distinct from that of some other cultures, for such declamation usually focuses on the character of its subject with little narrative treatment of his exploits or accomplishments. Instead, Hausa praise song consists of a series of modes of address or praise epithets for that person, listing royal titles, allusions to parentage or offspring, or names relating to one's skills and accomplishments.

Like a proverb, the praise epithet functions by the juxtaposition of two images. It involves calling a person by a nickname that indicates something about that individual, thus implying a metaphoric connection between the two. "Bull Elephant" (*toron giwa*) is a common appellation for an emir, implying his position as the mightiest, the most impressive and powerful among men. The image of a bull elephant, full of strength and impressively large, contributes to the sense of importance the poet wishes to convey about the emir. The Hausa term *girma* (large) is commonly used to designate large size, importance, age, or respectability; that is, a person can be *girma* in many traits other than physical size. Although *girma* is not mentioned with the praise epithet *toron giwa,* it is implied by that expression's implication of massiveness. The many implications of *girma* are implied by *toron giwa* because they both share allusion to massiveness.

Occasionally, as with *karin magana,* the full praise epithet is abbreviated, eliminating the name of the subject. In these cases the referent is understood in context, as the elided second noun phrase is understood in the abbreviated *karin magana.* A praise epithet's referent, however, is usually more clearly recognized than is the elided portion of the *karin magana.* For example, as appositives for the Emir of Kano are delivered in a song performed for him in the palace, their point of reference—Sarkin Ado Bayero—is clarified by the context and without the repetition of his full name. Defined by Hill as a form of *karin magana,* a praise epithet is characterized by its brevity: "Its praise or blame may be rendered clearly by a single noun that represents the subject of praise" (Hill 1972, 27). *Toron giwa* always refers to the emir.

Just as there are standard *karin magana* and innovative forms created by talented performers, so there is a wide variety of types of praise epithet that may be used to describe an individual. Maizargadi's work is perhaps most representative of the plenitude of standard praise epithets in royal praise song (*wakar yabon sarauta*). They compliment the patron they describe and support the political administrations these individuals represent. Maizargadi's position as Kano's royal *zabiya* demanded of her work a focus on the emir and his family, guests, and associates. She regularly depended on many different descriptive phrases in describing the subject of a song. When she described the Emir of Kano, Alhaji Ado Bayero, she sometimes referred to him as *sarki* (king, emir), *mai gadin birnin Kano* (Kano's guardian), *mai gidan birnin Kano* (Kano's leader), *mashasha* (mighty leader), *toron giwa* (bull elephant), *jarma yanka mutane* (slayer of men), *toya matsafa* (burner of fetish groves; i.e., crusader for Islam),[19] or *magajin Kano* (heir to Kano). These descriptive phrases, familiar to her audience, referred only to Alhaji Ado Bayero, the Emir of Kano. But they will also be used to refer to his successor when that day comes; the epithets belong to the office, not the man. When they were used in another setting outside the palace, Maizargadi continued to use them only in reference to her patron, the emir. The only time these phrases may be used to describe someone other than the Emir of Kano is when they are applied to another emir, perhaps in another town. Hauwa Mai Duala, a royal *zabiya* from Ningi who visited Kano, employed such descriptive phrases in a song she performed as homage to both the Emir of Kano and the Emir of Ningi, as a gesture of respect for both her own patron and her host in Kano. These praise epithets are royal praise epithets. While royal praise singers may use them freely to describe their own patron or the patrons of others, they may not use them to describe less important individuals. Since the royal praise epithets are so clearly connected with certain individuals, there is no question about their referents except as determined by context.

Common terms of address for praise epithets include allusions to parentage, using the term "son of" (*dan*), "daughter of" (*'yar*), or "grandchild of" (*jikan*) with a parent's or grandparent's name. In addition to patronyms and matronyms, paedonyms (identification through one's offspring) may be used to describe an individual: *'uban* (father of) and *'uwar* (mother of) are typical examples.[20] Such epithets are frequently used in reference to royalty, especially in royal praise songs and king lists. Alhaji Ado Bayero, the Emir of Kano, is known as *dan Abdullahi* and *dan Bayero* (son of Abdullahi Bayero, former Emir of Kano), as well as *jikan Abbas* (grandson of Muhammadu Abbas, eighth Emir of Kano). The epithet *'uban Ado* (father of Ado) refers to Abdullhai, his father, while Alhaji Ado Bayero himself is described as *baban Usumanu Ahmadu* (father of Usumanu Ahmadu). By citing as many appositives as she can in this manner, Maizargadi adds dimension to the image of her patron.

Maizargadi's praise epithets for the emir's family members often are simply descriptive phrases, linking them with their paternal family members. One of the emir's wives is described as "Fulani Abba, daughter of the town official of Katsina" (*filani Abba, 'yar mai garin Katinsa*).[21] Another person is "Saude, daughter of the Sultan of Sokoto, commander of the faithful" (*Saude, 'yar Sarkin Musulmi*). While these connections confirm the Emir of Kano's relationship to royalty in Katsina and Sokoto, the technique of using such common terminology may be part of songs describing anyone, royal or not.

That individuals are often described in relationship to their family members is indicative of the importance of family among the Hausa. Orientation within a family milieu and its attendant obligations is so important that the Hausa have a special word for the concept: *zumunci* (family ties). But the cataloguing of family connections to describe an individual serves another purpose as well. Listing someone as the parent or sibling of many other individuals is indicative of that person's wealth of relations. While social status is largely determined by one's economic wealth, it is also highly dependent on family membership, which can be illuminated through praise epithets. Maizargadi's principle subject is indeed "the slayer of men" (*jarma, yanka mutane*), but the image one derives from her descriptive phrases depicts the emir as a man whose claim to kingship is buttressed by his strong family ties and associations; genealogy is very important in Hausaland and in Arab-culture countries.

Another common praise epithet construction involves the term "master of" (*mai*) in the grammatical agentive construction. *Mai* alludes to ownership or control over something. The *mai gadi* is a master of guarding; *mai gida* is the master of the house; the *mai gari,* the master of the town (see note 21 in this chapter); *mai gemu,* the owner of a beard (and thus a mature man). The emir's mother carries the title *mai babban daki,* literally the head of a large important room, like her own.[22] The former Emir of Katsina, Alhaji Muhammadu Dikko, became known for his friendly associations with Europeans, particularly the British, thus earning him the praise epithet *mai Turawa* (master of the Europeans, one of them). Royal retainers of the emir are known by epithets for their functions: the royal mat-spreader is *mai kilishi.*

Mai is not gender specific; it attests to anyone's control of or connection to a group of people, a town, a geographic area, or a skill. It is a term that may be affixed to any number of nouns to indicate superiority. *Mai Makka, Mai Madina* (Masters of Makka and Medina) is Maizargadi's epithet for the Prophet. *Mai Kano, Mai Zaria* (Masters of Kano and Zaria) are the emirs of these towns. Emir Ado Bayero is known as *Sarkin birnin Kano* (King, Emir of Kano). By linking all these praise epithets, Maizargadi broadens her imagery, including local towns as well as the destinations of devout pilgrims, in mutual association. The term *mai* is used to create a praise epithet of sacred, royal, or common degree; the status of the individual described depends upon the quality of the word or phrase affixed to *mai.*[23]

Similarly, the term *sarki* (king, or emir) may be used with sacred, royal, or pedestrian import. *Sarkin duniya* (King of the World) can refer only to God, *Mai Makka* and *Mai Madina* can refer to the Prophet, and *Sarkin Kano* describes the King of Kano. While these are not fixed standard praise epithets of the type described as nicknames for the emir, they are fixed descriptive epithets that can only refer to certain individuals. When affixed to more quotidian terms, *sarki* functions much the same as *mai,* denoting mastery of a craft or high status in a certain area. The best soccer player may be known as *sarkin wasa,* king of play, or an accomplished student may be called *sarkin littattafai,* king of the books. Other phrases may be used seriously or sarcastically: *sarauniyar kyau,* beauty queen; *sarkin tuki,* reckless driver; *sarkin dawaki,* chief of mounted squadron; *sarkin kuka,* crybaby.[24]

Praise epithets are also common to written poems. In Hauwa Gwaram's "Song of Condolence for Tafawa Balewa and the Sardauna of Sokoto," she alludes to Nigeria's political leaders as the "stairs of Nigeria," leading the way in the nation's upward, progressive movement: "Three influential people have passed from us; / Stairs to the well-being of Nigeria" (*Jigajigai uku sunka wuce mana; / Su ne matakin lafiyar Nijeriya*; v. 12). Similarly, in her "Song of Condolence for Tafawa Balewa and the Sardauna of Sokoto," Hausa Gwaram employs the term "stairways" to describe individuals who are important to the nation, particularly the Emir of Kano, Alhaji Ado Bayero: "Emir of Kano, Alhaji Ado Bayero, / He is a tower of strength here in Kano" (*Sarkin Kano, Alhaji Ado Bayero, / Shi mataki ne a nan Nijeriya,* v. 47; *mataki* is literally a stairway). The emir's personal example and leadership, she implies, shall lead Nigeria upward in a progressive movement. Every Muslim is familiar with the upward path to heaven that leads one on the way to God, and the concept of the path of Truth is central to Islamic philosophy. The parallel between seeking salvation and Nigeria's path toward cultural progress is clear.

While many praise epithets are associated with men, an undocumented network of associations exists among women as well. Such associations are indicated by praise epithets that attest to the social status of individual women. These praise epithets are of the same wide variety as those that are applied to men. Some are descriptive, such as *'uwar babban daki* or *'yar sarkin Musulmi,* referring to specific individuals. Others may be applied to any context: *'uwar soro* (lit., head of the ground-floor room; senior wife), *'uwar bene* (lit., head of the upper-story room; head wife). Women's royal epithets and praise epithets commonly associated with women beyond those cited here have yet to be analyzed in detail. Such a study will likely reveal a great deal about the network of status relationships among women in the palace and in the town.

HAUSA WORDPLAY

Kirari as metaphoric expression is as common to Hausa communication as proverb; wordplay is the third most prevalent linguistic device for achieving ambiguity in speech. Wordplay involves the briefest of all such metaphoric expressions. Its effectiveness depends on the simultaneous evocation of two images by the use of one term. Brevity is perhaps the key to that effectiveness; it illuminates a broad range of imagery with very few words. Such verbal efficiency is metaphor in its sparest form: one word with a multiplicity of meanings. While praise epithets and proverbs rely on the recognition of relationships between disparate images, the effect of certain wordplay is to create delight in the distinction between homophones or near-homophones. This is achieved in several ways.

Many of the effective double entendre phrases in Hausa literature are founded on word division that renders several possible meanings. Wordplay in Hausa may depend on one term having several meanings or several terms in sequence being divided variously, rendering different sentences depending on where the divisions occur. Wordplay through ambiguous word division is demonstrated in a narrative involving a devout Muslim for whom the consumption of dog meat is forbidden. He and his non-Muslim host are from different, mutually antagonistic ethnic groups. When the host leaves his Muslim guest sitting at a table with food on it, he says to the Muslim, *Kada ka ci karena*—"Don't eat my [dog meat] stew." He is not only warning the Muslim against eating his food but is also identifying the food as dog meat, which he understands is forbidden to the Muslim. But the Muslim, accustomed to feeling antagonistic toward his host, hears instead a tease: *Kada ka ci, ka rena*—"Don't eat this, you wouldn't like it anyway." So the Muslim hastily gobbles the stew, complimenting the host when he returns. The host remarks that he is surprised to learn that Muslims eat dog meat, and finally the Muslim realizes how the warning phrase was meant—and how his attitude caused him to misinterpret it. Although this confusion is founded on ambiguity, the fundamental mutual antagonisms between certain groups are at the root of the misunderstanding.

Wordplay with foreign words is not frequently used in these poems, but occasionally it does occur. One of Hajiya 'Yar Shehu's works on the Biafran civil war ("Song of Explanation about Biafra") contains two examples in close proximity. Describing the leader of the first military regime in 1966 after the country's first coup, she reports leaders' names and the actions they took at the time. Odumegwu Ojukwu, head of the Biafran secessionists, drove non-Ibos from the area he had declared to be Biafra: "Then Ojukwu incited rebellion, / And he sent his guerillas" (*Sai Ojukwu ta ta da bore, / Sai ya turo 'yan amore*; v. 44). When she explained this passage to me, Hajiya 'Yar Shehu made it clear that she intended to express by the term *amore* the image of a large monkey-like animal, but *amore* is the Hausa term for a Fulani highwayman. Hajiya 'Yar Shehu speaks minimal English, so her definition of *amore* as both gorilla and guerilla may be a misunderstanding—or an intentional pun, in which case the joke is on me. In any case, the transformation is relevant and evocative.

Following this passage, which mentions Ojukwu's name, Hajiya 'Yar Shehu recounts her version of the date of the Biafra outbreak: "Then on the sixth, without doubt / Of July, this is the truth, / Biafra attacked / The government was there at its limit" (*Sai a ran shida babu shakka, na ga Yuli hakika, / Sai Biafra sunka afka, kan na gwamnati can iyaka*; v. 46). A prominent leader in the first military regime in 1966 was General Aguiyi-Ironsi, and although he was killed in the July 1966 countercoup, his name is linked with that of his opponent Ojukwu as symbolic of the era. Hajiya 'Yan Shehu's *a ran shida* ("on the sixth day") suggests the sound of the name Ironsi, as she pointed out. Surely this is not lost on the audience. Such subtlety is appreciated in many forms of Hausa communication.

A similar effect is achieved in Hausa Gwaram's "Song for a Visit to the Birnin Kudu Hospital," in which the term *mutuware* carries comparable implications in both Hausa and English. The *mutuware* of the hospital— from the Hausa (verbal noun) term for death, *mutuwa*—is the place where corpses are deposited after death: the mortuary. The similarity of the two words is coincidental, but many individuals who speak both Hausa and English appreciate the punning effect. While it may be argued that *mutuware* exists in Hausa as a borrowing from English, the root *mutu* (to die) is integral to the Hausa language, predating the colonial era and arguably derived from the Arabic. A term that clearly is a borrowing occurs in another line: *Mun je gidan mutuware ɗakin tautsayi, / Mun je dasifansare mui lafiya* ("We went to the mortuary, the emergency room, / We went to the dispensary, where one goes to be healthy"; v. 9). In this case, *dasifansare* is borrowed from the English "dispensary."

* * *

This chapter considers the figurative expression of metaphor through proverb, praise epithet, and wordplay in Hausa *waƙoƙi*. Where they occur, these figurative expressions are occasionally straightforward metaphors. More often they are new images created by the performer herself, though they are modeled on well-known forms of figurative language. Understanding that they are innovative creations couched in familiar form is central to an understanding of Hausa literary aesthetics.

Inordinate dependence on standard proverbs and epithets can change the tone of a work, marking it as antiquated or perhaps less relevant in the context of modern literature of the region; a work that is overburdened with these traditional verbal images may forego a natural style (Hofstad 1971, 30). Chinua Achebe's novels are known for their inclusion of a plethora of Ibo proverbs; the language of the Hausa material examined here is more subtle in style and therefore more natural to its audience, whose inherent familiarity with cultural clichés makes subtleties of language not only possible but mandatory as features of consummate artistry. Poetry is judged by the author's ability to manipulate familiar cultural images, weaving them into known forms in a new manner that is expressive of the author's individual style. The author's facility with ambiguity in imagery is indicative of the quality of her work.

Studies of ambiguity in Hausa poetry indicate that this device is necessary to criticism in a hierarchical society. An entertainer must be able to couch criticism in terms with satisfactory surface meaning; members of the audience who share with the performer an awareness of the subject's situation and the existing criticism of the subject will understand the criticism. In one discussion of Algerian Muslims' perceptions of their own society in a repressive era, "only poetry showed signs of life—one suspects because the thoughts Algerians wanted to express were too bitter or too seditious to express, except transformed as metaphor" (Allan Christelow, personal communication, 1997). Similarly, David Ames points out that in Hausa culture "symbolic statement is especially developed in song lyrics and formal poetry—two art forms which are closely related" (1970, 142). The ambiguity inherent in metaphor is the keystone of successful Hausa praise singing and has become an integral part of the written as well as orally composed *waƙoƙi* performed by Hausa women in Nigeria.

Hajiya Faji playing the *kukuma*, 1979

Profile Four: Hajiya Faji and
Hauwa Mai Duala, Hausa Singers

ajiya Faji, who moved to Kano from Bornu State with her first husband, was in her sixties when this study was undertaken; she died
sometime between 1992 and 1996. Hausa women do not sell in the market except by proxy, but in Bornu State, Hajiya Faji's home, it is common,
so she had a market stall for a while after she moved to Kano. Neither of
her parents was a musician, so when she came to Kano with her first husband and decided to abandon her market business for music, she paid a

man to teach her for approximately thirty pounds sterling. Faji accompanied herself on the lute whenever she performed, as she did frequently for
political rallies during the 1979 presidential campaign. At the time I knew
her, she was married to a truck driver who was away for long periods of
time, an arrangement that suited them both well and left her free to perform whenever and wherever she wanted. She was paid to support candidate Nnamdi Azikwe with praise songs and often raised her hand in cheerful support of "Zik!" a minority candidate in Kano, just like Bornu-bred
Faji, who was also an outsider in Kano. Nnamdi Azikwe was the 1979
presidential candidate of the National People's Party (NPP) and had served
as president of the First National Republic in 1963.

After she learned to play the *kukuma* as a young woman in Kano, Faji
gave lessons to others, teaching both youngsters and adults, especially young
women. During my fieldwork she tried to teach me to play the *kukuma*.
While teaching me fingering technique for the *kukuma*, Hajiya Faji said,
"You can do it—You'll learn by watching" (*Kin iya. Kya koya daga dubu ni*;
March 18, 1979). She said she learned to play the *kukuma* in this way. The
fingering technique she learned and used on the bowed lute involved damp-
ing the string with the flat of the first joint of the fingers, not the fingertips,
as is done with other stringed instruments. The fingers are depressed and
released in rapid succession while the lute is being bowed. The two middle
fingers of the left hand ("big fingers," *manyan 'yan 'yatsa*) and the index
and little finger (*kananan 'yan 'yatsa*) control the production of various
sounds ("the voice of the *kukuma*"—*muryar kukuma*). Her simplest bowing technique was a pattern of two short and two long strokes, with one
long stroke being an open, or unfingered, note. Only after mastering the
muryar kukuma is one ready to learn the vocal accompaniment, for the
words of the song repeat the tones played on the instrument. Thus, the
message of the work is conveyed through the music as well as in the lyrics
of the song. The final stages of learning involve "public" sessions at which
a novice can participate among many musicians without spoiling the performance. Once again, at this stage the student learns through practical
application, adjusting technical skills to fit the group's performing style. In
addition to her individual performances, Faji played with a group of women
in the Kano palace harem for a wedding celebration (March 18–23, 1979,
see my audiotape collection reels 1–3, Indiana Archives of Traditional Music,
Accession number 81-100-F/B) and at KNTV in May 1980, where her
songs were recorded for broadcast on a popular television show.

Hajiya Mai Duala of Ningi, who was in her sixties when I knew her,
was a longtime friend of Maizargadi. In Kano in September 2002 I was
told she had died, but no one knew the exact date. Mai Duala was the
official *zabiya* for the Emir of Ningi and, like Maizargadi, she also performed outside the palace for private, nonroyal celebrations. Her material,

also like Maizargadi's, usually included testimony of allegiance to her primary patron in praise songs for wealthy patrons.

Hajiya Faji rarely traveled outside Kano to perform, but she did appear in public often, playing her *kukuma* and singing for political rallies, in this manner supporting her current patron and his political party. She also performed when invited to the Kano palace for a women's celebration, for recording sessions at the television station, and for political rallies. Once they had moved to Kano from Ningi, Mai Duala and her friend Maizargadi each stayed in her own part of Kano, close to primary patrons, although they occasionally visited one another. Because of their advanced ages, Faji and Mai Duala enjoyed more freedom to move around the city than younger women, but ultimately for all these women their status as professionals overshadowed any restriction of mobility on the basis of gender.

FIVE

The Social Functions of Hausa Women's Creativity

WESTERN AND TRADITIONAL INFLUENCES

Hausa women's poems reflect the cultural context in which they are produced, so they are replete with allusions to traditional and Western values that often conflict with one another. Just as Hausa performing artists derive a modern form by mingling stylistic features of oral and written poems, they also mix traditional and Western influences in the content of their poems, reflecting the complexity of daily life in Kano. Oral songs and written poems overlap in style, form, and theme. Among the Hausa, the song traditionally has been an instrument of religious advocacy and political concerns (Ames 1973, 151–152; Paden 1973). Written poems by Hausa women fulfill the same functions; Islamic traditions infuse literature with religious concerns, and political issues are central themes.

Founded on the Islamic orientation characteristic of Hausa literature, these poems comment primarily on the acquisition of knowledge, community solidarity, and historical accounts. Each of these concerns is of an Islamic orientation by virtue of its being related to religious obligation. First, as discussed earlier, literacy is necessary for studying the Qur'an and thus important to one's salvation; the acquisition of knowledge is a recommended path for all. Second, historical accounts, especially genealogies but also narratives of contemporary political issues and the individuals involved in them, reinforce the hierarchy of authority which until very recently has been closely linked to the religious community. Third, community solidarity is founded on a sense of brotherhood among people, specifically manifested in Northern Nigeria by association with religious brotherhoods and related to the pillar *zakat,* which advocates charity. Women's associations, which flourished in the last three decades of the twentieth century, were also known in the nineteenth century, especially in the example of the Jaji teachers trained by Nana Asma'u. Men's brotherhoods, which are associated with the Sufi Tijaniyya and Qadiriyya orders, had their origins in religious affiliations but moved into political operations in the twentieth century. Women's participation in these brotherhoods rarely has been acknowledged, despite their active status (Sule and Starratt 1991). It cannot be argued that there are no women in brotherhoods nor that there is an absence of women's organizations to parallel men's groups, only that women's activities have been insufficiently examined. Other exclusively women's organizations that are unaffiliated with the Tijaniyya and Qadiriyya have been oriented toward education and social services: Women in Nigeria (W.I.N.), established in the late 1970s, is an example. Very often poetry is both the means of disseminating information about and an instrument of instruction within the group. In these contexts, oral and written works critique the commingling of traditional and Western values, promote a sense of progressive development to benefit both individual and state, and report on historical and current events central to Hausa culture.

The orally composed works, like the written works, are sprinkled with opening invocations to God ("Let us begin in the name of God the Almighty, the Merciful") and invocations for God's aid. Then, in keeping with Hausa praise song tradition, they go on to exhibit varying degrees of criticism—from good-natured critiques to biting satire. When they are part of *bori* performance, the orally composed songs juxtapose reference to God with reference to spirits and requests for money; such simultaneous expression of the sacred and the irreverent occurs in performances of oral songs outside the *bori* environment as well. Opportunities for oral song performance cover the widest possible range of Hausa social experience, from the most exclusively private situation to a public setting with a general audience. These songs can be made to suit any social setting as the composer tailors her material to the individuals and the particular situation. The content of the oral performance, therefore, will describe the subject and situation for which it is created. The degree to which it is satiric reflects the relative levity or solemnity of the occasion and the relative status of the performer and patron. The more solemn or important the occasion, the more subdued the performance. Those who perform for circumstances at the extreme top and bottom of the social hierarchy (as in a royal setting and for *bori* rites) are accomplished musicians whose ability is well established. They provide the aesthetic model for other, newer artists who perform in public for less noteworthy circumstances. The content of works by consummate performers and novices may differ in quality but not in intention, for the aim is always to praise and criticize one's subject with as many diverse epithets as one can. While written works more often include narrative accounts set in poetic style, oral performances usually consist of laudatory and critical descriptions of their subjects. They are most readily employed for entertaining at purely celebratory events or as historical accounts of leaders or events that have occurred in the past.

The topics treated in the written works in this study are for the most part relevant to the secular world and oriented toward practical concerns. The acquisition of knowledge is discussed in these works in many varieties, and each work itself constitutes a lesson plan on a particular topic. Some of them advocate the unified effort of a community of the faithful, while other works are important as historical or political accounts. They include works such as a catalogue of the city wards in Kano, an account of the Biafran war, and memorials to fallen political leaders. While these topics are clearly secular in nature, they are set in traditional literary form and are embellished with phrases that reflect traditional Islamic trust in God's will.

Both oral and written works contain images of material modernization in Northern Nigeria. Conservative written poems describe material culture in a framework that praises the "progressive" nature of some Western influences (driving cars, universal primary education, the children's hospital, the benefit of a census) and the detriments the West has brought to traditional Hausa society (drugs, indecent attire, lack of respect). The least reverent—primarily the oral songs—criticize most freely the social conflicts created by such influences, their praise of attendant economic benefits notwithstanding. They are also critical of traditional mores. What is pervasive among these various treatments of diverse themes and images, however, is that women interpret social situations in relation to their own changing roles in Hausa society.

EDUCATION

The Prophet Muhammad advised that seeking knowledge is a religious duty; a famous *hadith* recommends, "Seek ye knowledge, even unto China."[1] In Northern Nigeria, a traditional system of Islamic education was in place in the seventeenth and eighteenth centuries. In the nineteenth century, jihad leader Shehu Usman ɗan Fodiyo supported the education of women. He advocated the obligation of men to facilitate the education of their wives and daughters, reminding people that the Prophet Muhammad said that a man who educates his daughter will receive twice the heavenly reward of a man who educates only his sons. When the British colonized Nigeria in the early twentieth century, Islamic schools still included women scholars.[2] The War on Ignorance (Yaƙi da Jahilci) is the name of a movement that originated around 1950 when leaders of the Northern Region realized that years of resistance in the north to the kind of Christian missionary primary and secondary schools that had proliferated in the south had resulted in an economic disadvantage to northerners. The movement flourished in the 1960s. Their lack of English literacy meant that northerners were not able to fill new jobs being created with the establishment of British banks and other foreign businesses. Suddenly, British-educated southern Nigerians, many of them Christians, were flooding into the north for employment opportunities. As the British prepared to leave Nigeria just prior to independence in 1960, it became clear that those with literacy in English would have jobs in the commercial sectors and that they would be the ones to qualify for government positions in the new independent polity that was about to unfold. Realizing their disadvantaged position, northern leaders began a regional program to educate, an effort whose aim was as much to bolster their own party's popularity as it was to fulfill more altruistic goals. Both the government and individuals participated in promoting the cause of literacy. Sa'adu Zungur, one of the first widely published poets to write on secular topics, began in the 1950s to write about the need for Western education among the Hausa, while Mu'azu Hadeja was one of the first published poets to write on social and religious themes around the same time (Hofstad 1971, 28). In 1963, the Sardauna of Sokoto, Ahmadu Bello, initiated a "jihad against ignorance" organized by a committee of northern men who strove to foster unity along religious lines (Paden 1973, 184). Bello, who was the premier of the north, promoted a government based on Islam.[3] His political endeavors were coupled with a public campaign against illiteracy, which was couched in terms of religious obligation. Local government campaigns for self-awareness, self-improvement, and appropriate participation in public endeavors began under his influence and spread throughout the north. The program fostered urban and rural adult literacy classes, health and nutrition courses, instruction in social services, and later, in January 1974, the promotion of free primary education. In the years 1979–1982, I visited many of the adult education centers, where women constituted the majority of students. Poets Hauwa Gwaram and Hajiya 'Yar Shehu were young adults during this period, and the influence of these campaigns is evident in their poems, many of which were written in support of these programs. Several songs treat these issues from a perspective of fulfilling one's religious obligation through the acquisition of knowledge, a concept that became clear with the realization of Bello's role as a spiritual as well as political leader in the north.

A severe but highly dramatic portrayal of the dangers of ignorance is narrated in Hauwa Gwaram's "Song for the War on Ignorance" (circa 1974). Nomau, the main character of the work, represents the stereotype of the uneducated farmer whose life is fraught with difficulty because he cannot read, write, or calculate simple money transactions. His ignorance invites abuse by others, and in that way he inadvertently encourages their participation in evil. He is cheated by traders on the street, robbed by gamblers, and investigated by those who (inaccurately) write his messages for him. Nomau takes the wrong road, both literally and figuratively. Following a lengthy catalogue of his misdeeds, Hauwa Gwaram summarizes: "He took a road one shouldn't and was arrested / He brought it all on himself by not fighting ignorance" (v. 24). Fighting ignorance is like jihad in its true meaning, the struggle against negative impulses and the effort to perfect oneself. This obligation of jihad as a personal struggle for perfection is incumbent upon every Muslim, and so, by extension, Nomau's is a religious failure. This would be very clear to Muslims in the region. The metaphor of taking the wrong road is also closely connected to religious obligation, for a Muslim is obligated to follow the *sunna,* or the example of the life of Mohammad. *Sunna* also is understood to mean "path" or "way," so the implication is clear to Gwaram's audience. The metaphor also implies that the need for worldly knowledge parallels the need for religious knowledge; both ensure success. Gwaram criticizes Nomau for not having sought religious knowledge: "May God protect us from failing to seek advice from teachers / Do you hear? Such is the failure to fight ignorance" (v. 26).[4] She is addressing a woman in this verse; *Kin ji?* is "Do you hear?" with the "you" in feminine form.

Nomau's ignorance is connected to his lack of piety, for he ignored the opportunity to acquire literacy skills in a Qur'anic school, just as he failed to pursue other opportunities for self-improvement. Primary schools and adult education classes offer paths away from ignorance too:

> 45   Adults and children, we are called to class,
>   So we can understand everything and live without ignorance.
> 46   Children should go to primary classes and seek education,
>   Adults should go to classes too, for the war on ignorance.

Nomau ignores all forms of education, and his unhappiness is the consequence of failing to strive actively to acquire knowledge. In this poem, Hauwa Gwaram emphasizes the need to acquire knowledge by any of many possible means, thus satisfying one's moral obligation. She compares Nomau's blind ignorance to that of his ancestors, who suffered from lack of opportunities for education:

> 5   In times of ignorance [before Islam], people wouldn't admit to
>   Sickness, because of ignorance.
> 6   They ground together potash, herbs, and bark,
>   To spread all over their bodies, in ignorance.

Nomau's refusal to pursue any of his several opportunities for education constitutes a moral failure on his part, for he has not progressed beyond the situation of his ancestors. Early in the work Gwaram has warned: "You know about taking up the rope of knowledge, and about ignoring it, /

Everyone who leaves wisdom [aside] endures bad fortune" (v. 4). But Nomau eschews the "rope of knowledge," which could be his lifeline to salvation and upward mobility. Ignorance, like sin, Gwaram implies, is a poison that debilitates Nomau and ruins his life: "Stop and listen, ignorance is filth. / The poison it has and that of a snake are no different" (v. 50). The War on Ignorance movement assigned to each citizen a responsibility to improve his own situation. When Nomau makes no progress in his own life because of failing to pursue the advocated means toward upward mobility he is compounding his lack of piety with social irresponsibility. He is simultaneously a sinner and a bad citizen.

This poem always inspires great amusement, incredulity at the subject's unfathomable stupidity, and much head-shaking. Its popularity may be based on its portrayal of a character who may be ridiculed with impunity. Nomau is a stereotype through which Hauwa Gwaram hopes to advocate for self-help. Those who join in condemning Nomau's habits are transforming a negative role model into a positive one by disapproving of those habits. Thus, the critical nature of the work, in which the audience takes an active part by expressing disapproval, is executed to positive ends—the revelation of the path to moral righteousness through the acquisition of knowledge.

In thematic contrast, Maimuna Choge's Bayero University Hausa Conference performance (1980) provides a platform for satiric rebuttal to Hauwa Gwaram's highly moralistic views on education. Choge's praise of Western university education is belied by the bawdy execution and irreverent import of such praise. Her performance opens with a brief doxology praising God, followed by praise to Inna. While *inna* is a common term for mother, it is also (along with *iya*) a name for the principal figure of the pre-Islamic *bori* cult (Nicolas 1975, 151–152). Thus, Choge's arrangement begins with the irreverent juxtaposition of both God and non-Islamic possession-cult goddesses, setting the tone for her performance. Throughout the evening, Choge maintains a running parallel of reverent and irreverent references, juxtaposing contrasting images of many types through her work, for example by addressing the audience indirectly by invoking God to grant them money. The patron pays the praise singer, yet God is the universal patron whose generosity provides everyone with what is needed to live. Implying such a parallel between the human patron and God is an irreverent suggestion to begin with; the sacrilegious tone it represents is reinforced by the repetition of the exhortation, "May God grant us money!" which recurs almost as a leitmotif in the work.

Choge expresses ambivalence about the merits of Western culture. She is being paid to praise the university students at this conference, which she does at great length, commenting on their prospects for material gain, high status, and professional incomes. She extends her praise to an extreme, saying "All those who do not hold the pen do useless work" (l. 47). Choge suggests by her commentary that there is no better-paying or higher-status job in Nigeria than a white-collar one. Then she turns to the subject of professionalism in general, reminding the audience of her own relatively exclusive position; her own material accoutrements rival those of the educated elite. Choge's second perspective is a direct contradiction of the first, transforming her previous comment on the value of education into satire.

Finally she is explicit, stating her position relative to that of an educated individual: "And for a long time he has held the pen; for a long time I have been well off" (l. 75). The two professions represent the highest and lowest on the social scale, but Choge's point is that there is little difference between the two. They both involve sufficient economic gain. Here is none of Hauwa Gwaram's altruistic belief in the virtues of acquiring knowledge for the inherent betterment of an individual's character. Choge finds neither spiritual nor moral virtue in the acquisition of an education. Instead she draws a parallel between educated professionals and performers of orally composed songs; each type of performer, she implies, participates in his or her profession primarily for economic gain and its attendant status.

The audience's response to Choge's performance indicates that they delight in her irreverent imagery and behavior. When she shakes her body provocatively, they shower her with whistles and shouts of approval. Although nearly all members of the audience are involved in academia, they understand Choge's remarks about economic gain. She can say what respectable scholarly individuals cannot: that an altruistic approach to one's work is a fine stance, but it will not feed one's family. These audience members sincerely believe in the social benefits inherent in education, but like scholars everywhere they are fortunate to be among an elite that can benefit from a loftier and less physically stressful livelihood than most individuals must pursue. They understand that, and they accept from Choge criticism of their profession that they prefer not to voice themselves. Choge delights them with risqué humor, satiric commentary, and provocative behavior, but under it all there lies a truth that her audience recognizes and must accept. Their rising status is an indication of progress only as it represents their only economic gain. It is not necessarily the pursuit of knowledge for moral salvation that Hauwa Gwaram advocates.

POETRY AS A TEACHING DEVICE

Several of Hauwa Gwaram's poems were written as teaching aids when she worked for the Kano State government, teaching adult education courses on nutrition and child care for women in the 1960s. In "Song for the

Course at the Children's Hospital and for Public Involvement," Gwaram advises women about food preparation and water sterilization, personal hygiene, and household responsibilities (vv. 8, 15, 16, 26–30). She appeals to women directly to help educate themselves by attending a clinic on public health and maternity care (vv. 2–5). Advising women to bring their friends to classes, she urges them to trust in Western medicine and the efficacy of regular medical checkups at the clinic (vv. 18–20, 35, 39–40).

From one perspective, Hauwa Gwaram's participation in this adult education program seems indicative of her explicit approval of these forms of Western intervention in traditional society. At the same time, however, her attitude, her activity, and her writing all reflect the nineteenth-century example of Nana Asma'u, whose activist role in educating women on the same topics was also accomplished through the use of poetry. Both Hauwa Gwaram and Hajiya 'Yar Shehu consistently cited Nana Asma'u as their role model, the works produced by these two contemporary poets share the same concerns evidenced in Asma'u's works. Such parallels are not co-incidental; they surely are connected to the rights guaranteed to women by Islam and, more important, to women's awareness of those rights, which cannot be denied.[5]

Hauwa Gwaram's participation in the adult education program is indicative of her explicit approval of attitudes about women's discrete comportment, for women did not have to meet publicly for these classes; the meeting place itself was secluded from men, and women needed the permission of their husbands to attend. Ultimately, however, attendance at these classes ensured for Kano women—and especially for Hauwa Gwaram herself—a greater freedom in the name of a morally upright pursuit, the value of which could not be questioned by devout, reasonable Muslim men.

Hausa women at all levels of education and socioeconomic status regularly are engaged in income-producing activities. These range from crafts to white-collar employment. Traditionally, Hausa women were the spinners for huge commercial cloth markets. Today they maintain independent incomes by cooking snacks or making craft items that their children sell for them on the streets or in the market. In this way, a woman in seclusion may participate in the market economy without violating her social obligation to remain in the home. The obligation to remain secluded does not extend to upper-class urban women who are white-collar professionals. In Kano, there are many examples of highly educated professional women who serve in jobs in the public sector without being expected to be secluded in the home. Women are attorneys, doctors, broadcasters, journalists, and educators in public schools. In addition, huge numbers of rural women work in the fields, go to market, fetch water, and gather wood, among other activities, in public. Some of the classes offered to women included craft classes to establish or improve their skills, while others dealt with literacy skills to ensure against their being cheated in trading (vv. 36–38, 41–43).

Hauwa Gwaram advocates women's acquisition of skills associated with Western education systems, and she encourages women's participation in the endeavor to educate other women. What Gwaram suggests—the progressive development of each individual's skills—can benefit the state as well as the individual by raising income levels and standards of living, thus buttressing the nation's economy. Every suggestion, however, is made within the context of Islamic philosophy. The jobs and skills women are encouraged to acquire are all domestic, in keeping with traditional Islamic tenets specifying a woman's primary responsibility to her family and home.

Binta Katsina's oral composition "Song for the Women of Nigeria" echoes on one level Hauwa Gwaram's plea for "progressive" behavior. On another level, it is anarchistic. She expresses a belief in the potential professional equality between Nigerian men and women and encourages women to teach, to do clerical work, and to work for the government. She assures women that what is traditionally "men's work" can also be their own, advocating that women pilot airplanes, drive vehicles, and run machines (ll. 300, 344, 358, 360). These jobs require literacy skills that are best acquired at public schools outside the home. Her song clarifies the need for Nigerian women in the public work force and supports the desirability of literacy among women. In these respects Binta Katsina's song expresses a "progressive" approach to economic and educational matters.

Attendance at secondary schools requires women to travel outside the home, a situation that presents a twofold problem between traditional Hausa men and women. First, the Hausa woman who is secluded in the home would have to relinquish seclusion, a sign of high social and economic status, to attend classes, and, later, to work outside the home. This is a situation that could constitute a loss of social standing for both husband and wife. This dilemma can be solved very easily by the use of hijab, the "full veil" (as discussed in one of Hauwa Gwaram's poems) that assures respectability for the woman who moves about in public. The second part of the problem is one faced by many young Hausa couples that have tried to become more "Western" by circumventing the first dilemma with the rationale that pursuit of a higher degree constitutes a sign of higher social status itself. While this reasoning mitigates the first concern, a new potential problem is created with regard to women's fulfillment of their religious obligations to oversee the domestic sphere, although most families at this level can afford to hire domestic help. A woman who is preoccupied with her profession cannot fulfill her religious obligation to her family and home.

Binta Katsina's song, purportedly commissioned by a national government eager to get women into the workforce, advocates what may be a progressive new role for many Nigerian women. Those who enjoyed these songs most thoroughly and displayed greatest interest in its revolutionary news were, as might be expected, younger women university students. Even they, however, pointed out the difficulty of carrying out such radical role changes. Women who try seriously to follow the spirit of Binta Katsina's song find that the difficulty of juggling domestic responsibilities and professional pursuits is nearly insurmountable, even with domestic help. And the calumny incurred for abandoning those domestic responsibilities is even worse. This is the classic double bind known to women in the West.

One of the beneficial legacies of Western influence on educational systems among the Hausa is the concern about establishing enough primary school systems to educate all children. The consensus among Hausa people is that such education is beneficial to all, though they may disagree on the importance of university or post-primary (secondary, technical, teacher-training) education for young women. The concept of universal primary education is not without its problems. It can seriously damage the economic welfare of a lower-class family in several ways. First, the children who attend classes during the day have less time to help with household chores, sell market items, and run errands. Second, *free* universal primary education has not yet been instituted; parents must pay school fees; buy books, supplies, and school uniforms; and provide lunches or money for midday meals. There is great concern about standards in schools and therefore a great increase in the number of privately funded schools that charge high fees. People are also concerned about pass rates, which tend to be low universally.[6] Families could deal with the first problem more willingly if the economic burdens were reduced by the institution of free primary schools, the subject of Hauwa Gwaram's poem "Song on Universal Primary Education."

Appealing to individuals of all walks of life, Hauwa Gwaram seeks to foster a sense of solidarity on this issue (vv. 2–13). The length of her catalogue emphasizes the magnitude of her appeal; no one is omitted in what she hopes will be a unified effort for the benefit of all. As is common with such lists, the penultimate and final citations are magnified by their positions; in them, Hauwa Gwaram speaks of women's roles in the effort toward free primary education and finally, like every devout Muslim, she leaves the matter in God's hands:

17   Prior to this [time], few women were teachers;
      Well, now we will try to make some improvements.
18   May God give us the power to achieve our hearts' desires,
      And see teachers who give universal primary education.

Hauwa Gwaram's explanation of women's roles is made important at the outset by its strategic and emphatic placement near the end of the list, but it is further enhanced by this juxtaposition to stanza 18's line, "God give us the power to achieve our hearts' desires." Implicit in this line arrangement is the wish to promote women's active participation in the teaching profession.

COMMUNITY SOLIDARITY

Hauwa Gwaram's "Song of Self-Improvement and Community Work" conveys a sense of community responsibility and nationalism. She begins with the smaller unit, expanding her range of imagery to cover areas outside the immediate neighborhood and outside the town, finally extending the view to include the nation itself. She comments on the benefits of improved living conditions—proper waste collection, insect eradication, and road repair (vv. 19, 20, 22, 47, 48)—emphasizing the positive results of such organized efforts to improve the environment. Gwaram fosters an awareness of one's neighbors and their contributions to the group effort to improve living conditions in the area, repeating the phrase "They help themselves through community work." The unspoken follow-up to this is "and so can you," bearing the implication of an individual's responsibility to his neighbors. Using the catalogue technique, Gwaram expands her imagery, mentioning all 126 wards of Kano's Old City sector and extending her verbal map to include areas in metropolitan Kano and in outlying rural areas beyond Kano's geographic limits. Implicit in such wide-scale geographic narration is the impression that community work can benefit all groups, not just those in the urban areas. The sense of community solidarity guaranteed by Islamic brotherhoods is thus expanded to a feeling of unity on a broader scale.

In regard to women's roles in such an effort, Hauwa Gwaram specifies the function of adult literacy and craft courses as an important aspect of community work. Women teach and learn through these classes, which are sponsored by the community itself. Ultimately they are for the benefit of that community:

> 61   Well, here is our cause, women, we are making efforts
>   We've striven mightily and we are continuing with community work
> 65   We teach occupations to women, so they can all do some work;
>   Literacy too, through community work.

Hauwa Gwaram's emphasis on the need for a unified effort among both men and women signifies a new perspective on women's roles in regard to public activity. The strict traditionalists advocate the seclusion of women in their homes, while Gwaram's commentary suggests that Kano women may extend their circles of influence to those outside the home. She maintains a conservative perspective, however, by restricting the kind of work women are encouraged to pursue as part of the community effort to domestically related skills.

Both Hauwa Gwaram and Hajiya 'Yar Shehu advocate the acquisition of knowledge on a community scale through cooperation in the nation's census effort. In songs on the 1972 national census, they try to dispel suspicions about being counted for tax purposes. Explaining that the purpose of the census ultimately is to benefit the people themselves, Gwaram warns them that mistrust on their part is founded on ignorance: "All who refuse to count / Because of taxes are foolish" (v. 12). Hajiya 'Yar Shehu points out that those who refuse to participate are no better than the trickster figure of Hausa narratives, the spider Gizo:

7   Oh, God, the Wise, Your wisdom suffices.
     Make us understand so that we may explain the truth,
8   Lest we fall into the bad ways of the loose-mouthed Gizo,
     Who, when he couldn't bear something, just shouted louder.

Such association of humans with animals is derogatory—only an animal is excused from being informed on social issues and from behaving with discretion. Association with Gizo the trickster, however, carries a doubly serious accusation, for Gizo is more than an animal lacking reason. He is an animal who, having acquired some human attributes, misuses those potentially redeeming qualities to abuse and destroy those around him. Gizo's concerns are for his own welfare, not for the betterment of his associations. His lack of generosity is as well established as his ignorance, and thus the two qualities are related. Gizo is the prototypical irresponsible citizen.

Those who are responsible for counting individuals in the Kano area owe a great debt of social responsibility to the people they count. Their accuracy is deemed a direct reflection of the sincerity of their nationalistic feelings, as is the cooperation of those they count. Hajiya 'Yar Shehu's admonition to listeners to count every individual, regardless of age, sex, or health, emphasizes that failure to do so signals a failure of citizenship. Every individual has a moral obligation to participate in the government's acquisition of this specific information, which will eventually benefit all citizens by guaranteeing the equitable division of funds and ultimately contribute to the nation's progressive development (vv. 30, 31).

An accurate count depends on the counters' literacy skills and the cooperation of the populace. Among individuals of both these groups, the success of the effort is contingent on a clear understanding of the purpose of the count and a fervent sense of responsibility toward the government. Dispelling ignorance on a local and ultimately on a national scale is the mandate of every citizen, whether she is being counted or doing the counting. Each one is in part responsible for the success of a united effort. This attitude also reflects the Muslim's obligation to the community at large, the *umma*. By appealing for cooperation on the basis that it is good for the community, Hajiya 'Yar Shehu cannot help but imply that the obligation to cooperate is in part religious as well.

Like the poems on the census, Hauwa Gwaram's "Song of Preparing to Drive on the Right" and "Song of the Naira and Kobo, the New Currency of Nigeria" inform the public of nationwide policy changes. The first poem concerns the change from left-hand to right-hand driving, while the second is an explanation of the change from British currency to Nigeria's own monetary system. These poems serve several purposes: they inform the public, they couch the news in religious as well as public-policy terms, and they implicitly celebrate the feeling of nationalism that flourished with Nigerian independence from Britain in 1960.

In "Song to Prepare to Drive on the Right-Hand Side," repeated invocations to God constitute over half the work's content. Gwaram's repetitions of God's laws are paralleled by her repetitions of the authorities' laws of the road, creating a relationship between the importance of following God's laws in life and following the government's laws on the road. This poem draws upon an assumption of an individual's obligation to God to inspire a comparably strong obligation to the state, making one's responsibility as a citizen concomitant with one's responsibility as a member of the Islamic congregation. Knowing the laws of the road facilitates one's own safety and the safety of those around the driver. But as is the case with Islamic law, knowledge of the laws is ineffective without implementation.

Hauwa Gwaram's poem on Nigeria's new currency was written to inform the public of the change of monetary systems which occurred in 1973. She states that the purpose of the work is to inform everyone, rich and poor, urban and rural, Muslim and non-Muslim, about the new currency (vv. 5, 28, 29, 40, 41). Describing the legal tender, Hauwa Gwaram reminds Nigerians of their country's rich resources, which are depicted on the coins and bills (vv. 4, 15–17, 21, 23, 25, 27). The exportation of palm oil, groundnuts, cocoa, cotton, and petroleum oil is Nigeria's own form of material tender in the world market, from which is culled the income for import trade. The government crest appears on all currency (vv. 8, 23), and the coins no longer have the center hole that was characteristic of British colonial currency. These are completely Nigerian coins, made and distributed by an independent Nigerian government and guaranteed by that government (vv. 7, 8, 23).

Implicit in all these poems about social change is the belief that the literate person is best able to participate in the progressive development of the nation. In urban areas, billboards advising people to drive carefully and advocating health care often accompany advertisements for commercial products. People who read these billboards and those who can read the newspapers can be best informed of social changes like those conveyed in these poems. In fact, poems are often used in advertising; short jingles tout the best attributes of products. Certain nation-building projects like the census and currency changes are successfully implemented only with the aid of literate participants. While the written poems in the previous section of this chapter advocate the acquisition of literacy skills, these poems implicitly demonstrate the ways that such skills contribute to the fulfillment of individuals' responsibilities as good citizens and the importance of each citizen's contribution to a community effort which is ultimately for the benefit of the nation as a whole.

HISTORICAL AND POLITICAL POEMS

Written and oral poetry has been more than a vehicle for the static recording of historic events throughout the last half of the twentieth century in Nigeria. Independence from British colonial rule in 1960, the establishment of a civilian government, a coup and military takeover, a three-year civil war, assassinations of political leaders, and the country's democratic elections in 1979 all have been described in popular poetry. Poetry has been important as a political instrument in the struggle, focusing public attention on certain political positions and influencing the public's attitudes.

The most dramatic moments of the twentieth century in Nigeria have involved the deaths of the noted and beloved figures of Alhaji Sir Abubakar Tafawa Balewa and Alhaji Ahmadu Bello, the Sardauna of Sokoto, in 1966. They are commemorated in *ta'aziya* poetry, the genre that expresses condolences. This traditional form of expression of bereavement for the deceased involves praising the subject's finer attributes; this is commonly the poetic style used by Hausa poets to honor fallen political figures. Hauwa Gwaram's "Song of Condolence for Tafawa Balewa and the Sardauna of Sokoto" describes Alahji Sir Tafawa Balewa, a northerner who was federal prime minister, and Alhaji Ahmadu Bello, Sardauna of Sokoto and premier of the Northern Region, both beloved figures who were murdered in the coup of 1966. Her poem explains their roles as victims of the political upheaval of the period. She mentions them together with former Emir of Kano, Muhammadu Sanusi, who was deposed in 1963 by Ahmadu Bello (v. 13), and describes Ahmadu Bello's efforts to unite the north by traveling to "Kacako . . . Gwaram, Sumaila . . . Dutse . . . Birnin Kudu" (vv. 24–25) to ameliorate the unrest of the time. Subsequent stanzas relate that Ahmadu Bello's advice to his people was always to follow the tenets of Islam (vv. 26–32), an intention made clear by the previous discussion of his efforts to institute the war on ignorance movement in the north. Major Hassan and General Yakubu Gowon were active in the 1966 countercoup against secessionist Biafra after General Aguiyi-Ironsi was overthrown. Hauwa Gwaram describes these events (vv. 41, 43) as well as the installation of Alhaji Ado Bayero as the new Emir of Kano and the leadership of Alhaji Audu Bako as the Kano State governor (vv. 47, 53).

Hajiya 'Yar Shehu's "Song for Alhaji Sir Ahmadu Bello, Sardauna of Sokoto" gives a far more extensive account of Ahmadu Bello's travels (vv. 32–40), which some believe served the solidarity of the north by better informing the *sardauna* of the state of Islamic affairs throughout the rest of the world (Paden 1973, 189 passim). Hajiya 'Yar Shehu's work more closely resembles oral praise songs in its inclusion of praise epithets such as "the king of truth" and "father of the north . . . bull elephant" (vv. 10, 41). Ahmadu Bello's role as the leader of Islam in Northern Nigeria—the pillar of the north—is legitimized by repeated references to his lineage, a technique also common in oral praise songs. He is linked to Fatima Zahara, the Prophet Muhammad's wife (v. 6), and to Shehu Usman dan Fodiyo, leader of the region's nineteenth-century jihad (v. 8). Twentieth-century Ahmadu Bello's connection to Mohammadu Atiku, his great-grandfather, caliph (1832–1842), and Sultan of Sokoto (v. 16) in the nineteenth century, strengthens Bello's connection to a family with a significant role in the region's governance.

Another *ta'aziya* praises Murtala Muhammad, who took over after Lieutenant Yakubu Gowon was ousted in 1975. Muhammad himself was assassinated in 1976. The condolence poem Hauwa Gwaram wrote for him is brief, but in it she describes some of Muhammad's accomplishments (vv. 18–21), appeals to God to forgive and welcome him (v. 11), and implores all people to bear their bereavement with the fortitude that is expected of devout Muslims (vv. 11–13).

The poems of Hauwa Gwaram and Hajiya 'Yar Shehu draw direct links between religious and political authority in the north. Indeed, the confluence of traditional and Western values is involved in a complex way in the integration of religious and political history in Kano. Since Usman dan Fodiyo's nineteenth-century jihad, Islamic ideology has been integral to the emir's policy and to regional governmental policy in the north. While never strictly a theocracy, the tendencies toward such a structure make it logical that oral and written works function to promote theocratic ideology. That feeling continued through the end of the twentieth century, as these poems indicate. In March 1981, the idea of an Islamic state was expressed by Alhaji Sir Abubakar, then Sultan of Sokoto, who said: "In Islam there is no distinction between religious and political leaders because Islam, being a way of life, governs the day to day activities of its followers."[7] Fundamentalists have emphasized the role of Islam in politics. The 'Yan Izala movement caused tremendous controversy in the 1970s and 1980s. The 1981 riots had their basis in disagreement about the role of orthodox Islam in Kano, and the early years of the twenty-first century have indicated a rise in fundamentalist sympathies in the region; they have continued to rise since the 1990s. It is a disagreement that continues; religious issues remain pertinent to politics in the region.

Every Kano leader since the nineteenth-century jihad has been a Fulani emir, whose authority is affirmed through Islam.[8] "Song for the Fulani Emirs" is a traditional poem originally transmitted orally but written down and revised by several authors. As Hauwa Gwaram explains in a preface to her version of the work:

> Well, this poem is about the Fulani emirs, and it is written by me, Hauwa Gwaram. That is, I heard it from Alhaji ɗan Amu, the [former] Imam of Kano, who composed it in Arabic. As for me, I went to visit Sidiya, a wife of the [former] Emir of Kano, Alhaji Inuwa. We read it together. We studied until we mastered the song. She said she got it from the head wife in the white compound. That's it . . . I too said that she gave it to me. I went to ask at the house of Alhaji ɗan Amu for permission [to work with it], and I wrote it in Roman script, in order to study it in that form. I have added Emir Sanusi, Emir Inuwa, and Emir Ado Bayero because it was originally written before they took office. And in recent times we had Emir Abdullahi too. So. Let us begin in the name of God.[9]

Reworking and revising another author's work is common in Arabic poetry, and the tradition continues in Kano. Like the songs recounting new urban development in Kano, the "Song for Fulani Emirs" contains narrative segments that explain the contributions of emirs to the city: the mosques, hospitals, schools, and libraries built and the technological advances that have been made (vv. 55–56). Hauwa Gwaram's description of Alhaji Ado Bayero, current Emir of Kano, is also complimentary (vv. 89–90). But he is most thoroughly described in relationship to Abdullahi, his father, and Hauwa Gwaram compares the two repeatedly (vv. 84–88, 91–93).

In Hauwa Gwaram's version of this work, the entire line of Fulani emirs in Kano since 1806 is recounted. The work is a king list and a partial genealogy, since there are familial connections between several emirs. Hauwa Gwaram's version represents a transitional song style: it is a written composition that includes description and praise of the development of Western technology under recent emirs, but it is also a composition in the oral song style, resembling royal praise song performance by women praise singers in the emir's court.

Hauwa Gwaram's "Song for the Fulani Emirs" includes all thirteen emirs of Kano cited in order, with only a few inaccurate lengths of reign.[10] Her tendency to describe through narrative marks Hauwa Gwaram's version as typical of written poems in Hausa. She also includes several epithets that are common to oral praise songs. For instance, she refers to Dabo and Abbas as "brave warrior" (*sadauki*); Abbas is also known as "the lion" (*usudu*).

Royal women praise singers such as Maizargadi naturally refrain from criticizing their patrons. Instead, their praise songs express loyalty to the traditional Hausa leader just as lavishly as the written poems. The form those praises take, however, is different, involving less narrative explanation than in the written poems. They consist of a lengthy catalogue of praise epithets (*kirari*), which constitute by their number and variety a multifaceted perspective on the subject of the work. In this case, praise epithets are direct reflections of support for whichever current Hausa leader is the patron of the performer. Maizargadi's "Song for Alhaji Ado Bayero, Emir of Kano" describes Emir Ado Bayero's wealth (ll. 47, 69, 70–71, 74), but she proclaims his wealth for another purpose than mere blandishment. By recounting his possessions, inheritances, and distribution of gifts, she binds the concept of wealth to the obligation incumbent upon every devout Muslim to distribute that wealth (and she hopes that some will come her way, too). Charity (Ar., *zakat*) is a pillar of Islam that requires the recognition that all wealth and fortune comes from God and therefore is not to be hoarded but shared willingly. Maizargadi expresses appreciation for the emir's magnanimity: "You gave me a gift, and it was not a loan" (l. 81). The emir is depicted as a patron, the leader and protector of Kano, with praise epithets that are reserved for him alone (ll. 15, 17, 62). His foresight in helping his people deal with changes that result from greater contact with the West is implicit in references to his capable leadership abilities.

The message repeated most often in this work, however, is the right to inheritance enjoyed by Alhaji Ado Bayero. This is not a technical right, because a council of kingmakers selects emirs. Succession by a son does not happen automatically; many vie for the position. Alhaji Ado Bayero's father, Alhaji Abdullahi Bayero, was the tenth Emir of Kano, who enjoyed a long (27-year) reign and was well liked by his people. Alhaji Ado Bayero is not the only one of Alhaji Abdullahi's sons to reign after him, but Maizargadi reminds the audience of Alhaji Ado Bayero's personal link with authority. She repeatedly refers to him as his father's son (vv. 66–67), perhaps feeling she must reinforce his right to the position. In a passage of consecutive lines, Maizargadi repeats a list of groups over which he has control through inheritance, attesting to the fact that Ado has "inherited the house" of each one (ll. 69–71).[11]

Maizargadi's song is typical of her other performances. She combines praise for many aspects of her patron's character—wealth, generosity, concern for modernization, attention to people's welfare, family relations. By juxtaposing images of the emir's inherent right to authority and his individually achieved capabilities, Maizargadi conveys a sense of his total competence, of Ado Bayero's unquestioned suitability for the position as the Emir of Kano.

Because the content of oral songs reflects the occasion of their composition, they are historical documents; they recount the names and relationships of people present for the celebration. When Hauwa Mai Duala, a praise singer from Ningi and an old friend of Maizargadi's, visited Kano for the naming ceremony of one of Maizargadi's grandchildren, she performed a song for the women who attended the celebration. The song reflected the makeup of the audience and the occasion and was representative of the kind of royal praise song that is generally associated with performances inside the palace. As a guest in Kano, Mai Duala's praise of Kano's Emir Alhaji Ado Bayero is expressive of her appreciation for the hospitality extended to her. Simultaneously, she praises her own patron, the Emir of Ningi, Garba Inusa. But shortly after her opening doxology to God (l. 1) and brief reference to Alhaji Garba Inusa (ll. 2, 3, 10), Mai Duala launches into a catalogue of the women known by or related to those present at the ceremony or somehow connected to the Emir of Kano. Since this naming ceremony is the place for women to gather, women are the focus of the work.

In the first 100 lines, Hauwa Mai Duala establishes the groups to which she refers—the women of the palace communities in Kano and Ningi. She cites a sister of the Emir of Kano (ll. 18–22, 60, 62), the Emir of Kano's new daughter (ll. 44–45) and one of his wives (ll. 95, 96, 98), as well as her own friend Maizargadi (ll. 128, 135, 158, 163) and Maizargadi's friend Binta Baturiya (the name by which I was known in Kano) (ll. 87–89, 115–120). Women of the Ningi palace community are mentioned in relationship to the Ningi emir's royal status; he is identified as the descendent of various women (ll. 36, 37). Throughout the work, Hauwa Mai Duala repeats allusions to women of the Kano and Ningi palaces and to emirs of Kano and Ningi. Clearly this is a song by and for women.

Meanwhile, Hauwa Mai Duala has introduced another important figure in Nigerian news, [former] President Shehu Shagari, who had been in office for only seven months at the time of her performance (lines 150–151). In addition to the highest-titled individual in the nation, Hauwa Mai Duala cites several individuals by their royal titles: attendant to the emir (*barde*), the attendant to the ruler (*mai gari*), royal mat-spreader to the emir (*ɗan kilishi*), the senior son of the emir (*ciroma*), and the senior son or brother of the emir (*galadima*). Quotidian epithets are also part of Hauwa Mai Duala's song, and many of them refer to women. *Mai Babban Ɗakin Kano* (lit. "head of the big house") refers to the emir's mother, who was visited often by Maizargadi, Mai Duala's friend. *Uwa mai bene* ("rightful mother of the second story") alludes to the head wife, who sometimes enjoys the privilege of sharing the upper-story room with her husband. A woman called Rekiya shares the same status; she is described as *Rekiya mai sauwa* [*soro*], which has much the same meaning as *mai bene*.

The predominant imagery of Hauwa Mai Duala's song directly reflects the environment in which the work is performed. Though the song is primarily an expression of allegiance to those male political and community leaders named, Hauwa Mai Duala's performance is set among women in an exclusively female setting, the inner compound. Her constant repetition of praise for women is expressive of a woman's milieu; this song is not appropriate for a mixed public audience; it is geared to the private portion of a naming ceremony in which women celebrate separately from men. Hauwa Mai Duala's performance is simultaneously a declaration of political loyalties and an expression of the network of women who are the individuals of Hauwa Mai Duala's most immediate concern.

* * *

Praise songs and poems composed by contemporary Hausa women reflect a pervasive concern for literacy and the religious and social obligations of the devout Muslim, especially women. The works express an obligation toward and participation in the urban community that is manifested in the teachings of local self-improvement projects sponsored by government policies: the war on ignorance (*yaƙi da jahilci*), free primary education (*ilmi kyauta*), association, community (*jama'a*), and community work (*aikin gaiya*). General Gowon announced a policy of free primary education (universal primary education) in January 1975, and *aikin gaiya* was familiar in colonial days as a way of getting roads built.[12] Hauwa Gwaram's and Hajiya 'Yar Shehu's poems on these topics explain to a general public the intentions of these programs. The works often address social problems such as drug abuse or social changes such as new driving laws and currency changes. They report historically significant events such as the civil war, census reporting, and the establishment of local mosques, clinics, and parks (like the Kano Zoo), and they name the principal figures in those events. Songs—especially those performed for *bori* events—are always performed for the sake of entertainment, and yet most are also blatantly didactic. Their quality is not just technical; it is also determined by the depth of information they convey. Like beautiful pottery that is also functional, these songs are pleasing to the ear as well as useful in their didacticism.[13] For a song to be popular in Hausa culture, it must have message as well as melody.

The poems that Hausa women write and extemporize are not explicitly feminist tracts, but the existence of these songs speaks to the changing roles of women in Hausa culture. These songs are testimony to Hausa women's awareness of social and political events and personages. Both oral and written works share the intention to transmit information to all members of Hausa society, whether women or men, urban or rural, professional or nonprofessional. In Hausa culture, oral performances are indigenous theater that fulfills a multiplicity of needs for education, entertainment, and the communication of news about current events. The forces that have molded northern Nigerian culture have been refined and transformed into new social standards that affect current perspectives. These women's songs and poems represent widely varied perspectives on contemporary culture; considered together they contribute to a portrayal of culture in transition.

Hausa women's poetry offers clear perspectives on traditional and Western education, the regulation of mores and values, and the maintenance through *waƙoƙi* of certain historical and political perspectives. It represents women's artistic voices, whose impact has not fully been recognized in the areas of education, politics, and social history among the Hausa. To ignore the social function of these literary works is to deny their purpose in Hausa culture; to ignore women's perspectives on these issues is to hear only half the sound of contemporary Hausa voices.

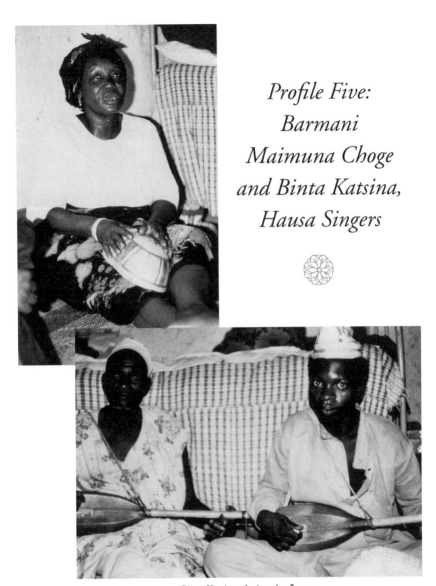

Profile Five:
Barmani
Maimuna Choge
and Binta Katsina,
Hausa Singers

Binta Katsina playing the *kwarya*
and two of her accompanists playing the *garaya*, 1979

In the 1980s, Barmani Maimuna Choge of Funtuwa was in her forties. She was born in 1945 (Furniss 1996, 141, citing Mashi 1982). She performs extemporaneously, and her performances involve a great deal of narrative and nonverbal notation. Choge's performance is raucous entertainment; she makes use of body movement, gesture, and suggestive metaphor to convey her satiric message. Her bawdy allusions and spirited performance style make her a popular entertainer. Choge is backed by a group of women—Rakiya, Zulai, Hajara, and A'ishatu—who drum on calabashes (*kwarya,* s. *kore*) and sing choral responses. Choge lives with her husband and family in Funtuwa but spends considerable time on the road and traveling to performances and to local radio and television stations for recording sessions. When I visited her in Funtuwa, I found her husband at home with the children while she was away, performing on tour.

Choge's Sufi affiliation involved her participation

> from an early age in the performance of Sufi religious litany singing, known as *kidan amada,* also known as *kidan ruwa/kidan kwarya[,]* "drumming on an upturned calabash in water" (Mashi 1982). . . . Performed often by groups of women [in seclusion,] this repetitive style of litany singing involves an act of devotion through the mentioning of saints, particularly of the Tijaniyya or Qadiriyya sect. (Furniss 1996, 141)[1]

This *zikiri* singing is still popular in the region, according to sources in Sokoto and Kano in September 2002. Music in Sufi celebrations is central to a range of devotional activities from *zikr* (Ar., repetition of "remembrances," recitations of the names of God) to mystical concerts known as *sema/samaa'* (Turkish, Ar.). Although the *samaa'* performance is more common in Asia than Africa, the *zikr* can often be heard in Northern Nigeria, especially during the month of Ramadan. Some Muslims reject the possibility of music and song as integral to devotional practices, but others argue that music and song celebrate God.[2] Maimuna Choge's familiarity with Sufism may account for the freedom she exhibits, both in her performance style and her travel throughout Northern Nigeria. In both style and venue, Maimuna Choge's performances demonstrate a philosophy that corresponds to a Sufi belief in gender equity and the need to seek higher understanding of the purpose of life. But as is evident in the analysis of her performances, Choge's work is not restricted to staid devotional activities. Indeed, the freedom with which she performs belies the stereotype of Muslim Hausa women as subdued, subordinate citizens. On the contrary, Choge's performances celebrate life, challenge the status quo, and confirm the Sufi belief that "the soul has no gender." As of September 2002, sources in Sokoto confirmed that she was still performing.

Hajiya Binta of Katsina, in her sixties in the 1980s, died in 1995. She performed extemporaneously with the accompaniment of two male chorus members—musicians who played the one-string plucked lute (*garaya*) and the upturned calabash gourd (*kwarya*) as percussion. She sang and accompanied herself on her own *kwarya.* Binta Katsina was known for *bori* music and her work "Song for the Women of Nigeria." It has been said that this song was sponsored by the National Party of Nigeria, which was interested in promoting the participation of women in public activities. Binta Katsina also performed for wedding and naming celebrations. When she performed at private functions such as wedding and naming celebrations, her audiences were secluded Muslim wives, restricted by custom to the private inner courtyards of their adobe homes and the homes of their friends for celebratory occasions. In the 1980s, she performed this song that urged the Muslim women of Northern Nigeria to take charge of their lives:

> Women of Nigeria!
> Women of Nigeria!
> You should try to understand,
> You could do every kind of work.
> Women of Nigeria, you will do every kind of work,
> You should be given the chance to take charge.
> You can do office work,
> You can do administrative work,
> You should be given the chance to take charge.

The secluded, less educated women of Binta Katsina's audience are the subject of her song, but the song advocates that these women participate actively in the public domain. Now, as in the 1980s, some women work in the public sphere as broadcasters, journalists, architects, and lawyers. Although her message may appear to run counter to the stereotype of a Hausa Muslim woman, Binta Katsina's long popularity was testimony to both the appeal of her message and the complexity of contemporary women's roles in Northern Nigeria, where the gender equity described in the Qur'an has been compromised by traditional Hausa patriarchal interpretations of Islam. That Binta Katsina was illiterate herself indicates clearly that artistic ability does not depend on literacy.

Nonroyal singers are unusually itinerant, independent women who travel from town to town, accepting invitations to perform for public events. Maimuna Choge traveled from her home town of Funtuwa to Kano, Zaria, and smaller towns along the way whenever she was hired for celebratory occasions. Binta Katsina moved around Northern Nigeria for performances from Sokoto to Kano, Zaria, and other towns beyond her home in Katsina for naming, wedding, *salla,* and *bori* ceremonies. These two women were favorites of the Bayero University student body, by whom they were invited often to perform for the annual Hausa Conference.

These women were unconstrained in choosing their performance venues. Choge and Binta Katsina were successful performers and independent businesswomen, managing their own professions. By virtue of becoming ungendered in the process of performing, they enjoyed what is perhaps the greatest degree of freedom for Hausa women, even though their freedom of movement was still restricted in comparison to that of male singers, who often travel outside the northern regions of Nigeria and even outside Nigeria itself to perform and record their music. Women who are paid performing artists use this artistry as a mechanism for exempting themselves from the status quo for Hausa women. Women singers may not travel as widely as men do, but they are free to cross cultural boundaries determined by both gender and status, which men are not able to do.

SIX

Oral and Written Hausa Poetry

> Song is the measure for poetry.
> —al-Marzubani (cited in Adonis 1990, 14–15)
>
> Recitation of poetry is a form of song.
> —Adonis 1990, 15

PRE-ISLAMIC ORIGINS OF POETRY:
THE WRITTEN DERIVED FROM THE ORAL

The communication of aesthetic works through the spoken word often is distinguished from written composition. Scholarly studies in both Arabic and Hausa poetics treat oral performance and written works separately, but the two cannot be separated entirely because they function within the same cultural context. To some degree, all Hausa poetry is oral, because both written and oral works are chanted or sung in public performance. Since oral recitation is the standard means of presenting written works, it is impossible to speak of oral or written poetry in Hausa culture without describing both. Their delivery styles, forms, and contents are integrally connected.

Traditional oral poetic style among the Hausa dates back to the beginning of its social history, which coincides with the region's legacy of Islamic and Arabic influence. It is customary for sociolinguistic studies to cite Arabic-language "borrowings" in Hausa, explaining that these derive from trans-Saharan trade relations in the last three centuries. But Hausa's deep linguistic structure offers substantive evidence of the establishment of Arabic-language influence in the region dating back at least four centuries. Arabic has contributed far more than mere "borrowings" and for far longer than was previously felt. This underlines the pervasive, long-term influence of Arabic language and culture in Hausaland. The standards of written poetry among the Hausa are derived from Arabic literary form, with their origins in orality, song, and music. The root of the Arabic term for song, *nashiid,* means the raising of the voice; the Arab adage "Song is the measure for poetry" (al-Marzubani, cited in Adonis 1990, 15) indicates that song traditionally was the means of measuring rhyme and meter. "Meters are the foundations of melodies, and poems set the standard for stringed instruments" (al-Marzubani's *al-Muwashshah,* p. 39, and Ibn Rashiq's *al-'Umda fi Mahasin al-Shi'r wa Adabihi wa Naqdihi* [cited in Adonis 1990, 14–15]). Poetry's synonymy with recitation and song also is evident in fourteenth-century historian Ibn Khaldun's observation:

> In the early period singing was a part of the art of literature, because it depended on poetry, being the setting of poetry to music. The literary and intellectual elite of the Abbasid State occupied themselves with it, intent on acquiring knowledge of the styles and genres of poetry. (Cited in Adonis 1990, 15–16)

At the same time, oral recitation has long been the basis for Islamic education: "Oral instruction was the rule not only in the teaching of hadith, but also in other sciences and arts" (Schimmel 1994, 130). Oral poetic recitation is well integrated into Islamic life and Hausa culture.

Among the Hausa, both oral and written works share common ground in the fact that they are delivered orally. Extemporaneous oral poetic performances are both decried and lauded by audiences who revel in the bawdiness of the works. More conservative written works also are recited, not just passed around in published form. In fact, it is only through the oral recitation of a written work that its authorship and credibility can be confirmed; a reliable scholar's stamp of approval on a manuscript is necessary for its authorship to be verified. Such approval can be conferred only through a successful formal reading, a recitation in which no mistakes are found, based on the memorized version known to the scholar. The implication of this process is that it is only in hearing it that the veracity of a poem can be determined.

POETRY IN HAUSA HISTORY

Hausa written poetry (*wakokin rubutu*) depends in large part on influences conveyed through the commercial trans-Saharan caravans that came to Kano from Tripoli and Tunis as early as the ninth century with exotic spices and written manuscripts to exchange for tanned animal hides, slaves, kola nuts, indigo cloth, and other indigenous products. But the North African product that was most influential was unquantifiable and freely given—Islamic culture. Arabic literacy and Islamic cultural values long have pervaded Hausa culture, particularly in the creation of written Hausa poetic form.

During the millennium between the ninth and nineteenth centuries, Hausa culture was Islamicized through mercantile trade and scholarly movement. Hausa merchants depended on learning the accounting skills of their North African Muslim counterparts and in the process began to become familiar with Arabic through Islamic writings, beginning, of course, with the Qur'an. Arab architecture, modes of dress, and values infused Hausa traditional culture most readily among royal and mercantile classes, where Arabic literacy and numeracy skills associated with Islam were necessary for political and commercial success. Hausa merchants depended on learning the accounting skills of their North African Muslim clients, and the steady stream of scholars from Timbuktu into the region increased the degree to which Arabic literacy was important in Hausaland.

Islamic influence is not restricted to circles of the literate but has great impact on the lives of the nonliterate Hausa as well. Hausa traders and peripatetic scholars with Arabic literacy as early as the sixteenth century told and were the subjects of stories, wrote letters and made lists for a paying illiterate public, and perpetuated oral traditions about Arab origins of early settlers in Hausaland. Arabic literary influence is first evident in Hausa cultural records during the reign of King Muhammad Rumfa (1463–1499), who is credited with establishing Islam in the region by building the first large mosque in Kano and instituting the celebration of annual post-Ramadan festivals, such as Eid al-Fitr. The innovations of King Muhammad Rumfa in Kano's royal court in the fifteenth century are remembered to this day in oral histories in verse. His most influential act was to establish Arabic as the language of the courts, and he is renowned in oral traditions as "the Arab King, of wide sway!" (Palmer 1967, 111–112). By the sixteenth century, the move toward literacy led to the establishment of Hausa language in Arabic script (*ajami*),[1] and Arabic language and concepts began to shape Hausa communication at its deepest semantic level. The Fulani Muslim clerics who moved into the region (circa 1400s C.E.) from the western Futa Toro (Senegal) and Futa Jalon (Guinea) regions were perhaps most influential in spreading literacy. Hausa kings were not scholars themselves but relied on the literacy skills of these clerics, whose skills in Qur'anic verse laid the foundations for literary structures in Hausa culture while also allowing for communication and negotiation with their North African visitors. Meanwhile, Hausa royal praise singers declaimed for their kings, announcing the arrival of royalty at an event with shouted praises of the king's attributes and genealogy. Hausa oral traditions are replete with literate characters whose scholarly acumen functions as the magic that can resolve the tale's dilemma. Thus, Arabic literacy has been common in the region for at least four centuries, even if it has been the privilege of only a minority of the population. The medium of communication is Hausa, but Islamic precepts and Arabic language are integral to discussion.

In the seventeenth and eighteenth centuries, the Islamic cleric class became even more influential in the development of Hausa culture and language. Although most of the population was neither literate nor well versed (literally or figuratively) in formal Islam, the degree to which the rising Muslim cleric class influenced the social order early on was significant as literacy and religiosity became closely aligned. Contemporary scholars are divided on the social order of Hausa society prior to the nineteenth-century Sokoto jihad; some feel that society was divided between peasantry and the elite royal and mercantile classes, while others make a convincing argument that the Muslim cleric class was the predominant social influence (Furniss 1996, 285). In any case, the influence of literate religious figures resulted in the simultaneous spread of both Islamic doctrine and literacy.

As Islam's appeal to the general populace began to rise, Hausa leaders increasingly felt threatened by shifting loyalties in a populace moving rapidly toward Islam, whose literal meaning, "acceptance of the will of God," was seen by royalty as a threat to loyalty to the king. Indeed, resistance to the incipient influence of Islam led to a nineteenth-century conflict between a traditional Hausa leader and the charismatic Muslim preacher Shehu Usman dan Fodiyo. Eventually the perceived competition between God and king led to a local king's suppression of freedom to worship and armed conflict. The Shehu's campaign to confirm his right to preach Islam and reform syncretic versions of the faith resulted in a military campaign, the Sokoto jihad. Fodiyo's aim in resisting the oppression of his followers by Hausa leaders was twofold: first, to free Muslims (especially recent converts) to practice openly, and second, to replace traditional animist rites and their lascivious celebrations with orthodox Islamic modes of decorum. Fodiyo's jihad resulted in the nineteenth-century reformation of Islam in Northern Nigeria and the replacement of its Hausa non-Muslim kings with Fulani Muslim emirs. The use of poetry, especially the *qasida* form, was central to the accomplishment of these sociopolitical goals. Classic Arabic-form *qasida,* a verse with end rhymes that is set in one of the classical Arabic verse meters, is a hymnic ode that predates Islam (Hiskett 1975, 154; Schimmel 1994, 144). The *qasida* has long been associated with both pre-Islamic and Arab-Islamic cultures. In the Ottoman Empire, it was a primary means of expressing loyalty to the monarch—the panegyric ode. The importance of the pre-Islamic *qasida* as one of the foundations of Arab-Islamic poetry is evident in studies that speak of the Ottoman *kaside* as a "gift to the monarch," and therefore it is never trivial, as can be the case with modern Western poetry (Stetkevych 1993 and 2002; Andrews 1993, 166). In the Hausa context, the *qasida* has been called the "classic vehicle for panegyric" and the "means and product of 'calling people to the religion of God'" (Hiskett 1975, 18–19, in Boyd and Furniss 1993, 240).

In nineteenth-century Hausaland, the *qasida* led to a focus on panegyrics of God, over and above the non-Muslim kings whose un-Islamic behavior was criticized in verse. Such verse forms were to become the vernacular of sociopolitical commentary in the culture. More than simply a form for the expression of criticism, the *qasida* soon became the means of instilling inspiration toward reformed behavior, moving beyond didacticism to a sense of purposiveness in the wake of the nineteenth-century Sokoto jihad (Boyd and Furniss 1993, 251). Members of the Fodiyo clan used *qasida* extensively to persuade through panegyric, expressing the laudable qualities of Muslims whose lives should be emulated (Boyd and Mack 1997; Mack and Boyd 2000). Through the prolific output of the Fodiyo clan in the context of reformation, the term *qasida,* which originally referred only to panegyric, came into broad usage in Hausa culture: "As purposiveness became an all-pervading characteristic of Hausa poetry so also the term *qasida* became a general term for all verse constructed in the stanzaic and metrical forms associated with Arabic poetry" (Boyd and Furniss 1993, 251). *Qasida* works were performed in public venues, where the message reached many more ears than eyes. Poetry became an instrument of sociopolitical change and was accessible to both the minority who were literate and the majority of illiterate citizens.

The jihad also brought a flourishing of Qur'anic education and the establishment of Arabic literacy skills and poetic modes as the prime vehicle of communication among scholars. Indeed, the nineteenth-century jihad had to establish a new, Islamic worldview if it was to be successful in the long term. Poetic verse was central to accomplishing this aim. The Fodiyo clan's prolific literary output marked the Sokoto jihad as a movement of intellectual, as well as politico-religious, reform.

Religious concerns were integral to the curriculum of Qur'anic education, but they were not its sole focus. Contemporary concerns needed to be part of the reintegration process that would confirm the jihad's success in Nigeria. It was not enough to tell people about God, they also needed to be instructed how to pray, what to wear and eat, how to conduct themselves, and how to think about their history. The oral dissemination of these verses was central to the regularization of the lives of jihad battle refugees and was instrumental in reforming Islam in Hausa culture. Prime among the Fodiyo scholars was Nana Asma'u, whose poetry was instrumental in the resocialization of widows and orphans. She recognized the oral nature of Hausa culture, so she wrote the works she felt should reach the people at large—the Qur'an, *Sufi Women,* and *Be Sure of God's Truth*—in Hausa instead of in her first language, Fulfulde. This rendered them immediately available to the masses; most were not literate and spoke only Hausa. These works were meant for oral delivery, so both the itinerant teachers ('Yan Taru), and their students, young women secluded in their homes, committed the poems to memory. Singing these works constituted the lesson plan and served as a lesson that students could integrate into their own experience, even without writing it down.

FEATURES OF ORAL POETRY

An oral performance of either extemporaneous or written material can occur only with an audience to hear it, but an extemporaneous performance has much greater freedom of expression; performers can use intonation and nonverbal gestures to embellish the words, providing a subtext of implied meaning. Moreover, oral poetry is distinguished from written poetry in that it seems to be more than the sum of its parts; the poem must please the listener by manipulating words to create unexpected relationships between them. The oral poem plays with language, not only by lengthening vowels and intoning words in uncommon ways but also by incorporating gestures, body language, and facial expressions that imbue the song with layers of meaning (Scheub 1977a, 1977b). Extemporaneous oral Hausa poetry might even be compared to contemporary Western rap music, since both rely on the expertise of the singer to perform rapid-fire strings of phrases that rhyme or otherwise blend together in a cohesive whole. Certainly in both cases the performer depends on a repertoire of set phrases in his or her own performance vocabulary, but the delivered piece will be unique with each performance because of nuance (verbal and nonverbal) and adjustments of content for a particular audience.[2]

Hausa oral poetry is unique to Hausa culture and is vibrant and in constant flux. Certain related features between Hausa oral and written poetry are evident, such as formulaic doxologies, greetings, and colloquialisms. But what makes oral poetic performance appealing is its unpredictability, and that is what drives enthusiastic audience support for public performances in a wide range of venues. Whether women performers appear at a university, a political rally, or for segregated audiences of women in private settings, the audience relies on being surprised, challenged, and happily shocked by the songs that express what cannot be said in polite company.

OPENING AND CLOSING DOXOLOGY

The *basmala* is the invocation *Bismillahi ar-Rahman, ar-rahim* ("Let us begin in the name of God, the All Merciful, the All Compassionate"), which is the formulaic opening to any activity—a meal, a trip, any undertaking. These words, which preface every Qur'anic chapter except Chapter 9 are based on the root *r-h-m* "which [term] also designates the mother's womb, and thus convey[s] the warm, loving care of the Creator for all His creatures" (Schimmel 1994, 222–223). The repetition of this phrase at the beginning of any endeavor conveys "to the Muslim a moderate optimism" (Denny 1984 in Schimmel 1994, 223). God's help is always invoked and anticipated. It is said that one who writes the *basmala* beautifully is guaranteed a place in heaven (Schimmel 1994, 124). The *basmala* is revered, but it is also commonly found throughout the culture, on bumper stickers, necklaces, tiles, postcards, and decorative design in textiles (Schimmel 1994, 152). Thus, is it not surprising that an opening invocation to God is a standard part of poetic composition. Hausa women always open both oral and written poems with formulaic doxologies.

Not only is the particular *basmala* fundamental to a Muslim's worldview, but the idea of expecting a formal opening is integral to it as well. The *fatiha* (lit., the "key" or "opening") is the first verse of the Qur'an. It is perhaps the most frequently recited portion of the Qur'an, integrated as it is into each of the five daily prayer sessions familiar to Muslims everywhere. It is not surprising that in the written material discussed here, Hauwa Gwaram and Hajiya 'Yar Shehu habitually begin their works with:

1   Beginning in the name of God I will compose a song,
      For women to come to the library to learn an occupation. ("Song for the Opening of the Course at the Old Library in Sabon Gari")

1   Oh God, may He be praised, Predestinator and Just One,
      Help those who built the mosque. ("Song for the Opening of the Second Friday Mosque in Kano")

One or two lines' duration is most common, but occasionally the praise is continued for several stanzas, as in Hajiya 'Yar Shehu's "Song on the Census of the People of Nigeria":

1   Let us begin in the name of God, I begin in the name of the Lord,
      God the Almighty—May He be exalted—the King of Truth.
2   You are omniscient, You hear all, You know all.
      Protect us from evil, from the world's wicked ones.
3   For the sake of Mohammad, the leader of all on earth,
      And of the afterlife too, if You grant it to him,
4   For the sake of the Prophets, the Companions, those who were sent,
      And for all the relatives of the Apostle, the exemplary one.
5   Grant me protection,
      You who are our defense, which cannot be eroded.
6   I will compose on the census of the districts
      Of the North and of all our country together.

Just as one does not move directly into conversation without first greeting a friend at length, so too the poem cannot begin without an appropriate acknowledgment of the role of God in every endeavor.

Although doxologies are discussed in the literature as standard features of written poems, it is rare that they are discussed in the context of oral works, which often are considered to be reflective of Hausa tradition outside the ambit of Islamic influence. But Islam pervades every aspect of Hausa culture, so it is not surprising that extended praise in opening doxologies is a regular feature of extemporaneous songs; this is suprapraise that extols the virtues of God before the singer even begins to speak about the patron at hand. In these performances, the singer repeats epithets for God for four to six lines and continues to include invocations interspersed throughout the rest of the song.

The opening doxology is so standard an element of orally composed songs that even music for the non-Islamic *bori* cult begins with an invocation to God (King 1967, 110). In oral performance, the invocation comes at the beginning of the song and sometimes at the beginning of each new piece, as one song flows into another. Maimuna Choge's several songs for the 1980 Bayero University Hausa Conference were part of a continuous performance, but their individual introductions were signaled by a change in rhythm and a series of introductory doxologies. The following examples are excerpts from various songs that are part of one continuous performance:

1   In the name of God, let us begin in the name of God,
2   Let us begin in the name of God, I begin in the name of the Merciful, I will praise God
3   Creation is His, the Lord of life gave life to a thousand, gave life to three thousand, Lord without equal!
4   God Who rules even the evil spirits, hide my secrets from my enemies! [transition to new song]
204   Children, may God give long life to your families
205   Hey, conference [attendees], may God give you knowledge
206   Now may God reward [us], may God bless us,
217   Only God, buttocks, God, buttocks
266   Praise be to God, I will tell you about the wicked wife.

As the reader may expect, the juxtaposition of the words "God" and "buttocks" is extremely irreverent, and one suspects the audience laughter reflects embarrassment. That the sequence of words appears to create a non sequitur indicates the importance of nonverbal communication in these works; the juxtaposition of these disparate images seemed quite in keeping with the overall performance during its delivery. Binta Katsina's oral performance on the same occasion involved the same kind of transition from song to song, each introduced by a change in musical rhythm and invocations to God:

1   Let us begin in the name of God, the Lord God
2   God, Master of the east and the west
3   Who rules over south and north

4   May God set things right, the blessings of God set things right,
5   Oh king of night and day, important one,
6   Blessings of God, the paramount King, oh God,
7   I draw from the east, I draw from the north
8   From the east I beg, all seven heavens,[3] I beg
9   You know the seven, may God set them right, the seven, oh God repair the
        impossible,
10   Because I know of no one else like God
11   Let us begin in the name of God, who will set things right, the blessings of
        God the paramount King
12   Oh King of the night and day will set things right
        [transition to new song]
285 God, our Lord, our Prophet, God's Messenger
286 Help the women of Nigeria
287 God, our Lord, our Prophet, God's Messenger
288 Help the women of Nigeria

In these lines, the repetition of praise epithets to God creates a pattern that
establishes a focus on God throughout the work.

The closing doxologies of written works involve thanks for the guidance and wisdom to compose the poem. They occur several stanzas prior
to the poem's end. In Hauwa Gwaram's "Song for the Association of Women
of the North," the closing doxology occurs three verses before the end:

45   It is finished with praise to God, here I shall stop,
        The song about women of the association of the North.

Into the final and sometimes the penultimate verse of the other poems, praise is repeated and a signature is woven in to inform the
audience of the work's author, as in Hauwa Gwaram's "Song of Warning to Those Who Take Drugs I":

42   Seeing something in another is enough to cause fear,
        May God protect Muslims; let them stop taking drugs
43   May God give us good luck, oh God, protect us,
        God protect us from this wickedness of the addicts
44   It is finished with praise to God, here I shall stop,
        Hauwa Gwaram I am; I do not take drugs.

That women continue to include doxologies in secular works when men
are giving up the practice may be indicative of women's tendency toward
greater adherence to traditional practices, especially in relation to endeavors that might otherwise be inappropriate for them.[4] The practice reflects

Hauwa Gwaram and Hajiya 'Yar Shehu's strict Qur'anic literary backgrounds and couches their work in a religious framework that is above criticism.

In a Muslim culture like that of the Hausa, it is natural for individuals to wrap up any event with thanks to God, so both oral performance and written pieces are marked by the standard closing doxology phrase *Alhamdu lillahi* ("Thanks be to God"). The pattern of closing doxologies is not as regular in extemporaneous songs, where endings are contingent upon performance circumstances. The song's end or transition to another tune is signaled by a combination of factors—waning audience interest, the performer's fatigue, or an externally determined stopping point, which can all mark the proper moment to end or change an oral performance. Since oral song is composed extemporaneously, there is no impetus to progress through a given amount of material as in written works. The repertoire is not fixed; it can depend on audience response. The nature of oral composition precludes explicit endings as regular features, but entertainers are often heard to mutter *alhamdulillahi* as they turn away from their audiences at the end of their performances. In written works, the phrase is woven into the rhyme scheme of the final verses, marking the formal end of the poem.

CHRONOGRAMS

A chronogram, or *ramzi,* weaves the date of the poetic work into the end of the work itself by using certain Arabic characters that have calculable numeric value (Hiskett 1977, 169; Schimmel 1994, 76–83). A *ramzi* in a poem in the Hausa language written in Arabic script would consist of a line in which the numerical value of the letters carries meaning for a date in time; the numerical system used by Hausas writing in *ajami* differs from that used by those writing in standard (Egyptian) Arabic, which means that Hausa has its own particular means of calculating the *ramzi* (Hiskett 1975, 169 passim). The Hausa *ramzi* technique deepens a poem's meaning by giving the words a second meaning associated with a date.

While the creation of the *ramzi* is not possible in poems in Latin script where numerical value is not assigned to letters, authors sometimes simply include composition dates in their closing doxologies: "On Thursday I wrote this, / The tenth of May I finished. / In seventy-three I wrote this poem: / Whoever heard it liked it / Let's go visit the zoo" ("Song for Abdu Bako's Zoo," v. 33). Occasionally the date of the event the poem celebrates is included at the beginning of the poem:

2   On Monday the seventh in the second month,
   We went to visit the health care workers. ("Song for a Visit to the Birnin Kudu Hospital")

3   On the twentieth day of sixty-nine in December,
    The Emir of Kano, Ado, opened the mosque. ("Song for the Opening of the
    Second Friday Mosque in Kano")

    On the tenth of January we want
    To open a course for women to learn an occupation.
    In nineteen hundred and seventy-four
        We want to teach women an occupation. ("Song for the Opening of the
        Course at the Old Library in Sabon Gari"; vv. 3 and 4)

The inclusion of dates of composition or mention of occasions for the performances are not standard features of extemporaneous songs, though the women who perform them often do include themselves in their commentaries, weaving in signatures of authorship in the only manner suitable to the oral literary form, self-reference.

REPETITION IN DECLAMATION
AND WRITTEN WORKS

Repetition is a central mnemonic device that depends on metaphoric transformation to prevent it from becoming boring. Schimmel discusses poetic repetition in high Islamic poetry as involving the circumambulation of a central idea, focusing attention on it from all directions, just as the pilgrim in Makka devotes her focus to the Kaaba. Using a repeated rhyming word or phrase (*radif*), the poet "tries to approach the Divine from all possible new angles to give at least a faint idea of His greatness" (1994, 115). Muslims familiar with the Qur'an and poetic expression related to it would understand the value of such repetition.

For Hausa poets, repetition is central to both declamation and writing; the art of praise singing and expository performance as well as the composition of written works depends on the repetition of ideas for metaphoric effect. The most common types of interwoven phrasing depend on the complete, partial, or implied repetitions of lines, phrases, and terms.[5] The complete repetition of a line often punctuates more subtle repetitions, and sometimes a call-and-response interchange is effective in producing the repetition of images. Popular religious songs throughout the world share similar characteristics: the Turkish *ilahi* involves repetitive four-line stanzas, the Indo-Pakistani *qawwali* includes alternating voices of the leader and chorus, and in Sindhi and Panjabi languages the "theme is given by an initial line which is then repeated after every one or two lines by the chorus" (Schimmel 1994, 114). Repetition is the universal cornerstone of poetic style.

In performance there are several ways in which such complete repetitions are expressed. The most straightforward manner is the performer's repetition of the same phrase in close sequence. Hauwa Mai Duala of Ningi uses this technique in her oral performance:

12 Mother of the Emir, mother of all the town,
13 Mother of the Emir, mother of all the town.
15 The giver of robes,
16 The giver of robes,
42 Spear-throwing that mocks brave men
43 Spear-throwing that mocks brave men
   The new baby girl in Kano, 'Yar Mamman
45 The new baby girl in Kano, 'Yar Mamman ("Song for the Emir of Kano and
   the Emir of Ningi")

Occasionally a complete repetition will occur within one line, that is, within one breath-phrase, such as: "Mighty Aminu, mighty Aminu" (l. 75). An appended or deleted exclamation may mark the only difference between two identical repeated phrases, as does "Thanks be to God" at the beginning of this example:

38 Thanks be to God, I saw the Emir, the leader of the people of Katsina,
39 I saw the Emir, the leader of the people of Katsina.

Maimuna Choge's "Praise Song for the Hausa Conference" demonstrates the use of repeated phrases directly relevant to the work's theme. In this work, which deals with the varieties of lucrative professions, she uses a complete repetition of "God grant us money" nine times over 199 lines. While this may seem a small percentage of recurrence, the figure is implicitly inflated by the repetition of the term "the money" in many other phrases, like these two:

152 My playing goes where the money is,
157 The real playing goes where the money is

Choge's repeated references to money and a patron's (whether God's or a human's) generosity run through the work. Repetitions of "May God grant us money" refocus for the audience the partial image that is reinforced each time she mentions "the money" in another line. The complete repetition's key term, "the money," suggests the larger phrase whenever it is repeated in another line.

In close proximity to mention of "God, You gave us money"[6] is the recurrent "A nice thing!"[7] Such repeated juxtaposition of these two complete repetitions identifies them as mutually related. By constantly placing the two phrases close to each other, Choge suggests to her audience the positive value of having money.

Central to another semantic thread running through the work is the repeated reference to one of Choge's musicians: "Ladi, calabash drummer." In the twelve complete repetitions of this form of address, Choge focuses attention on her chorus and their drumming. She addresses herself to them and to Ladi in particular in another complete repetition that refers to the purpose of their performance:

84   This is drumming for the students
93   This is drumming for the students
95   This is drumming for the head of the shari'a court, and for Muntari, son of his house
116   This is drumming for Muntari
149   This is drumming for the students
183   This is drumming for the scholars
185   This is drumming for Muntari, that's it, for Muntari, son of his house, hey!

These remarks are always set in close proximity to references to Ladi.[8] This is Choge's oblique manner of relating several images to one another. The audience is repeatedly informed of: 1) the reason for the performance ("This is drumming for . . ."); 2) Ladi's role ("Ladi, calabash drummer"); and 3) the desired effect of all their work together ("God grant us money"). Thus, the complete repetition of whole lines serves two purposes: it holds an image before the audience by its constant repetition and it connects those repeated images to a larger one by juxtaposing the two ideas, creating a single impression by the combination of many smaller images.

Interwoven phrasing through partial repetition creates a different complexity. The simplest repetitions are of two types: one type includes semantic change within a series of lines that are grammatically the same, while the other type involves grammatical changes in the phrases with shared semantic identities. The creation of a list introduces each new object in the same way, allowing semantic change within an established grammatical form. In the following excerpt from Maimuna Choge's "Praise Song for the Hausa Conference," the particle "and" links many lines in a catalogue:

41   And you, Audu's wife, who spends the night drumming
42   And you, who beats on the large calabash
43   And you, daughter of the government, high shakes and low shakes, Choge's work
45   For God's sake, let me pray attentively
46   It's during stormy weather that one drinks water from the pot
49   And you see Choge
50   While I praise with my begging voice
51   And Ladi, the calabash drummer
52   And our Hausa Conference

53 And my guests, and the children watching Choge
   Choral response
54 For God's sake let me pray well
55 While I praise with my begging voice
   Choral response
56 And those who play the large calabash
57 And you, you are a daughter of the government, with my work I will beg you
58 And I give thanks
59 When they see Kwaire they'll put down a gift
60 While I praise with my begging voice
61 And I give thanks
62 And a gift for the night of drumming
63 And I remember God
64 Drum abundantly! Driver,
65 If you put me in a car
66 Take me to the city to play
67 Let's consider modern times
68 He's put on a lace shirt
69 Moreover, on his wrist he wears a watch . . .

The repetition of "and" gives structure to the work at the same time that it links a multiplicity of terms. Then, building on a repeated phrase, various terms are added to the basic list, as in this example from the same work:

69 Moreover, on his wrist he wears a watch
70 Moreover, on his eyes he wears glasses
71 Moreover, on his feet he wears shoes
   Choral response—Let's buy a white cloth and act like European
   Let's buy a bottle and decorate the room [like Europeans do]
147 Me, I won't despise the drummers
148 Me, I won't despise the small children

Fundamental to these partial repetitions is the persistence of a particular grammatical structure. Whether subject, verb, or object is replaced, it is replaced consistently within the list—there are no midlist switches in which, for example, a noun phrase is substituted for a verb phrase.

Deviation from this rule of consistency occurs when the dimensions of a partial repetition increase. A partial repetition may maintain its catalogue quality while undergoing transition within a stable milieu. Consider this example from Choge's performance:

18 May God increase [your] intelligence
19 And advance [your] way to enlightenment
20 May God advance the way to higher status

21 May God advance the way to promotion
    Choral response
22 Greetings! Put on perseverance like a shirt! Be God-fearing!
23 May God ensure abundant prosperity!

In this case, Choge maintains stability within change in several ways. "God" is repeated at the beginning of lines 18, 20, 21, and 23 and follows a progressive action ("increase," "advance," "ensure") in each line. The object phrase is patterned; there is stability within its transformation. In line 19, "way to enlightenment" replaces "intelligence." Then a portion of the new phrase is maintained ("a way to[ward]") while a portion is changed (to "higher status" and "promotion") in the two following lines. In line 23, "prosperity" replaces the most recent "a way to[ward]" construction and is repeated for emphasis in the same line. The effect of all this is to create a new repetition of terms ("abundant prosperity") within the milieu of an earlier repetition ("May God increase"). What the audience hears several lines later has been prepared for by the previous sequence: (line 37) "Hey! May God advance the ways to enlightenment, may God advance the way toward promotion." The delivery of that line lasts for only a few seconds, but in that brief time the audience is implicitly reminded of the several intricate partial repetitions that have preceded it.

Partial repetition in Maimuna Choge's work demonstrates the device of syntactical slot replacement. In the following lines a portion of the structure is maintained while another portion is repeatedly substituted with varied, albeit grammatically comparable phrases:

84 This is drumming for the students
93 This is drumming for the students
95 This is drumming for the head of the shari'a court, and Muntari, of his
      household
116 Like this drumming for Muntari
149 This is drumming for the students
183 This is drumming for the scholars
185 This is drumming for Muntari, that's it, Muntari, and for his house, hey!
      ("Praise Song for the Hausa Conference")

These repeated phrases are not sequential but are spread throughout the work, just as is evident in South African poetic style (Kunene 1971, 92–94). The phrases constitute appositives rather than contributing to a narrative development: students (*'yan ilmi*; lit., people of knowledge), scholars (*'yan biro*; lit., people of the pen), Muntari, and "son of [Muntari's] house" (*dan gidansa*) refers back to similar individuals in the audience, any one of whom could be the subject of the song. Maimuna Choge uses the sporadic recurrence of these partial repetitions to different effect than oral poets of heroic verse, since she is concerned with the continued recurrence of an image rather than the progressive development of a narrative.

The structure of Binta Katsina's "Song for the Women of Nigeria" likewise offers a kaleidoscopic perspective on her subject. The complete repetition of "women of Nigeria" occurs alone (i.e., in its own breath-phrase) twelve times over eighty-seven lines. It is also appended to other repeated phrases, sometimes occurring at the front of the line (thirteen times) and sometimes at the end (five times). The types of phrases connected with "women of Nigeria" are grammatically comparable, as is expected in syntactic slot repetition. The following sequence offers six varied grammatically comparable phrases modifying "women of Nigeria":

304	Women of Nigeria, you could do every kind of work
305	You should do every kind of work
306	Women of Nigeria, you could do every kind of work
307	Women of Nigeria, you could do office work
308	You can do paperwork
309	You can do paperwork
310	Women of Nigeria, you could take charge of the school
311	Women of Nigeria, you could take charge of the school and hang on to it
312	You could be government officials
313	Women of Nigeria, you could do every kind of work
314	You could do every kind of work
315	Here, women of Nigeria, you could do the typing work . . .

The objects of verb phrases throughout the song—more than are shown here—all refer to kinds of professional work that women should be allowed to do: paperwork, typing, clerical work, running the schools, customs work, office work, government work, ministry work, driving, running trains, piloting planes, and police work. In short, Binta Katsina asserts that the women of Nigeria should be able to do every kind of work (*kowane aiki*). Her song is composed of the constant rearrangement of a set number of related noun phrases, verb phrases, and object phrases. Verbal aspects are directive, often imperative, inspiring motivation in their positive, energetic delivery. Thus, in relation to their functions, these sets of noun, verb, and object phrases maintain a grammatical consistency, while they establish a multiplicity of images in each category.

On another level, however, the balance of grammatical consistency with semantic variety is reversed. The effect of repeated related images is to evoke an overview. This occurs in the preceding example as the noun-object phrase "every kind of work" eventually comes to represent all other noun-object phrases. A sense of active participation is the qualitative effect of the accumulated verb phrases. As the work's message is unfolded during performance, the condition of repeated grammatical structures with semantic variety is transformed to a state of semantic consistency grounded in that grammatical variety. That is, the implication of women's unlimited professional potential is conveyed through a variety of suggestions expressed in a similar manner. The constant reworking of these phrases bombards the listener with the impression of an endless array of possibilities for Nigerian women's professional opportunities.

The second major type of partial repetition is perhaps most evident in lists of praise epithets. These involve grammatical change and semantic consistency. Maizargadi regularly depended on many different, well-known descriptive phrases for the subject of a song. When she described the Emir of Kano, Alhaji Ado Bayero, she used any of the following expressions to describe him: emir, king, Kano's caretaker, Kano's leader, son of Abdullahi [Bayero], mighty leader of Kano, bull elephant, reformer (lit., burner of the fetish groves), heir of Kano. These descriptive phrases, familiar to her audience, clearly refer to Alhaji Ado Bayero, the Emir of Kano. In addition, she used local terms of praise: head of those in Medina, head of Kano, head of Zaria, and the healer. And finally, because her audience was Muslim and very familiar with the ninety-nine names of God, she incorporated some of these praise names of God, which represent the zenith of praise epithets: the Merciful, the Omniscient, the Almighty.

Other examples of this type of partial repetition were exhibited by Hauwa Mai Duala of Ningi, who applied local praise epithets in descriptions of God:

23   God, the divider of falsehood from Truth
24   The true king, the master of today and tomorrow
25   The king, controller of men's movements
26   The king of men's inheritance . . .
27   Adamu Ado Bayero, Ado, descendent of Muhammadu
28   Leader of the army of Kano, who acts without delay ("Song for the Emir of Kano and the Emir of Ningi")

By their position, however, these praises represent a transition from focus on God to a focus on the emir. The term *sarki* may be translated as "king." By opening her sequence with "God" in line 23, naming God as the king of various conditions, and then moving on to describe the human king in Kano, Hauwa Mai Duala moves the king-related imagery from religious to secular by her sequence of partial repetitions, progressing ultimately to a description of the new subject of her song, the King of Kano.

Ambiguity inherent in the term *sarki* along with the familiar Hausa agentive aspect allows one to speak of a king of many contexts: God as king of the universe, the emir as a local king, indeed, anyone who is master of something, such as king of the beggars. In this sequence, partial repetition ostensibly maintains one semantic focus while undergoing grammatical change. On a deeper level, a transition in focus from God to man occurs simultaneously and yet without causing offense.

Partial repetition that involves grammatical change and semantic repetition is common to praise epithets in Hausa declamation. Many different names or descriptive phrases are applied to one individual or image. Partial repetition involving grammatical stability through which is effected semantic change is also at the heart of the popular Hausa declamatory device of cataloguing: citing possessions, growth, and relations at great length conveys concepts of wealth, fecundity, and heritage. Most partial repetitions, however, are located between the two extremes discussed above. They commonly involve slight grammatical variations and subtle semantic change. In such a fashion, the song itself is advanced while it is held together. Lines change enough to prevent audience boredom, yet they continue to resemble each other enough—both grammatically and semantically—to convey similarity in design and intent and to maintain the work's rhythm. It is these many variations of partial repetitions in combination with complete repetitions that constitute the arrangement of Hausa oral poems.

Occasionally portions of complete repetitions are combined in one line that creates a phrase of several partial repetitions. In Maimuna Choge's "Praise Song for the Hausa Conference," several lines represent a combination of patterns that precede them. Following several repetitions of "begging voice" (lines 55 and 60) and "see Choge" (lines 38 and 43), Choge combines the two patterns in line 77: "While I praise with my begging voice . . . and you see Choge." The idea of thankfulness in repetitions of "and I give thanks" (lines 58 and 61) is combined with reference to the Hausa Conference crowd (lines 15, 24, 52, and 79) in line 81: "We thank the Hausa Conference, hey!" Choge and the chorus refer to "money" in lines 80, 89, 92, 101, 103, 111, 125, 139, and 141; in lines 51, 82, 94, 98, 113, 136, and 142, they refer to "calabash drumming"; and in lines 88, 102, 112, and 124, they refer to "a nice thing": this is brought together in line 145: "Today I said [to us, money] Chorus— . . . calabash drumming, a nice thing!" Such combinations seem almost too obvious to mention as features of patterning and repetition, and they are certainly based on a commonsense approach to the topic. Yet such repetition in pattern is allowed in song where it might be redundant in a written work and is rendered necessary to the rhythmic delivery of the work. These patterns are not consciously planned, as they probably would be in a written work, but they occur spontaneously and reflect a performer's individual style. Indeed, the ability to make repeated patterns in this way is a singer's necessary talent.

In a different manner, Choge creates two separate patterns from a line delivered early in the song, in line 15: "Hey! Our Hausa Conference, I say, you should pray, little girl." Throughout the rest of this performance, she creates a pattern in reference to "the Hausa Conference crowd" (lines 24, 52, 79, 81, 99, and 106) and "you should pray, little girl" (alternating with "daughter of Amanawa") (lines 29, 83, 104, 140, 163, and 194); the term conference (*ƙungiya*), itself feminine in gender, is the "little girl" to whom she refers.[9] ("Little girl," "daughter of Amanawa," and "Kungiyar Hausa" can all be considered appositives.) In these examples of combined partial repetitions, significant portions of several different established patterns are repeated together in one line, suggesting several patterns occurring at one moment.

IMPLIED REPETITION

Overlaying these various repetitions are implied repetitions whose effect lies in their phonological similarities. The most rudimentary of these repetitions has a subtle catalogue effect, creating an appositive image:

4   Beloved Friend
5   Beloved spirit of the world. (Hauwa Mai Duala, "Song for the Emir of Kano and the Emir of Ningi")

Here the repeated use of "beloved" relates the second line to the one preceding it. "Beloved" (*habibi*) is often used in religious poetry in reference to the Prophet Muhammad, the "Beloved of God," so in this case the epithet "Beloved Habibi" is implicitly repetitious: "Beloved Friend."

Maimuna Choge's "Praise Song for the Hausa Conference" contains a catalogue repetition to which is appended a phrase that, by virtue of its phonological similarity, echoes part of the catalogue that precedes it:

69   Moreover, on his wrist he wears a watch
70   Moreover, on his eyes he wears glasses
71   Moreover, on his feet he wears shoes
73   Today I said to him, Garba's son, the one with light-skinned women

"Moreover" (lit., "then," "next," "so") and "today," "here," and "now" do not share the same meaning, but the latter is a phonological echo of those that precede it: *ran nan* (today) echoes the repeated *san nan* (moreover).

In the same song, Choge plays on similar sounds in *saya* ("to buy"), *tsaya* and *tsai* ("to stop"), and *tsegumi* ("gossip"), all of which occur in one line. *Sai ta* ("let her") also resembles the sound. Line 32, *Sai ta tsai da gulma, ta sayi tabarma, ta tsaya bata gida da tsegumi,* translates as "Let her stop making mischief, let her buy the mat, let her stop ruining her home with gossip"; in the Hausa, one hears similar repeated sounds. In another sequence, Choge develops a rhythmic pattern of sounds in a few lines:

143	*Ga shi, mun tashi, mun yi rawa,*	Look, we got up, we've danced
144	*Na kira sunanki, na yi rawa*	I called your name, I danced
195	*Mun je, mun tashi, mun yi rawa*	We came, we stood up, we danced
196	*Har na je Faranshi na yi rawa*	Even when I went to Niger I danced[10]
197	*Dutsen-ma na je na kwana rawa*	To Dutsen-ma I went and I spent the night dancing.

In the first example above *ga shi* and *tashi* resemble each other phonologically, as does the repetition of *yi rawa*. The second example involves the phonological repetitions of *mun je, na je, mun yi rawa, na yi rawa,* and *kwana rawa.*

If a catalogue involves the introduction of phonologically similar items on a list, it constitutes an implied repetition. The latter is actually distinct from a partial repetition or catalogue, however, because it focuses on phonological resemblance rather than on grammatical or semantic similarities. Binta Katsina's "Song for the Women of Nigeria" contains an implied repetition within a partial repetition toward the end of the work. She sings:

367	*Biyayya kun iya*	You can be obedient
368	*Soyayya kun iya, da biyayya 'yan Nijeriya*	You can be loving and obedient, daughters of Nigeria
369	*Soyayya kun iya, da biyayya kun iya*	You can be loving and obedient.

In addition to the partial repetition of the line as *kun iya* recurs, Binta Katsina alternates between *biyayya* and *soyayya*. Their phonological similarity constitutes an implied repetition, as does their partial similarity to *iya*.

In the selected lines that follow there are several partial repetitions:

8	Hey! You Hausa Conference students, I have come to your place without anger
15	Hey! Our Hausa Conference, let me say that you should pray, little girl
24	Hey! You see the conference crowd is seated
52	And our Hausa Conference crowd,
79	You see the Hausa Conference crowd. Let us do the low shake to enjoy ourselves!
81	We thank the Hausa Conference, look out!
85	You see the Hausa Conference
87	Let me do the low shake to enjoy myself, look out!
99	See, the Hausa Conference students have come
100	If only they do the low shake, they will feel fine
101	Let them do the high shake with money!

106   Well, here we are at the Hausa Conference
110   And let me do the low shake to feel fine
111   Do the high shake with money, hey!
122   Let us do the high shake so we'll feel fine
123   One does the low shake . . .
      (Chorus: . . . for money!)
124   A nice thing!
152   My playing goes where the money is
157   The real playing goes where the money is ("Song for the Hausa Conference")

Two types of implied repetition are involved here. First, *kun ga ƙungiyar Hausa* ("You see the Hausa Conference crowd") represents an implied repetition within one line because *kun ga* ([you] see) suggests the sound of the separate term *ƙungiya* (conference). Second, the reduplicated terms *ƙasa-ƙasa* (the low shake) and *sama-sama* (the high shake), whose alliterative nature elicits audience attention, are the phonological (and in this case, lexical) models for the implied repetition *wasa-wasa* (playing, whether instruments or in joking or in sports), which has been suggested earlier by the appearance of *wasa* (to play) in line 152.

NONVERBAL PERFORMANCE AND REPETITION

Superimposed on these many repetition patterns is the performer's active style, her nonverbal punctuation of the work. The importance of body movement in the performance of oral poetry dates to its origins in pre-Islamic poetry, during a time when poets recited while standing or sitting and relied heavily on hand and body gesture. The sixth- and seventh-century poetess al-Khansa's tendency to rock and sway in performance (Adonis 1990, 16) brings to mind Maimuna Choge's energetic and suggestive use of body gesture to punctuate her songs. In the sequence cited above, she attunes her body movement to the irreverence of the material she delivers. A significant implied repetition in her "Praise Song for the Hausa Conference" involves her repeated use of the exclamation *wai!*, for it suggests a term that she uses verbally and alludes to again through body movement that would bring to a Hausa-speaking audience's mind the term *duwaiwai* (buttocks) as she tosses her massive hips to emphasize the low shake and the high shake. Though she does not use the term *duwaiwai* in this song, she does say, "Wait, let me shake my hips" (l. 86). These, along with her numerous references to *ƙasa-ƙasa* (the low shake), to prostitutes, and to *kwanciyar faifai* (spreading one's legs) allow that the suggestive tone in her voice when she exclaims *wai!* may have a more specific reference than simply being a general exclamation. Implied repetition, in some ways an elusive topic, must be considered, for it is at the heart of the double entendre in Hausa verbal creativity. The Hausa riddle relies for its effect on the conjunction of noncognate homophones, as do many proverbs and word plays, which are common to Hausa. In this case, body movement provides yet another level of repetition of a concept.

Each repetition of *ƙasa-ƙasa* ("the low shake") is embellished with a shake of her buttocks, and each *sama-sama* ("the high shake") is accompanied by a toss of her breasts. Because each *ƙasa-ƙasa* or *sama-sama* is followed by some form of *sha daɗi* ("be happy!") or *nairori* ("money"), the phrases become mutually associated. As she develops this pattern, she is able to elicit howls of embarrassed laughter from the audience with the mere mention of *sha daɗi* or by gyrating as she exclaims nothing more than *wai!* (hey!). The effect of nonverbal implication is eminently clear in this passage; Maimuna Choge creates such an obvious repertoire of key phrases cued to certain body movements that after a few repetitions of the verbal and nonverbal in conjunction, the use of only one is sufficient to suggest the other. In this way, the performer plays on her audience in an efficient manner, minimizing her dependence on the spoken word.

Much more conservatively, Maizargadi's public performance style is expressive of her praise song material and her position as a performer in a royal milieu. In praise song performance for an emir there is no place for hip shaking, dancing, or otherwise indiscreet behavior. Instead, Maizargadi moves slowly and with dignity, shouting sets of lines before each step. She jabs at the sky to punctuate her song at especially important references to the emir, a technique that is nearly identical to that of a man who also performs solo praise poetry in the palace, Alhaji Ɗan Amu of Kano. The style of another court *zabiya*, Hauwa Mai Duala, involves techniques of interaction with another performer, who cues Mai Duala's lines. In the following sequence, her partner, signaling the beginning of Mai Duala's line immediately after that cue, utters each term on the left:

80	Mighty	Mighty Usman
81	Ahman	Ahman travels the world over, there has been trouble in the world, and it has not been a nice place
99	Usuman	Usumanu
100	Nagogo	Nagogo
103	May God have mercy on Dikko's soul	May God have mercy on Dikko, friend of the colonials
104	May God have mercy on Dikko's soul	May God have mercy on Dikko, friend of the colonials
105	May God have mercy on Fulani	May God have mercy on Fulani, and forgive her
114	I am thankful to	I am thankful to Alhajiya Juji ("Song for the Emir of Kano and the Emir of Ningi")

In a variation of this cuing device, she does not repeat the cuer's phrase, but continues where the cuer leaves off:

95	Abba	Good friend of Fulani Abba
100	Nagogo!	[For] Usumanu Nagogo Abba, she did the drumming . . . (Hauwa Mai Duala, "Song for the Emir of Kano and the Emir of Ningi")

These direct and oblique cues are standard extemporaneous performance devices among those performers who work with another individual or with a chorus.

Maimuna Choge treats her musicians as a chorus, relying on them for cues leading into lines that she elides. Early in the performance they simply repeat her lines (the chorus's lines are in the left-hand column):

1	In the name of God, let us begin in the name of God	In the name of God, let us begin in the name of God
3	Creation is His, the Lord of Life gave life to a thousand, gave life to three thousand, Lord without equal!	Creation is His, the Lord of Life gave life to a thousand, gave life to three thousand, Lord without equal!
4	God who rules even the evil spirits, hide my secrets from my enemies	God who rules even the evil spirits, hide my secrets from my enemies (Maimuna Choge, "Praise Song for the Hausa Conference")

Maimuna Choge and her chorus continue these complete repetitions, the chorus repeating many of Choge's lines.[11] Throughout the performance, however, the chorus functions as more than just an echo chamber for Choge's lines, for she relies on them in the same way she relies on response from the audience. The chorus responds to her remarks and occasionally finishes off her lines. In the following excerpt, Choge delivers the numbered lines; the rest constitute choral response:

90	That I might reach Kano . . .
	. . . to buy things
	Let us buy white cloth, and behave like Europeans
	Let us buy a bottle and decorate the room [like Europeans do]
91	Ladi, calabash drummer
145	Today I said [to us, "money!"]
	. . . calabash drumming, a nice thing! (Maimuna Choge, "Praise Song for the Hausa Conference," ll. 90–91, 145)

Choge's numerous references to "Ladi, calabash drummer" display a tendency to address the chorus directly. She also gives advice to the audience, using the metaphor of the conference as a young girl. Here Choge complicates things further by using the plural form of the third-person pronoun (*ku*) with a singular object (*'yar Amanawa*) at the end of the line. The effect is the personification of the conference members collectively as a young girl (Amanawa is a region in the north near Kano):

15   Hey, our Hausa Conference, I say you should pray little girl
29   Hey, you should pray girl
83   You should pray, daughter of Amanawa
104   You should pray, daughter of Amanawa
137   May he be exalted! daughter of Amanawa
140   You should pray, daughter of Amanawa
163   You should pray, daughter of Amanawa
194   You should pray, daughter of Amanawa (Maimuna Choge, "Praise Song for
      the Hausa Conference")

Ultimately she uses both the chorus and the audience, playing one against the other. Choge turns first to her chorus member, saying,

24   Hey, you see the crowd is seated.

Then she addresses the audience itself:

36   Hey people, get up and shake off the dust, or if you refuse, then leave [to the
      patron] the victory!

She addresses a musician—"you, Audu's wife"—and then describes a member of the audience:

68   He's also put on a lace shirt
69   Moreover, on his wrist he wears a watch
70   Moreover, on his eyes he wears glasses
71   Moreover, on his feet he wears shoes
72   And he holds the pen properly
73   Today I said to him, Garba's son, the one with light-skinned women . . .

In Maimuna Choge's constant movement between the audience and chorus lies the potential for ambiguity in these performances. She addresses chorus members and particular audience members; ultimately the Hausa Conference audience itself is personified as a little girl. There is safety in this technique of creating a subject through personification, even where no real person exists. Finally, she reminds the chorus to thank the audience:

24 Hey, you see the conference crowd is seated
52 And our Hausa Conference crowd
79 You see the Hausa Conference crowd. Let us do the low shake, we'll enjoy
     ourselves
81 We thank the Hausa Conference, look out!

Such incessant movement between audience and chorus ensures that Maimuna Choge has control of her scenario and grants her the limelight. She is creating audience all around her, constantly shifting physical and verbal positions. She is riveting the audience's interest by including them in such shifting foci and by making everyone respond as audience and chorus; they are all observers and performers.

* * *

Repetition is central to the organization of all Hausa songs, whether they are written or extemporaneous. Since all songs are composed with the intention that they be delivered orally, even the written works exhibit patterns of repetition that are recognized features of oral songs. Awareness of patterned repetition as a prime organizing feature of oral poetry is not new, but this discussion concerns the special ways in which it functions among Hausa women singers (see also Scheub 1974–1975).

In these songs complete, partial, and implied repetitions are the organizational features of the material. Cataloguing, on which much Hausa declamation depends, is founded on the technique of repeated images. Such listing is the cornerstone of declamation, expressing a sense of abundance of many kinds—wealth, family size, intelligence, honor, devotion, power, bravery, and other positive qualities of character. Other sources of repetition, such as grammatical parallels or semantic similarities among phrases, are integral features of cataloguing. Within the parameters of these repetitions and catalogues, the language employed in Hausa songs is not significantly different from that of colloquial Hausa: there is no formal poetic vocabulary reserved for such expression apart from a few archaic royal titles. Rather, it is the manner in which the colloquial language is organized, the way phrasing is interrelated, that is central to the work.

Repetition is also important as a mnemonic device for both artist and audience, through which the information to be conveyed is continually, albeit subtly, reintroduced. The repetition of identical images and phrases that suggest other phrases ensures cohesion within the piece. The technique allows the artist to rely on standard phrase forms, constantly honing them to her needs, while the audience depends upon her variations grounded in basic patterns to apprehend the song. In addition to the types of phrase repetition considered here, music functions as a mnemonic device in Hausa songs, especially in spoken epithets whose tone patterns can often be recreated when played on musical instruments. Beyond reconstruction of tone patterns, music functions mnemonically by providing the tune in which the song is performed. Certain of the written poems in this study were delivered orally in identical tunes, despite their significantly different scanned metric patterns.[12] Whether sung or chanted, the song's imagery is limited to the vocabulary that suits the tune.

Occasional publication in local Nigerian newspapers and university literary journals notwithstanding, Hausa songs are very much ephemeral forms, rarely written down. Yet both written and oral songs share features of declamatory style. This belies a distinction between composers of songs based on their degree of literacy. A Western definition of literacy may be inappropriate in a Muslim culture, where orality is of prime importance to one's spirituality. The word is God; the Qur'an is "recitation of the word of God." The angel Gabriel's admonition to the Prophet Muhammad to "Recite! In the name of thy Lord . . . Who taught [the use of] the pen . . ." (Sura 96:1, 4) indicates that proclamation and writing are equally important to the dissemination of the word of God.

If there exists a definable distinction between composers of oral and written works among the Hausa, it may be one of class distinction, which determines the delivery style chosen by the artist. Aliyu na Mangi, one of the most prolific Hausa composers of written poems, was blind from birth. A literate Hausa poet is not likely to engage in extemporaneous performance, which is closely related to the style of random public begging. Nevertheless, as Maimuna Choge's performance at the Hausa Conference at Bayero University indicates, literate people are delighted to be entertained by artists of oral songs. That a Hausa woman performs oral songs in public sets her apart from those who write and declaim songs in private and from secluded Hausa women, who behave with seasoned discretion when venturing out in public. Choge's public performance not only takes her out of her home, it also draws attention to her and provides a platform for her to speak boldly to her audience. In effect, it allows her to behave like a man. Thus, as a socially aberrant woman, the female singer may perform bawdy songs that are too sexually explicit or (perhaps even more dangerous) too politically risqué for any other milieu. Indeed, bawdiness is almost expected from these women. The singer makes use of body movements, nonverbal gestures, and facial expressions to convey and cover her meaning. These singers are not prostitutes, although they are regarded as playing a role outside the mainstream of society; they use their bodies to different effect and certainly derive financial gain from their extremely physical performance style.

Repetitions, interwoven phrasing, and the device of cataloguing are

discussed here in relation to performance styles because they are inseparable in effective performance. The manner in which they are combined
determines audience appreciation. Repetition is at once a tangible structural device and an aspect of the ephemeral aesthetic of the performance. It
is a means of advancing the work, making it a dynamic performance, and
giving variety to imagery while binding various images in a multifaceted
unity. While important to the written works, effective repetition assumes
its greatest dimensions in oral performance; the verbal and the nonverbal
combine in a many-layered network of interrelated images that ultimately
cohere into one.

Part 2

SONGS AND POEMS

POEMS IN TRANSLATION

WISDOM AND WARNING (HIKIMA DA WA'AZI)

For other works by Hausa women singers, see the University of Kansas website at www.ku.edu/~hausa.

WRITTEN WORKS

ORAL WORKS

MODERN TIMES, CURRENT EVENTS
(ZAMANI DA LABARI)
WRITTEN WORKS

OCCUPATIONS AND SELF-IMPROVEMENT
(SANA'A DA AIKIN GAIYA)

WRITTEN WORKS

CONDOLENCE AND PRAISE (MADAHU DA YABO)

WRITTEN WORKS

ORAL WORKS

Praise Song for Alhaji Ado Bayero, Emir of Kano • 247
(Waƙar Alhaji Ado Bayero, Sarkin Kano)
Hajiya Maizargadi, 1980

Praise Song for the Emir of Kano and the Emir of Ningi • 252
(Waƙar Sarkin Ningi)
Hauwa Mai Duala, 1979

HISTORICAL CHRONICLES

WRITTEN WORKS

Song for Kano State • 257
(Waƙar Kano Sitat)
Hauwa Gwaram (no date)

Song for the Fulani Emirs • 261
(Waƙar Sarakunan Fulani)
Hauwa Gwaram, circa 1976 (after Ɗan Amu)

Song of Explanation about Biafra • 268
(Waƙar Bayani)
Hajiya 'Yar Shehu (no date)

Poems on Wisdom and Warning

SONG ON WOMEN'S PROPER ATTIRE
BY HAUWA GWARAM

1   In the name of God I shall sing,
May the Lord increase my wit,
Give me the wisdom to compose the song,
To receive the style of this song,
        A full veil is best for women.

2   Excessive laughter and gazing on nakedness,
Is wicked among Muslims,
As are showiness and disrespect,
False accusations and ignorance,
        A full veil is best for women.

3   I will explain about those with babies on their backs,
When they travel with babies thus,
They should loosen their cloth and turn away to nurse,
When the child has drunk, they can turn back around,
        A full veil is best for women.

4   If it is ordained that another summons you,
And you must go outside where you will be seen,
Then let them see you in your full body cloth,
Don't display the beauty of your body [publicly],
        A full veil is best for women.

5   Whether you are outside or in your own room,
Wrapping your headtie is proper,
Only your daughter can go without a headscarf,
Be respectful in your home,
        A full veil is best for women.

6   You know, faithful women
Don't loosen their wrappers when they sit,
Among their co-wives and them,
There is no quarrelling, much less deception,
        A full veil is best for women.

7   The true believer, the one who is saved,
     Takes heed and improves her lot,
     She doesn't wander about naked,
     She doesn't go about begging,
             A full veil is best for women.

8   Repent, if you would have a chance at salvation,
     Prostitutes, with beer and tobacco,
     Don't let them lead you to drink to excess,
     Just hurry and repent,
             A full veil is best for women.

9   Refuse to marry during your waiting period,
     Strive to follow the Holy Word,
     Try to learn about religion,
     Lest you become one who ignores your prayers,
             A full veil is best for women.

10   You must come and repent,
     Before death comes,
     Seek proper spouses, not
     Tricky tobacco-mouths,
             A full veil is best for women.

11   We see improvement is difficult,
     And now evil ways have flourished,
     Healers are few in number,
     And truth is even getting scarce,
             A full veil is best for women.

12   Let us be energetic, lest we fail,
     For good character is distinguished,
     You swindlers, go hide yourselves,
     The truth is hidden from you,
             A full veil is best for women.

13   Qur'anic students, pray for us,
     That we may find the success known to Nana A'i,
     Let us pray against calamity,
     The ignorant one does not pray,
             A full veil is best for women.

14   You know of upright women,
     Both in public and in seclusion,
     Give them goodwill, give her work,
     Their thrifty planning benefits the household,
             A full veil is best for women.

15   They will tie their wrappers properly,
       Covering themselves from head to foot,
       No one can describe them,
       Much less admire the beauty of their bodies,
             A full veil is best for women.

16   So fear the day of reckoning,
       [When everything will shatter,]
       The good and the bad,
       And the heart's secrets will be known,
             A full veil is best for women.

17   We will have to read out our deeds,
       Done abroad and at home,
       Prostitutes, when they read out your works,
       Damnation will be yours, because of His power,
             A full veil is best for women.

18   Everything given to her to do,
       [The upright woman] will do it well,
       No matter where her feet tread,
       Whether among innocents or sinners,
             A full veil is best for women.

19   I cried and was full of regret,
       And self-pity, lacking zeal,
       "Oh God, give me the strength,
       To correct my sins,"
             A full veil is best for women.

20   My sisters, listen to us,
       I will explain our warning,
       She whom God favors will hear us,
       While the apostate will ignore us,
             A full veil is best for women.

21   Whatever comes to us,
       God, give us peace of mind,
       As for our sins,
       May God ease our troubles,
             A full veil is best for women.

22   I will stop here and rest, sisters,
       Continue to be pure,
       I will clothe myself properly,
       A body cover is mandatory,
             A full veil is best for women.

23   May God forgive us our sins,
    He has mandated that our men,
    Provide for us with patience,
    May He ease our troubles,
      A full veil is best for women.

24   You see Hauwa Gwaram has spoken,
    It is she who has given you a song,
    On women's clothes and customs,
    Honor our traditions and customs,
      A full veil is best for women.

    Thanks be to God.

SONG OF WARNING AGAINST INCURRING A DEBT
BY HAUWA GWARAM

1   I begin this song in the name of the Lord God,
Through Your kindness, our Father in heaven.

2   You made man, the spirits, and angels,
The wild animal in the bush and the domesticated one.

3   May God give me wisdom and eloquence,
I will compose a song for those who incur excessive debts.

4   Brothers and sisters, listen well and hear me,
I will warn women against buying on credit.

5   The thing you want to buy costs ten, they say,
They will sell it thus to test you on debt.

6   On the day one buys, [if someone sees the buyer,] she'll come back around,
That same day, she'll return to ask for a loan.

7   If there's no money to lend, she'll sit here at the house,
Until she's aggravated everyone, looking for a loan.

8   They start to fight, people gather and separate them,
They abuse each other because of debt.

9   After this she will take the matter further,
That is, going to court, and all because of debt.

10   Or she'll go and spend the afternoon at a party or at the hospital, ill—
Running from her creditor.

11   Some go out late at night
Buying and selling among the men, all for a debt.

12   Whoever listens to "Leave off!" will not refuse to consider
All that happens to chronic borrowers.

13   Better that you put your money in the bank, people,
Buying with cash is better than taking a loan.

14   I thank God, the Lord God, our One Master,
For making me hate indebtedness.

15   I've finished this little song, just a few verses,
People, restrain yourselves from excessive debts.

16   It is finished, with praise to God, here I shall stop,
Hauwa Gwaram I am, I don't have debts.

Thanks be to God.

SONG OF WARNING TO THOSE WHO TAKE DRUGS I
BY HAUWA GWARAM, 1973

1   Beginning in the name of God, I hope for success,
I will warn Muslims against taking drugs.

2   Oh brothers, come with me and be successful.
All who follow the Way—don't take drugs.

3   You know that taking drugs causes trouble.
If you are being decent, don't take drugs.

4   Muslim people, men and women of Kano State,
If you go to Makka, don't go with drug pushers.

5   Starting here at the airport, if they see you, you'll be in trouble,
Hoping for money, they'll bring you drugs.

6   If you go to Jedda, and if they see you, you'll be in trouble,
Because they will forbid you from buying, if you take drugs.

7   Drugs are forbidden, they make you lose your wits,
You leave your home and go into the bush because of drugs.

8   See the sorcerer "Mr. Tomorrow-Is-Not-Far-Away,"
And how a shameless person followed him and caused him
    to take drugs.

9   By God, if you buy drugs today you will not sleep at night,
But doze at your devotions, if you take drugs.

10   Teacher bought a bottle of drugs and stashed it away,
He took some and was unable to sleep because of drugs.

11   His students finished their lessons,
But he couldn't teach them because of the effect of drugs.

12   The teacher took his stick and left the house, running,
Only the dogs accompanied him, because of the effect of
    drugs.

13   His sweating bothered him, so he removed his robes,
He cast off his cap and tossed it away because of drugs.

14   He removed his hat completely, leaving only his headcloth,
And there was our teacher, all dignity lost, because of drugs.

15   The students gathered and were playing,
They set aside their writing boards because of the effect of
    drugs.

16   On the following day they came and did not find their
      teacher,
      He had gone to his brother's house, under the influence of
      drugs.

17   He became a raving madman, behaving abusively.
      His craziness was the effect of drugs.

18   The teacher's students began to disperse
      Because of the breakdown of the teacher, because of drugs.

19   As for the teacher, he got angry and left his house running,
      He didn't stay with the students, for they didn't take drugs.

20   He worried his relatives—they got together and renounced
      him,
      Children and adults, all abused him for his drug habit.

21   As for the teacher, he got angry and left his house running,
      He didn't stay with the students, for they didn't take drugs.

22   He was raving mad, he behaved abusively,
      He went to his brother's house because of the effect of drugs.

23   An honorable bearded teacher with sideburns and no clothes!
      A madman, and when you saw him you knew he was a
      crazed drug-taker.

24   Drugs cause him trouble; he sits on the roadside,
      He is begging for food—see the effect of drugs.

25   He spends the night hungry and no one gives him food
      Because no one pities him—such is the effect of drugs.

26   Then his brothers spread out and look for him,
      They go to the market to find him—see the effect of drugs.

27   They find him lying asleep in a tree,
      They awaken him and drive him home—see the effect of
      drugs.

28   They put him in the stocks—he is just like a donkey,
      He is a tragic sight—because of the effect of drugs.

29   Spirit possession folks and a traditional doctor try a cure and
      then leave him,
      He does not improve but has to return to the house of drugs.

30   You ask me their place; let me give you the news,
      Their home is hospitals everywhere—drugs!

31   The drugs' names I shall tell you, do not abuse me;
      Salare and *roka* are the names of the drugs.

32   I don't take drugs and I have no love for them.
      God protect us from drug-takers!

33   I say worthlessness and tactlessness and shamelessness
      And all lack of intelligence—all these are in drug-takers.

34   From those who abuse women and those who batter them,
      To those who murder their mothers—all because of drugs.

35   God protect us and purify our brothers,
      May he guide all Muslims to refuse to take drugs.

36   You are the son of a Muslim, grandson of a Muslim,
      Yet you wear tight shirts and wide pants and take drugs.

37   You have no shame or qualms;
      You ruin our State's good name because of drugs.

38   We will go to Makka for the sake of God,
      We don't want drugs, we won't take drugs.

39   Soldiers of Makka and Medina, hear me,
      Here is advice for you about drugs.

40   If you see drug-takers among our people,
      Stop beating them and imprisoning them for drugs.

41   Beatings and prison do nothing—
      Instead kill them like chickens, for taking drugs.

42   Seeing something in another is enough to cause fear,
      May God protect Muslims, let them stop taking drugs.

43   May God give us luck, oh God, protect us,
      God protect us from the wickedness of the addicts.

44   It is finished with praise to God, here I shall stop,
      Hauwa Gwaram I am, I do not take drugs.

               Thanks be to God.

SONG OF WARNING TO THOSE
WHO TAKE DRUGS II
BY HAUWA GWARAM, 1973

1 Let us begin in the name of God, may He be exalted, our
  Lord God,
 Protect us and our children from the evils of drugs.

2 As for us, we are disturbed because
 Our children are scattered about, taking drugs.

3 Shame and fear have no place with them,
 Just tight-tucked shirts and bell-bottom pants and drugs.

4 Pilfering and theft, betrayal of trust and deceitfulness,
 And they refuse to pray because they are taking drugs.

5 They've strayed from the path of religious knowledge
 And it has faded away while they take drugs.

6 Oh, government we all beseech you
 With bowed head, for we have no love of drugs.

7 Our doctor in charge at the dispensary,
 Help us—stop accepting drugs.

8 Drugs are forbidden among us, be sure of that;
 Give them to the horse or the dog, drug addict.

9 Local Government Authority, and leaders, help us,
 Tell the doctor he should not receive drugs.

10 The most pitiful thing you'll hear is that
 Small children are taking drugs.

11 There are men who are underhanded and deceitful,
 They trick women, you see, into taking drugs.

12 In streets and alleyways on their motorcycles,
 And there are those in cars, you know, drug pushers.

13 They abuse people and beat them,
 They are raving mad, they are taking drugs.

14 Now the djinns do no damage at all;
 If one sees a madman, one assumes he takes drugs.

15 Our Women's Association of Nigeria,
 Has declared it has no love of drugs.

16   As for me, what really frightens me is that
      At least half our students are taking drugs.

17   Leaves of weed they smoke everywhere,
      To be muddled and called drug-takers.

18   If you see a prostitute wandering all about
      It is leaves and *roka* she is smoking—drugs.

19   As for us, we beg you everywhere,
      In our Nigeria, stop trafficking in drugs.

20   On the playgrounds we must confront it;
      At the station in Kano they don't like drugs.

21   They even say now that working on a farm,
      Can only be done when one is drugged!

22   Water carriers are wandering around the town,
      Just dragging their cans—when they are taking drugs.

23   If you drink from a pot by the side of the road,
      Or even sweet porridge, it's likely it's drugged.

24   Kano Emir Ado Bayero, give us help.
      Governor and Magistrate, help drive out these drugs.

25   For God's sake, Magistrate, give us some help,
      Keep catching the crazy drug-takers.

26   And I beg you, our teachers,
      You who teach—give up drugs.

27   The students among you, when they see you drugged up,
      What will they learn from you besides the drug habit?

28   If you smoke leaves, you get a boy
      To light it and hand it to you—damn you, drug-taker.

29   This is the pitiful thing now, everywhere
      In both city and country, people take drugs.

30   If you talk to them, they say they're progressive,
      Enlightened, so they take drugs.

31   If the teacher takes drugs, of course the student does,
      And how much more the drug pusher himself.

32   Don't you feel ashamed, no matter whose son you are,
      Whoever you are, to be taking drugs?

33   Men, beware of your juniors, egging you on to take drugs,
Trying to steal your money for drugs.

34   You even bring a check to give them to take
To the bank, where they get money to squander on drugs.

35   Don't give drugs to children, to your sons or your wives,
Appeal to the saints, to end your drug-taking.

36   I have made my complaint to the head teacher
For God's sake, see me here with you because of drugs.

37   As for the teachers who take drugs, if one is brought to you,
Fire him, because of drugs.

38   Seeing something in another makes us fear it in ourselves,
If they see you thus they will stop taking drugs.

39   If the teachers will stop taking drugs,
Every other person will stop taking drugs.

40   May God grant us our heart's desire
To see teachers stop from gulping down drugs.

41   As for me, I invoke the blessings on the Prophet
      Muhammad,
And his family and the Companions—for the sake of drugs.

42   It is finished with praise to God, here I shall stop,
Hauwa Gwaram I am, and I don't like drugs.

        Thanks be to God.

SONG OF WARNING

BY HAJIYA 'YAR SHEHU, 1970

1   In the name of God, I will begin in the name of God,
The Lord God, the King of Truth.

2   You are the Almighty who hears and sees,
Death and our souls are with God along.

3   And I invoke God and our Prophet Muhammad,
He is the Almighty, the King of Truth.

4   Well I will sing about our country, Nigeria,
Adults and children, listen to me, all together.

5   I have no intention to criticize, much less to show envy,
I will speak honestly, though some may refuse the news.

6   They are always giving us warnings on the radio,
Concerning occupations or education, all together.

7   In this song I will start talking about our leaders,
All who have authority over Nigeria.

8   If you say the rat steals, you know,
Too that it's the stench of your locust bean cake that
draws him.

9   So here's the reason that I will explain to you,
And whether you take my advice or not, it's all the same.

10   *Hayye iye nanaye ayyururuy yuruy,*
You, Kosau, why do you laugh?

11   You told me someone took you to the town chief,
They say you refused to take either Tanko or Magajiya for
school.

12   You were forced to let them study in town,
So that when they've acquired knowledge you can rest from
your farm work.

13   Your work is farming, they don't know,
Theirs is only sitting on a chair, you hear.

14   You took them, they finished all the primary school and
passed out,
And then they were prevented from entering any of the
colleges, all together.

15   They finished with a primary certificate,
      And it was written that they "Passed," you hear.

16   Then they were told there would be an interview,
      And at this interview they were denied their rights.

17   They were pulled and were asked many questions,
      And then if they ace it, they still have to pay bribes.

18   Well you see Kosau, there is no one who knows about him,
      And he does not have the money to give as a bribe.

19   He has one farm and fifteen children,
      And except for farming, no other occupation.

20   Well, you see Tanko and Magajiya, all of them lose,
      For there is no one in the world who knows their father.

21   So for this reason, Tanko goes to town,
      Leaving mother and father with broken hearts.

22   After this he goes to the shops and companies,
      Even in the offices, but there is no work at all.

23   Tanko's education hasn't gone beyond primary school,
      And it is college people they want, you hear.

24   Well, you see, he won't stay at home where his father is,
      And here in the city there is no work for him at all.

25   His kind is beyond number in Nigeria,
      They get out of primary school and have no occupations.

26   Well you see, too little education is useless,
      One has a lot here in Nigeria.

27   Well, leaders, you must turn and look around,
      And help those who are not prosperous.

28   Their children and their grandchildren, pay attention to all
         of them,
      If they work hard, don't leave them to suffer.

29   Thus, for traders, open companies,
      Until everyone has enough, all Nigerians.

30   For there are many big young men without work,
      Pushing a handcart is the only work they know.

31   Thus in the markets you will see them with head cushions,
      Looking for something to carry, to earn a little soup change.

32   And see the blind ones together with the crippled,
None of them has a decent place here in Nigeria.

33   It is necessary to prepare a place for all of them,
With medicine and food all together.

34   Make a place for them, so they'll stop entering the towns,
For the sake of the welfare of Nigeria.

35   Make a place for occupations that can help the crippled
And the blind, all together.

36   Their children and their grandchildren attend to them,
Prepare places for reading so they can cease their aimless
roaming.

37   Be sure to give your annual charity to the government,
Men and women, all wealthy friends.

38   In this way, if everyone adds one little bit to the tax,
And it's collected for them, they can all be relieved of suffering.

39   But you refuse to do this, you detest them beyond hope,
Leaving them without the smallest reason, not one.

40   Thus are the orphans here, ignored, not helped,
They are just beggars, only beggars every morning.

41   Every fault here you should think about—how are you
responsible for it?
Search your thoughts to understand the truth.

42   Of all the students in other countries of the world,
From here, our country, stop and investigate the truth,

43   If you have a hundred, eighty will inevitably be
The children of kings, or of the wealthy.

44   They are the ones sent to seek knowledge,
This is what is done in every district.

45   The children of farmers cannot progress,
Even if they demonstrate diligence, they are argued out of
the picture.

46   Truth is bittertough, be sure of that,
But if one sticks to it, one will not suffer.

47   Well, here the public works authorities have their jobs,
be sure,
Each one does exactly what he is supposed to do.

48   Well, let's turn back to the strong young men seeking work,
Siphoned into society without a trade in Nigeria.

49   If a factory opens, you know,
You will see men waiting in the morning, more than a
    hundred.

50   If they are lucky, then about five will get work,
To the rest the employers will say, no work, you hear.

51   If you go to where they give out jobs,
The Labor Office, to ask questions,

52   You will see old and young men
Looking for work every morning.

53   You see, the blame is not with the strong young men
But with the work they would do in Nigeria.

54   The way it is now, there's little work
And no big companies in Nigeria.

55   Well, we must preserve work for them;
If they refuse it, then they can just be porters.

56   This is what we call the mother of happiness
She wears a veil to cover her head and face for protection.

57   By God, all of Africa knows
There's no country better than our Nigeria.

58   See our amazing groundnut harvest, and cotton
Cocoa and petrol, none exceeds us in the world.

59   And there are beniseed, rubber, iron ore,
And even coal, timber, and gold.

60   Whoever would prevent us should be left aside.
Let us do work and stop messing about.

61   Let us import engines, stop exporting.
Let us make our own until we become a nation.

62   Let us import engines that produce food products,
Both our clothes and our other belongings.

63   Let us import motors, even motorcycles and bicycles,
Farming engines and tanks beyond number.

64   University, college, and primary students
Should be sent to various countries to learn.

65   Let them study how to run different types of engines
      So we can have our own engineers.

66   All strong young men here in Nigeria,
      All will be trained in the work, which they will realize is not
          difficult.

67   Even the prostitutes, the homosexuals, the praise singer
      All will learn work to bring peace of mind to society.

68   And the pilgrims will hire a plane
      To do their pilgrimage work each morning.

69   Well, we should organize the market folks to establish a
          company
      So they can buy planes to ease our suffering.

70   Thus let us be freed from too much loss,
      And everything should be our own in Nigeria.

71   Well, this is all the government's work, you know,
      The right of all the country, and your obligation, every one.

72   If you are just, that is good, and God sees.
      If you cheat, He will punish you, no doubt.

73   Well, now the truth is, there's no work
      That will make Nigerians well off.

74   But the government and you businessmen
      If you make a persistent effort, there will be no more trouble.

75   I flow down on you people
      Well, here is my advice to everyone.

76   First you need to put your heads together,
      Joining your heads is protection against any conspiracy

77   So that you need not leave your door open to strangers,
      They are the hypocrites in Nigeria.

78   There are those who have amassed wealth
      They think they are better than anyone else in the world.

79   They don't pay attention to their own siblings, much less to
          anyone else,
      They put their noses up, ostentatiously.

80   They won't go to a naming celebration, much less a funeral.
      At their neighbors' homes they show off their riches.

81   And see the many houses of the prostitutes,
       They leave their wives at home and do not return until
         morning.

82   The cross-dresser is always doing business
       They will wash cups for beer money.

83   Well, I kneel down before you and ask
       For God's sake, for the sake of the Prophet, whom to follow.

84   We learn parsimoniousness for our state and thrift
       If we refuse, I swear we will be ridiculed.

85   If you see hopeless and irresponsible people drinking beer
       If you mention to them "God" they will laugh

86   All those with this kind of character, they are many in the
         north
       The rest of the folks will not leave wealthy women.

87   Of all the groups in the west, and those in the south,
       There is none that exceeds the north in preserving wealth.

88   Well, I return now to the farmers, you hear,
       There are those who waste their wealth.

89   Nomau, father of Ɗan Karo, father of Tsayyiba,
       It was he, Hafsu's son, father of Karima and Babiya.

90   Well, you see, being from Nomau, come and sit down to hear
       The conversation we will hear so you can understand the
         Truth.

91   Well, you tell me last year you reaped six hundred
       Bundles of millet and corn all together.

92   How many bags of beans and groundnuts altogether,
       And cotton—how many bundles of cotton all together?

93   Well, until I see you at the shops, looking for a porter,
       To carry for you, by God, you have had good fortune.

94   When I ask you how much grain and cotton,
       And beans and groundnuts all together,

95   I know, Nomau, you don't drink beer
       Nor gamble at all

96   Because I heard you say that your grain, cotton,
       And even your groundnuts all were sold.

97 Or did you buy cattle for the farm with the money,
    Or farm equipment, to let you rest from your hard work?

98 You told me you were to marry Citumi's granddaughter.
    And she harvested you to the point where you were broke.

99 From the beginning she told you that you could not reclaim
     what you gave her.
    She hid nothing, she spoke the truth.

100 You were the one who deliberately gave out all your money
     to convince her,
    You said she must, even though she refused.

101 Well, you see the effects of misusing your wealth,
    See what happened to Nomau, you hear.

102 His wife and children have neither food nor clothing,
    And even his home town, he left it altogether.

103 And the young men who are growing in the future,
    The businessmen or scholars, you hear.

104 University students and college students, listen,
    You should plan for the future and be prudent and live in
     peace.

105 If you are enlightened, work in your field
    And take care of your country and family in Nigeria.

106 Don't follow the worthless ones in town
    Who go to hotels and the cinema to drink beer.

107 They are lost and don't need to be questioned
    And they care nothing for the well-being of Nigeria.

108 I will give you the history of two friends, I am
    Clever that I rejected their overtures of friendship.

109 Even among cleverness there are some types that do not
     make sense.
    It is the type I always reject.

110 He sees that I am not sensible,
    He said to bring him all the money.

111 We bought a house and stopped paying rent,
    Once we rented the house, so we lived in peace.

112 One who refuses did not show his refusing character,
    He gave out the money so that they should live in peace.

113   From time to time cleverness shows its true character,
       They say he got a house and he settled down alone.

114   Since the beginning I have told you all,
       The end of the cleverness was a loss of all wealth.

115   Then I refused to let him have the house and ejected him
       And no matter how they tried, he'll say, he refused.

116   Thus friends, the impoverished fools,
       If they trip up you tell them, oh you refused.

117   I came to address you women who celebrate for your pretty
           friends,
       And you all listen to me all together.

118   Because there are those who waste wealth,
       If they get up to have a celebration for friends, you hear.

119   They buy tables, breakable plates, cupboards,
       Beds, mattresses, and pots of gold.

120   Even lidded enamelware, fancy boxes,
       All full of shiny lengths of beautiful cloth.

121   She explains these things are for celebration
       For her friend or daughter of a woman friend.

122   And then they pander to her, they say she's the best,
       They say she's better than that person and that person.

123   Then if she's married her husband is stuck with this,
       The celebrations of female friends, and all is on his neck, all
           together.

124   If he refuses to carry it all, you know,
       That's the end, she leaves him altogether.

125   Or she'll get into debt over cloth,
       That she buys for four dollars and sells for two.

126   She'll sell all her personal belongings,
       Until she ends up down the drain, soliciting.

127   For God's sake, women, don't be flamboyant,
       Treasure your friend, with whom you can laugh.

128   You need her for the generosity of her advice,
       Talk together in mutual trust, you hear.

129   If she has celebrations, help her,
       And you too, if you have to party, do it together with her.

130   It is not necessary that everyone know your secrets,
Much less have people gossiping about you.

131   Well, you see this, they prevent planning for the future,
They make people suffer.

132   Well, one fails to realize
He realizes that the stick gives trouble.

133   Thanks be to God, here I will stop,
I thank God, King of night and day.

134   The composer, listen and hear,
'Yar Shehu is the name, without question.

135   One hundred thirty five verses,
I have concluded in the name of One who does not seek
anything from anyone.

Thanks be to God.

SONG FOR THE WOMEN OF NIGERIA
BY BINTA KATSINA, MARCH 22, 1980

1   God, our Lord, our Prophet, God's messenger,
     Help the women of Nigeria,
     God, our Lord, our Prophet, God's messenger,
     Assist the women of Nigeria,
5   Women of Nigeria,
     Women of Nigeria,
     You will do every kind of work,
     Women of Nigeria,
     Women of Nigeria,
10   You should try to understand,
     You could do every kind of work.
     I'm giving you an office, women—you can do office work,
     Women of Nigeria, you will do every kind of work,
     You should be given the chance to take charge,
15   You can do the office work,
     You can do administrative work,
     You should be given the chance to take charge, to try, women
        of Nigeria,
     You can do all the typists' jobs,
     You know people, daughters of Nigeria,
20   Women of Nigeria, you could do every kind of work,
     You should do every kind of work,
     Women of Nigeria, you could do every kind of work,
     Women of Nigeria, you could be in the offices,
     You can do paperwork,
25   You can do paperwork,
     Women of Nigeria, you could take charge of the schools,
     Women of Nigeria, you could take charge of the schools and
        control them,
     You could be ministers in politics,
     Women of Nigeria, you could do every kind of work,
30   You could do every kind of work,
     Here, women of Nigeria, you could do the typists' work,
     You could do the typing,
     Women of Nigeria, you should do every kind of work,
     Which kind of boasting will they do?
35   Men, which kind of boasting will they do?
     You can do all the paperwork,
     You can be in the office,

You can hold the pen,
Well, what kind of boasting will they do?
40 Men, what kind of boasting will they do?
Women of Nigeria,
Let's give you the chance to take charge,
Women of Nigeria, let's give you the chance to take charge,
You can become the government,
45 Women of Nigeria,
You can do the paperwork,
You can do all the typing,
Women of Nigeria,
You can do all the typing,
50 Women of Nigeria,
What kind of boasting will you do?
Men, what kind of boasting will you do?
They can be in the office,
Give them a chair of their own,
55 Give them a chair of their own,
Women of Nigeria,
Let's give you a chair of your own,
Women of Nigeria,
You could do every kind of work,
60 You can drive cars, you can run machines,
You can fly airplanes, you can fly airplanes,
Women of Nigeria,
Thanks to the women of Nigeria. They've paid us and we
    thank them.
Thanks to the women of Nigeria. They've paid us and we
    thank them.
65 Hey, daughters of Nigeria,
Hey, daughters of Nigeria,
Thanks to the daughters of Nigeria,
Hey, daughters of Nigeria, you should do every kind of work,
You should do every kind of work, you should know every
    kind of work,
70 You can write papers, you can pound the typewriter,
You can fly airplanes,
You know how to be in the office,
You could do government work,
And you could be police workers.
75 You could do customs work,
Let's give you the chance to take charge,
Women of Nigeria,

Women of Nigeria, you know every kind of work,
You could do every kind of work,
80   And you could do all kinds of work,
God knows, women of Nigeria,
You can be loving and obedient, I tell you, daughters of
   Nigeria
You can be loving and obedient, I tell you, daughters of
   Nigeria,
You can be loving and you can be obedient,
85   I say to you out there, Nigerians,
We praise with thanks and blessings,
I say to you, daughters of Nigeria, we praise with thanks and
   with blessings.

SONG FOR THE HAUSA CONFERENCE
BY MAIMUNA CHOGE, MARCH 23, 1980

1   In the name of God, let us begin in the name of God,
(Chorus)
Let us begin in the name of God, I begin in the name of the
    Merciful, I will praise God,
Creation is His, the Lord of life gave life to a thousand, gave
    life to three thousand, Lord without equal!
(Chorus)
God Who rules even the evil spirits, hide my secrets from my
    enemies,
(Chorus)

5   Hey, welcome Inna's women, you who have nothing,
(Chorus)
Greetings, be generous for the sake of God
Now we will explain to you the news
Hey! You Hausa Conference students,
I have come to your place without anger
(Chorus)

10   Also, may God leave the man with his lover,
(Chorus)
You who have a sponge can wash. As for her with no sponge,
    what will she do?
(Chorus)
Hey, greetings.
I greet you all—and again!
I ask your pardon—and again! Women of Inna, you with
    only the basic necessities.
(Chorus)

15   Hey! Our Hausa Conference, could I say you should pray,
    little girl,
Hey, you see the students here arranged in rows,
Today fellows, please leave aside the pen
[May] God increase [your] intelligence
And advance [your] way to enlightenment

20   May God advance the way to higher status
May God advance the way to promotion
(Chorus)
Greetings! Put on perseverance like a shirt. Be God-fearing!
May God ensure abundant prosperity!
(Chorus)
Hey, you see the conference crowd is seated

25   Let everyone find a useful profession
Mine is to give serious advice repeatedly
If you are faithful to God, ladies,
Then each one should have a profession, ladies. The woman
    without a profession must be given in marriage.
(Chorus)
Hey, you should pray, girl.
30   You should do the drumming; what an important woman
    you are!
The whole world has found a profession,
Let her stop making mischief, let her buy the mat, let her
    stop ruining her home with gossip,
(Chorus)
Hey, I tell you, young women,
For God's sake shake your bracelets,
35   If you refuse, then leave [to the patron] the victory
(Chorus)
Hey people, get up and shake off the dust, or if you refuse,
    then leave [to the patron] the victory!
(Chorus)
Hey! May God advance the ways to enlightenment, may
    God advance the way to promotion
(Chorus)
Then you know the drumming over there, I say, see Choge's,
[unclear on tape]
40   [unclear on tape]
(Chorus)
And you, Audu's wife, who spends the night drumming,
And you, who beats on the large calabash,
And you, daughter of the government, high shakes and low
    shakes—see Choge's!
For God's sake, let me pray attentively,
45   It's during stormy weather that one drinks water from the pot
We are now in modern times,
All those who do not hold the pen do useless work,
(Chorus)
For God's sake, let me pray attentively,
And you see Choge,
50   While I praise with my begging voice,
And Ladi, calabash drummer,
And our Hausa Conference crowd,
And my guests and the children watching Choge
(Chorus)

For God's sake, let me pray attentively,
55   While I praise with my begging voice,
(Chorus)
And also those who play the large calabash,
And you, you are a daughter of the government, with my
    work I will beg you,
And I give thanks,
When they see Kwaire they'll put down a gift,
60   While I praise with my begging voice,
And I give thanks,
And a gift for the night of drumming,
And I remember God,
Drum abundantly! Driver,
65   If you put me in a car,
Take me to the city to play,
Let's consider modern times—
He's put on a lace shirt
Moreover, on his wrist he wears a watch,
70   Moreover, on his eyes he wears glasses,
Moreover, on his feet he wears shoes,
And he holds the pen properly,
Today I said to him, Garba's son, the one with light-skinned
    women,
His car is everywhere,
(Chorus)
75   And for a long time he has held the pen; for a long time I
    have been well off
(Chorus)
For God's sake, let me praise attentively,
While I praise with my begging voice . . . and you see Choge
Well, Audu's wife, and you, the drummers,
You see the Hausa Conference crowd. Let us do the low
    shake, and we'll enjoy ourselves,
80   May God grant us money.
(Chorus)
We thank the Hausa Conference, look out!
You Ladi, calabash drummer,
You should pray, daughter of Amanawa,
This drumming is for the students,
85   You see the Hausa Conference,
Wait, let me shake my hips to enjoy myself,
Let me do the low shake to enjoy myself, look out!
A nice thing!

May God grant us money.
90 That I might reach Kano,
(Chorus ". . . to buy things
Let us buy white cloth, and behave like Europeans
Let us buy a bottle and decorate the room [as Europeans do]")
Ladi, the calabash drummer,
May God grant us money
This drumming is for the students,
One will not do it for everyone,
95 This drumming is for the head of the Shari'a court, and
Muntari, of his household,
If I go to Malumfashi, I'll find Muntari there too,
Here I feel fine
Ladi, calabash drummer,
See, the Hausa Conference students have come,
100 If only they do the low shake they will feel fine,
Let them do the high shake with money!
A nice thing!
May God grant us money!
You should pray, daughter of Amanawa,
105 Since you see the students have come,
Here we are at the Hausa Conference
(Chorus)
We are drumming, we are singing,
See, the sons of emirs have come,
Wait, let me open my mouth,
110 And let me do the low shake to feel fine,
Do the high shake with money, hey!
A nice thing!
Ladi, calabash drummer
The time of night rain and our drumming,
115 Then I did drumming at Malumfashi
Like this drumming for Muntari
For the rulers of Malumfashi
(Chorus)
Hey, Ladi, the students have come
See them here, they are watching
120 Hey, Ladi, it is the Hausa Conference
See it, the students have come
Let us do the high shake so we'll feel fine
One does the low shake
(Chorus ". . . for money")
A nice thing!

125   May God grant us money,
        I beg the forgiveness of the married women
        For I will shimmy like European-style prostitutes
        For you know, in Funtuwa, in that city,
        There are European-style prostitutes,
130   Prostitutes in a European-style house
        Drink beer and smoke cigarettes—
        They wear white gowns and thrive—
        See that five-pound note I'm watching—
        You know no one will receive fifty—
135   For heaven's sake, you could put down a tenth of a penny
            [and no one would know,] for it's dark! Hey!
        Ladi, calabash drummer,
        May He be exalted! Daughter of Amanawa,
        See Audu's wife, a drummer,
        May God grant us money
140   You should pray, daughter of Amanawa,
        May God grant us money,
        Ladi, calabash drummer,
        Look, we've gotten up, we've danced,
        I called your name, I danced,
145   Today I said [to us, "money!"]
        (Chorus ". . . calabash drumming, a nice thing!")
        Everyone calls me, so I go.
        Me, I won't despise the drummers,
        Me, I won't despise the small children
        This drumming is for the students,
150   They summon the water carriers,
        And the water carriers call me, too.
        My playing goes where the money is.
        Dan Filani, water carrier
        As his life's work, he carries water
        (Chorus)
155   Father and son, water carriers,
        When they call me, the water carriers,
        The real playing goes where the money is—
        Moreover, I drink water from the tin,
        And even have some left for washing clothes, hey!
160   When one puts on his shirt,
        Who wants to wash?
        Ladi, calabash drummer,
        You should pray, daughter of Amanawa,

Come here, "madam," let's make local gin and we can go to
    the drinking house,
165   Ladi, of the drinking house,
Asabe, of the drinking house,
You Yalwa, of the drinking house,
A nice thing!
May God grant us money,
170   And you, Audu's wife, the calabash woman,
For God's sake give us a pocketful of money,
Health and money,
Let me come to Kano to buy things, let me buy myself a
    white cloth,
Let me collect my money and buy myself a bottle of Holy
    Mosque perfume,
175   Ladi, calabash drummer,
Let us perform a lot—
You know, lying down with open legs,
Ladi, calabash drummer,
Let us perform a lot
180   You know, lying down with open legs
A nice thing!
Ladi, calabash drummer,
This drumming is for the students—
One doesn't do it for everyone,
185   This drumming is for Muntari, that's it, Muntari and for his
    house, hey!
Important Aminu Muntari,
Nephew of Mairo Muntari,
If I go to drum in Katsina,
Then I will rest in Sa'i's house,
190   I will not tolerate slander of Sa'i,
Let me find Muntari and Jiminta,
A nice thing!
Ladi, calabash drummer,
You should pray, daughter of Amanawa,
195   We came, we stood up, we danced
Even when I went to Niger I danced,
To Dutsen-ma I went and I spent the night dancing,
Hey, today I say to the young women,
Learn how to spread your legs, look out!

Poems on Modern Times, Current Events

SONG ON FARMING AND ITS USEFULNESS
BY HAUWA GWARAM, FEBRUARY 4, 1974

1   In the name of God, whom I beg for insight,
    Now I will compose a song on farming.

2   People of the north, let's wake up and strive mightily,
    Let's roll up our sleeves in the matter of farming.

3   This calamitous drought that is sweeping over us,
    May God protect us from calamity in the affairs of farming.

4   Old and young, men, women, let us look for seed,
    Let us look for our hoes and go out to farm.

5   You market seller, and streetside hawker,
    You tailor, help yourselves by doing farmwork.

6   You who sell cloth in the market, you canteen owners,
    And tailors too, help yourselves by farming.

7   If you are embroidering the northern knot and fine patterns
    Of various sorts, help yourselves by farming.

8   You carpenter, making reading boards, hoe handles,
    Mortar, pestle, and wooden bowl; go and farm.

9   You who weave robes and make mats and you who do
        dyeing,
    Laundry men, blacksmiths, and tanners, go and farm.

10 You who build houses and make pots and the drummers,
    Go, you butchers and corn sellers, go and do farming.

11 Drivers and their apprentices and commercial haulers,
    You who auction things off, and sell shoes, go and farm.

12 You, whether a teacher or royalty,
    Wealthy traders and herbalists, go and farm.

13   Guinea corn and millet, wheat and maize,
Cassava and sweet potato and beans.

14   There's a storeroom for rice and cereal grass of both kinds,
Tubers, green tomatoes, guavas are all there for the farmer.

15   Tomatoes and pumpkins, onions and carrots,
Plus red sorrel and even hot peppers, all for the farmer.

16   Spinach, *karkashi*—greens, watercress, and okra,
Yams and papaya, groundnuts and sugar cane are in the garden.

17   Add Bambara nuts, mangoes, sesame, and pepper,
Cotton and tiger nuts, and gourds in your garden.

18   Grapes and pomegranate and *yazawa,* plus limes,
Tobacco, and henna are there in the farm office.

19   A cattle-drawn hoe and the new type of fertilizer, you know,
And seeds to plant are there in the farm office.

20   I'll tell you about the farmer, for everyone to know,
He is of fine character, like seventy men, the farmer.

21   He is careful, faithful, and God-fearing,
He tells the truth, he leaves himself in God's hands, the farmer.

22   He is cautious and generous; he is keen for success,
Polite and humble and devout, the farmer. [This verse is omitted on the accompanying CD.]

23   Zealous, observing family obligations and friendship, with help for all,
With respect for all men's rights, these are traits of the farmer.

24   Happiness, energy, thoughtfulness, religiousness,
Humility and obedience to our leaders—that's the farmer.

25   He is righteous and bears misfortune with fortitude,
Always turning his irrigation pole, Baba the farmer.

26   He's not envious or selfish or seeking quarrels,
There's no greed or deception or lies from the farmer.

27   No rivalry or senselessness, offensiveness or tyranny,
And he avoids argument, this good farmer.

28   Greed and quarrelling, and mean-mindedness are not his
concerns,
Religious learning, religious practice, and respect for royalty
has the farmer.

29   Anger and meddlesomeness are found only in other parts,
Gambling and card playing are only in nonfarmers' places.

30   People, consider the state of our world today,
Any thinking person should take up the hoe and farm.

31   Nomau and Himma and the rest of the other workers,
If I make a mistake, you must forgive me in this matter.

32   Thanks be to God, let me give many thanks,
Hauwa Gwaram I am, the composer of this song on farming.

33   On Monday I wrote this, the fourth day of the month,
Of February, in nineteen seventy-four, on the farmer.

34   I am the worker at the place for educating people,
The Old Library, that's where we meet.

35   At our home in Nasarawa, if you go inside [the city],
Behind Gidan Rijiya, you'll find all the farmers.

Thanks be to God.

SONG TO PREPARE TO DRIVE ON THE RIGHT-HAND SIDE
BY HAUWA GWARAM

1   Lord God, I beseech you,
And for the sake of your Prophet Aminu,
Leader of all the Prophets,
Who is honored by your presence,
       Let us prepare to drive on the right.

2   Oh help us,
For I have gone round our country,
Because we are without education, and
It is time to change our country's ways,
       Let us prepare to drive on the right.

3   I will explain about our country,
Our Nigeria,
Our parents and our grandparents,
We are all reconciled,
       Let us prepare to drive on the right.

4   Oh God, be just to us,
For You are the one who does justice,
Give us just leaders
Rather than leaving us to the corrupt,
       Let us prepare to drive on the right.

5   Lord God, King of all creation,
Who made everything there is,
Lord God, who forbids oppression,
Who disciplines all created things,
       Here we prepare to drive on the right.

6   Fortune has smiled on us,
Fortune has smiled on our Yakubu
To protect our country,
So that it becomes great,
       Let us prepare to drive on the right.

7   Lord God, who does not oppress,
Who knows not injustice,
Who established a government
That arrests those who do wrong,
       Let us prepare to drive on the right.

8 Our leader relies on God,
So become a witness to God's work,
There is no discrimination with God,
Whoever lacks, relies on God,
   Let us prepare to drive on the right.

9 Oh General, Supreme Commander,
Call us all together,
Lest we spill blood,
And our country becomes a desert,
   Here we prepare to drive on the right.

10 There is no God but God,
There is no king but God,
Brothers, there is no oppression
Nor enmity against oppressors,
   Here we prepare to drive on the right.

11 As they did in the Congo,
In Cotonou, Lome, and even in Niger,
As in Ivory Coast and in the Congo,
In Fort Lamy and in Malongo,
   They drive on the right.

12 Oh God make it easier,
Ease the difficulty of this task,
Motorcyclists, drivers,
Cart-pushers, don't forget,
   You must prepare to drive on the right.

13 Beloved Prophet, our pride,
And You, oh God, help us
Let us rise up and plead for our lives,
People, here is advice,
   Let us learn to drive on the right.

14 Let us read the section of God's word
That God may continue to protect us,
Let us say always, "God is One"
That He may protect all Believers
   If they are driving on the right.

15 Well, a bridge, a corner, an overpass,
A culvert, and put it in gear,
People, I warn you, don't slam on the brakes,
In the name of God, don't slam on the brakes,
   If we are to drive on the right.

16   The drummer changes the beat,
      So the dancer changes her step,
      People, here is my advice,
      Always pay attention, be alert,
              If you would prepare to drive on the right.

17   If you go where they've changed the roads,
      Look both left and right.
      If you usually speed, then change,
      In calmness, watch where you're going,
              If you are driving on the right.

18   Driving here is interesting,
      Here are even those teaching it,
      People with donkeys, some swaying on camels,
      And those with two wheeled pushcarts,
              Let us prepare to drive on the right.

19   Well, kings and our teachers,
      Local policemen and our country's police,
      Soldiers, and national police,
      And even the destitute, everyone among us,
              Let us learn to drive on the right.

20   Here is Kano, taking up a new practice,
      Be alert, boy, and you beggars,
      Car drivers, there's no trick to it,
      Bicyclists and motorcyclists,
              Prepare to drive on the right.

21   I implore those with kingly titles,
      Governor, District Officer, let us obey the law,
      Be on your guard, and be upright,
      Don't let the offender escape,
              Because one is driving on the right.

22   The governing board advises
      That you take care and preserve your own,
      Young man, boy and son,
      Hold on to him and explain that,
              You come to drive on the right.

23   Let us explain to everyone here,
      To be alert in our place
      The local authority, listen to us,
      Wants to train our Kano folk,
              If one is driving on the right.

24   People, we have repented,
      Holy men of our land, we follow you,
      Attend to your own jealousies,
      You who cut back our killing,
              If you are driving on the right.

25   There is no one who will say he did it,
      He will say only God has done it,
      There is no one to witness,
      No one lacks protection with Him,
              Let us prepare to drive on the right.

26   Oh God, give us an answer,
      Lord God, without a mother.
      Without a father or children,
      He has no relatives, there is no one like Him,
              Let us prepare to drive on the right.

27   It is important that we invoke God,
      For the many innumerable people of the law,
      Messenger of fasting time and celebration,
      Let us get up and pray,
              Let us prepare to drive on the right.

28   Oh blessings and goodness,
      I have tried to spread goodness,
      The Lord God knows I've planted goodness,
      Among all my brothers, goodness,
              Come and drive on the right.

29   My husband, I have praised him,
      Lord God, protect him from wickedness,
      The place for men and women with Him,
      Remains hidden until He reveals it,
              Come and drive on the right.

30   Lord God, enrich him,
      Provide for his needs,
      Let us get what we need,
      Until we go, grant us our desires,
              Come and drive on the right.

31   It is time for me to stop and sit down,
      It is finished, with praise to God,
      By God, I've made a song,
      I've implored with this song,
              Let us prepare to drive on the right.

32   If someone asks
      Who composed this song,
      Tell them it was Hauwa
      Of Gwaram, who arranged the song,
            Let us prepare to drive on the right.

            Thanks be to God.

SONG FOR THE NAIRA AND KOBO,
THE NEW CURRENCY OF NIGERIA
BY HAUWA GWARAM, 1973

1   In the name of God, I will compose a song,
    On our new currency, the naira and kobo.

2   Oh God Almighty, give me insight,
    For the song on our currency, the naira and kobo.

3   Naira and kobo, you are needed and appreciated,
    Welcome, welcome, naira and kobo.

4   Oh kobo, welcome, and naira too,
    Welcome, sit down here, naira and kobo.

5   I shall tell you about our old money,
    That is to be exchanged for the naira and kobo.

6   For instance, pounds, shillings, including florins and sixpence,
    Threepence pieces—all exchanged for the naira and kobo.

7   Well, see the government has arranged
    For us to have new money, the naira and kobo.

8   You know, the old money was easily squandered,
    [But] the kobo is foolproof [and easy to use!]

9   One kobo is called the same as it used to be
    With our old currency, [but now there's] naira and kobo.

10 Then we have a half-kobo,
    Don't forget, with the naira and kobo.

11 There are religious teachers who enlighten the people,
    I shall teach them about the new naira and kobo.

12 One naira equals one hundred kobo
    In change—that's ten shillings, with the naira and kobo.

13 The coins to equal twenty-five kobo,
    Are two *sule* and one *sisi* piece.

14 On the ten-kobo piece, that is, the *sule*,
    Are two palm trees, with the naira and kobo.

15 On the edge of the five-kobo, our old *sisi*,
    There's a picture of cocoa pods, with naira and kobo.

16 On the edge of the one-kobo piece are two rigs for
    Extracting petrol, with naira and kobo.

17   A half-kobo has on it a picture of cotton,
Two branches of it, with the naira and kobo.

18   You know there is no hole in these coins,
But only the government seal on the naira and kobo.

19   Paper money I will explain now
For the enlightenment of those who make change for the
      naira and kobo.

20   There is a paper for fifty kobo, that is, five *sule,*
It is light brown in color, with this naira and kobo.

21   With a picture of lumber on it;
Let no one cheat you with naira and kobo.

22   After that there is ten *sule,* or one naira,
Which is made of paper—naira and kobo.

23   That one is red and has groundnuts on it,
And there's a government seal for the naira and kobo.

24   After that, the paper for five naira,
Which is two pounds and ten *sule* with naira and kobo.

25   It is green and blue,
And it has on it a palm-oil tree, with naira and kobo.

26   After that, the paper for our ten-naira,
You know this is five pounds, but now in naira and kobo.

27   There are pictures of a dam,
Like Kainji on these notes, naira and kobo.

28   I'm helping you so you can understand,
The paper notes of our new money, naira and kobo.

29   Truly, without a doubt, if you listen to me,
No one can cheat you in changing your kobo.

30   From that first day of January,
In seventy-three, we will have kobo.

31   Around the tenth of July it shall begin in force,
In seventy-three, we will have kobo.

32   Look how the *sule* here in our country,
Is protected, this change to the kobo.

33   On Friday, the twenty-ninth
Of December, they are changing our currency to kobo.

34   Where are you dozers? Get up and hear me,
      Take it to heart—here's this new naira and kobo.

35   On Wednesday, the first day of January,
      In seventy-three, they convert to kobo.

36   In four days they will have accomplished,
      The change to our paper naira and kobo.

37   Thanks be to God, I have finished this song,
      On our new currency, naira and kobo.

38   With about forty-one verses,
      In the song of explanation about naira and kobo.

39   I am Hauwa Gwaram, I pray for us all,
      That we may be enriched with this naira and kobo.

40   May the religious teachers, the traders, and the emirs,
      May the prophet's descendents help us with naira and kobo.

41   Muslims and pagans and Christians,
      May we become enriched with naira and kobo.

         Thanks be to God.

SONG ON THE PILGRIMAGE
BY HAJIYA 'YAR SHEHU, 1959

"This is a poem about my first hajj trip. I tried to compose a song on this hajj, because this work on the hajj is an important obligation."

1   Beginning in the name of God, oh God,
        The Merciful One, oh God,
        I ask for help from God
        The Generous and Merciful God
            The God of all.

2   This song invokes God and gives greetings
        Upon the King of all creation,
        He exceeds all, it brings us closer to Him
        To give a sense of the Creator.
            Muhammadu, of the leader of all.

3   From God and the Prophet's Companions
        Mothers with their children
        Relations and loved ones
        Thus we perceive His love for us
            You forgive us God, master of all.

4   My request to You, oh God
        Protect us, all of us, God
        From all offense and envy
        For the sake of Your Messenger, master of a thousand prayers
            Your Messenger in the place of atheists.

5   I will compose a song on the hajj
        With You I search for my prestige
        In the same way I demand you scholars to listen
        I may mistake, but I will keep trying
            Please excuse me, I do not know everything.

6   On the seventeenth day of the eleventh Muslim month
        We got up in the morning without quarrels
        In the year of accounting, to witness
        On Monday we inherited
            With invocations to God, and smiles all around.

7   In the year nineteen hundred
        And fifty-nine, happily
        We left Kano as if in welcome
        You know Sabena's never late
            In work that needs quickness.

8   Our plane took off for Sudan
       Khartoum, which one calls Sudan
       In early afternoon we reached Sudan
       All our women and men, even the muezzin
           We prayed quickly for relief from trouble

9   From here we took off for Jeddah
       Which has long been the headquarters
       All planes headed to Jeddah
       All alhajis want to go to Jeddah
           It is the junction for every nation.

10   We disembarked here, fatigued.
       Someone gathered us, to talk about fatigue
       And lodging, and circumambulations, you hear.
       That you make there in Makkah, where they go
           They gather, the Alhajis, quickly.

11   Someone took us through customs
       The customs men called Jibiru
       And no one among them was arrogant
       Thus, without envy, much less evil
           Cheerfully, without anger in even one.

12   All our luggage was taken in the plane
       And as for us, we were full of zeal
       Someone took us to a small place
       We were grateful for our merciful,
           Generous Lord of all

13   At the airport we lodged
       The building is big and is just for accommodation
       It's a two-story building, no doubt about that
       The building can accommodate thousands
           Muslims, not non-Muslims.

14   We stayed in Jeddah with an excuse
       We went to the bank here, some went to one in the town
       We got our money for journey provisions and presents
       We spent all the two days preparing
           In early afternoon on Wednesday, quickly

15   We left Jeddah, we took to the road
       For Madinah we were traveling
       Our great gladness overwhelmed our fatigue
       At Badar we slept on the road
           At a place where martyrs died [in the seventh
           century of Badr].

16 In the morning we got up for prayer
    We sent our prayers to God
    The Merciful, we testify to God's might
    And we yearn to know the God
            Of our Prophet, Lord of all.

17 After this we got in cars
    Hired, not stolen
    And without wickedness, much less maliciousness
    Without envy, much less deception
            Only trust among us all

18 With Hajji Burai, our guide
    From here Nasidi, our friend
    They showed us where we should reach
    They put our congregation in order
            May God offer an unexpected gift.

19 We moved from Badar, we were traveling,
    With different types of stones, all over, you hear.
    Some were green, some were red, you hear.
    From here the driver turned
            He showed us where everything was.

20 And he said to us, "You should have a look."
    We spied the green dome
    We gave thanks, we were surprised
    We prayed that we might overcome
            And be victorious over the pagans.

21 We got off in Madinah, happy,
    And all our hearts were content.
    Thus all our photos were taken
    We were photographed without talking,
            Only happiness and laughter for each one.

22 We were dropped off at Bukhari's house
    And our loads were on a donkey.
    Someone brought him to Bukhari's house
    We said he should take us to the tomb
            Of our Prophet, leader of all.

23 From here then he said we should stop.
    We bothered him until he was annoyed;
    We reached a point of dispute.
    From here he gave us a small verse
            To guide us in visiting the leader of all.

24 From here he gave us a meal.
We said we could not eat.
All hunger, thirst, and sleep
All are there, but none of us feels them.
You carried us to the leader of all.

25 I settled down, sucking teeth in disgust.
He called me for oral praise
And he said to me, "Leave off your eagerness
Early afternoon I will take you to the Prophet's tomb,
Our Prophet, master of thousands of values."

26 From here I began to smile.
In the early afternoon he took all the community,
All the women and our men to prayer.
All, each one you see him, just smiling
No wickedness in the heart of anyone.

27 When we entered the place where Prophet's tomb is
We opened our eyes, even our mouths
In surprise and amazement.
Cleanliness stopped with God the Almighty
With his trustworthy one, the leader of all.

28 We prayed once with two prostrations,
We sat down and continued to pray.
Someone took care to call for prayer,
We arranged ourselves, row after row.
In the early afternoon we were there without any
hatred.

29 From here then Bukhari came to us,
He gathered us with one who would take us
To the Prophet, our sent Messenger.
The same with Bubakar our sent Companion.
Umaru, we knew who the Jews were.

30 And he followed us to the place
And here it was where he put us to pray
Two prostrations for the sake of God
We all prayed to God
For His forgiveness, God of mercy.

31 From here it was he took us to the tomb
Of our Prophet, we all were praying
We all greeted him without boastfulness.
From here then to the place of Abubakar.
Umaru, feared by the Jews.

32 We greeted them respectfully with genuflections
  We all prayed to the Lord.
  Here God forgave all sins
  Of Muslims from Ali to Sahabi.
    You forgave us, God our Master.

33 From here we moved on to the grave area
  We left Madinah, that's near the grave area.
  Usman and Fadima, you hear,
  Ibrahim, all of their grave sites are located at Madinah.
    The same with the wife of the Prophet
      Muhammad.

34 And on Friday we intended
  To go to villages where there were important verses to learn.
  For various visits, you hear,
  It's hard to move around because of fatigue,
    We returned home quickly.

35 We settled down in Madinah without a problem,
  Everything ahead of them was prayer
  And only fasting and saying prayers.
  We know of two Friday-like congregation prayers.
    At our Madinah there was no disrespect for anyone.

36 On Saturday we left Madinah.
  Some cried, some trilled joyfully,
  Among all in our company there was no quarreling.
  Each one spoke one word simultaneously
    Lord, the God of everyone.

37 There at Madinah we donned our pilgrimage clothes,
  Some put on robes like Ali's.
  From here we continue to say "Praise be to God"
  From the town of Ali, up to Makkah
    "Praise be to God" we were all saying.

38 On Sunday we reached Makkah
  And at the new moon, no doubt
  In the twelfth month, by God.
  On arrival, someone took us to our lodgings
    So we could do ablutions quickly.

39 Each among us was eager
  To get to the Kaaba to see the room.
  Someone gave us a kind guide.
  We followed him, he took us to the place.
    Everyone was surprised.

40   We all gave our thanks to God
And His Prophet of a thousand prayers.
And we prayed at the house of God
Some cried out, some just prayed.
        Their prayers to the King of all.

41   Someone took us to accomplish our work.
I made the circumambulations, as was our intention.
We went round seven times on the circuit
I touched the stone with my own lips
        Seven circuits to the knowledge of everyone.

42   We stayed here in Makkah.
Some had no place to stay
And it was very hot in Makkah
With no rain or planting season
        Until a miracle was given by the Generous One.

43   On Sunday we prepared again
To leave the hajj, we left the town
And then the visitors and the town people.
We went there, we were in the open field,
        We left Makkah without leaving one behind.

44   We settled down in the afternoon at Mina,
We spent the night in Mina.
Each one was happy.
Thus in our hearts there was no anger;
        Among all of us, none was angry.

45   We got up in the morning and on to Arfa site
With food and fruit
At the place where no one would again change clothes
In the afternoon; we stayed overnight in Muzdalifa
        According to the example of the Prophet, the master.

46   In the morning we left Muzdalifa,
We returned to Mina, to go on to Jifa,
Then Akaba, and on toward Jifa.
They did their work in order to fulfill the Arfa requirement
        We passed through Makkah without losing anyone.

47   In Dawafi we moved toward Makkah
From Safa to Marwa, no doubt.
On finishing, then leaving the town of Makkah
All returned to Mina, the town of departure
        An open space with no houses.

48   Here each one came to Mina
      Even the king of Makkah or of anywhere [else]
      It is necessary to settle down here in Mina
      For hajj work, all at Mina
                One agrees with all pilgrims.

49   All four nights were finished
      And here one distributed meat
      Three throws was enough to complete
      Each one you saw was about to pray
                Enter Makkah, without losing anyone.

50   On Thursday we were in Makkah
      In the early afternoon I left Makkah
      On the fourth day you left Makkah
      Of the month of Hajj, no one interfered.
                We said goodbye quickly.

51   From there in Makkah we reached Jeddah
      And spent one night reaching Jeddah.
      On Sunday we left Jeddah
      The first plane left Jeddah
                On Sunday it took us all.

52   Some we left forever.
      And from here in Jeddah we reached Sudan.
      Our plane stopped in Sudan,
      We rested there in Sudan
                And got back inside quickly.

53   We took off and were in flight
      When our plane pulled and stopped
      Someone said clouds made it stop.
      We were puzzled, we started reciting verses.
                Someone took us back.

54   Then our plane left.
      We left with worried hearts
      For our plane, lest it be broken.
      We came to Kano, got out, and said
                We give thanks to He Who made all.

55   This song that I wrote is finished,
      My hope is that we know the way to salvation,
      And our parents and grandparents in addition.
      May God take all of them into Him
                All Muslims and true believers.

56   Thanks be to God, here I will stop.
       I have reduced this song on the trying journey.
       The name of the singer, you hear,
       Of this reduced song, I say to you, is Hajiyaa
                'Yar Shehu, they should tell everyone.

       Thanks be to God.

SONG ON MODERN TIMES
BY HAJIYA 'YAR SHEHU

1   God give me skill, praise God, the Predestinator,
     God help me, the singer of the song of modern times.

2   Oh God, I begin my song in Your name,
     Drive out misfortune and wickedness in these modern times.

3   You are the One who hears, the One who knows, our Lord
        who predestines,
     Oh God, who knows our secrets, who hears all—exalt
        Him—who knows all!

4   For the sake of Muhammad, may he be blessed, our
        Messenger,
     For the sake of the Prophets, the Companions, and Tijani
        himself.

5   Help us—strengthen our religion,
     You are fighting the enemy Satan.

6   Because the breaking of marriage laws is so common,
     Some people have no faith.

7   So, important scholars, you should persevere in
     Your work to protect the laws of the Lord God.

8   This is something I must explain for you to hear;
     If you ignore me, one day blood will flow.

9   There are offenses being committed by those who should
        follow the laws
     Of the Prophet, our Messenger, the leader of the Faithful.

10   In the streets, in the alleyways, and in the dark corners, there
        worthless ones
     Refuse, idols—without faith.

11   If they saw married women, they always called to them,
     "You, Binta, you Hajiya, I'm in love . . ."

12   If they addressed one of good character, she didn't reply,
     If they got one without character, they'd both sin against God!

13   May God protect us from them! Say "Amen," people,
     Women and men, even children, all the Faithful.

14   Scholars and emirs, here is my message,
     I bow down before you, I tell you so you may understand.

15   If you read this, be patient with my mistakes,
I am your Qur'anic student, please don't reproach me.

16   It is by God's Word that you are tended,
Indeed, we are blind, like he who cannot see.

17   You will lead us until you take us to the town,
Deliver us from this evil of Satan's.

18   Well, He has ordained that I cry out to you so you may know,
Your duty is to protect the laws of the Lord God.

19   For God's sake, for the Prophet's sake, put your eyes
On the wicked who sin against the Lord God.

20   For this exceeds indignation and wonder—
Elders on the streets in only their houserobes.

21   They ignore the customs of the Messenger, the Prophet, our Messenger,
By God they are not full of faith.

22   Here are the prostitutes, their sisters, whom they lie with but do not love,
They followed him, their big friend, Satan.

23   They followed him, and he took them to the women who do not come out
During the day—only at night when no one can see them.

24   Instead of going to them, pass by and give them their place,
For the importance of God and religion.

25   You see them, they are hastening, calling out—
They are wicked people, spirits of Satan.

26   If you tell them God forbids fornication,
Especially with married women—that is the worst—

27   Well then, they will say to you that now there is progress,
And that it was God who brought about these modern times.

28   Well then, attend to the words of our great poet
Where he mentions some words exalting religion.

29   If the world had no religion,
Truly, it would not exist at all, much less these modern times!

30   My warning to women who follow the Sunna is this:
Preserve trust in marriage and religion.

31   Hang on to your men and ignore the worthless ones,
      Who deny the Apostle, the friends of Satan.

32   Those who are lost have neither shame nor fear
      Oh you wicked enemies of Adnan!

33   What will they give you that is of use here in this world?
      You cheat yourselves, sinning against the Lord God.

34   You harm your men, ruining your marriages,
      On the resurrection day you will be with the devils.

35   For God's sake, and for the sake of the Messenger, I
          implore you,
      Let us stop gazing at houses of temptation in modern times.

36   Let us stop watching spaceships and cowboys in the films,
      They are what causes one to follow Satan.

37   Indeed, you hear the words of the Lord God where He says
      Watch for signs of the end, and you shall understand.

38   It is finished, with praise to God, here I put my end mark,
      May God protect us from evil in these modern times.

39   The name of the one who composed this song is Hajiya,
      'Yar Shehu is the nickname, in Kano's Old City.

          Thanks be to God.

SONG ON THE CENSUS
BY HAUWA GWARAM, 1972

1   In the name of God, I will compose a song
On the approaching census.

2   People, the census time is only
Two months away.

3   Everyone should come together and prepare
For it, come prepare for it.

4   Support the teachers
And the counters when the time comes.

5   You must give the teachers
Answers to their questions; don't get angry with them.

6   Stop and see your names and
The names of your family members written down by them.

7   Even if a child is born that very day,
Don't hide him, but mention his existence.

8   Tell about him, even if he has as yet no name,
To do this is good.

9   All who refuse to do this
Do a disservice to their country.

10   If one has many praise names,
Include them all only to damage your country.

11   By counting, the government
Will prepare everything, it will improve things.

12   All who refuse to count
Because of taxes are foolish.

13   Remember times past, years long ago,
We counted ourselves then, don't forget.

14   For the census I was a teacher in Bici,
I was fighting ignorance.

15   And with no trouble
Among us, we collected [the names].

16   Now that each one is enlightened,
Let us get on with it.

17   Chickens, dogs, goats, and hyena
      Are all yours, don't forget.

18   As for me, I wrote to the office
      Of the census—look at it, you know how to read.

19   "We your teachers will help
      You do it. Give us [the tools] and we'll get to it."

20   "By God, if you give us every name
      He will be glad to see it."

21   Hauwa Gwaram has composed this song,
      On the census and its worth.

22   It is she who catches the mad
      Dog that grabs her stirring stick.

23   I don't despise a simple bed of stalks
      And a mat of leaves—don't forget.

24   May God help us to finish everything
      All of us in peace, without mishap.

25   I praise God, it is finished here,
      I will stop thus to rest.

26   Yusufu Aliyu my close friend
      In the Hikima Kulob has composed this song.

27   Hauwa Gwaram has revised it,
      And she has done her best.

28   Thanks be to God, I thank God,
      Who is always with us, let's not forget.

29   And the teachers of the Hikima Kulob say
      They want to do the census,

30   Because there are among us those who are careful,
      Attentive, and of good character.

31   It is the careful one who will count
      Until he knows the whole story.

32   Let him investigate fully and evaluate the material,
      If he is to research the full story.

      Thanks be to God.

SONG ON THE CENSUS OF THE PEOPLE OF NIGERIA
BY HAJIYA 'YAR SHEHU, 1973

1   Let us begin in the name of God, I begin in the name of
       the Lord,
     God Almighty—may He be exalted—the King of Truth.

2   You are omniscient, You hear all, You know all,
     Protect us from evil, from the world's wicked ones.

3   For the sake of Muhammad, the leader of all on earth,
     And of the afterlife too, if you grant it to him.

4   For the sake of the Prophets, the Companions, those who
       were sent,
     And for all the relatives of the Apostle, the exemplary one.

5   Grant me protection,
     You who are our protective wall, which cannot be eroded.

6   I will compose on the census of the districts
     Of the north and of all our country together.

7   Oh God, the Wise, Your wisdom suffices,
     Make us understand so that we may explain the truth.

8   Lest we fall into the bad ways of the loose-mouthed trickster
       Gizo,
     Who, when he couldn't bear something, just shouted louder.

9   Here is my warning for kings and teachers:
     Stand firm, to defend the north.

10   Whatever of the eyes or mouth or ears,
     Whatever oppresses you shall be suspended.

11   Wasn't it to you that Shehu 'Dan Fodiyo gave his banner
     For the trust of all the north, united?

12   Because it is thus, get up and help,
     In counting all our states together

13   Lest they bring in cockroaches or lice
     And shake them out among us and we have trouble.

14   May God have mercy on those former great ones,
     Sarki, [protect us from] all the fears in the north.

15   Lest we hear Satan's shouting,
     And the trickiness of those who eschew the Truth.

16   Let not ignorance entangle us,
      Clinging to our legs, yes, and our necks.

17   If someone comes to count us, let us be sure to come
      And report to them all our family members.

18   Men and women, even the small children,
      Including the babies who are but one day old.

19   And even the old people who don't go outside,
      For God's sake report all of them, don't miss one.

20   Because leaving one out is not wise,
      It is expelling him from among the people of Nigeria.

21   He's lost trap and bird, too,
      And left with vain regret here in Nigeria.

22   God save us from doing this, brothers,
      The remedy for it is to tell the truth.

23   Reject all those who give bad advice,
      They are the enemies of the state, hypocrites of the north.

24   They are saying we will be taxed,
      Because they want to spoil the whole operation of the north.

25   And if one is lax in making preparations, caring only for
          wealth,
      One subverts everything here in the north, and we'll be in
          trouble.

26   No one's counting you for tax purposes, you know,
      Children and women are not to be included among the
          taxpayers.

27   Nor the handicapped or old people, none of them
      Would be included among the taxpayers.

28   This counting is for something different,
      It is for knowing the numbers of people in Nigeria.

29   And to know the number of people in the states
      And the state that is most populous in Nigeria.

30   If one divides the revenue, it will get the largest share,
      It will benefit abundantly, the money will go to the
          taxpayers.

31   With money for agriculture
      And hospitals and schools for all people.

32   When they get the biggest portion of all—
So let's not cheat the north.

33   To whoever says they will tax us,
Say to him, "Tax is wealth, you hear?"

34   The sick and the mad will not pay—
Truly, tax is from the healthy people.

35   It is easy for him on the farm, you know—
He pays a tithe on what he earns.

36   And the market people pay once a year,
While there are [also] innumerable working people.

37   From whom every month there is withheld,
Sixpence from every pound sterling.

38   You teachers, men and women, do your best—
Give the names of your children, all together.

39   Children, grandchildren, and relatives, leaving out none,
Including even those away from home in some other place.

40   All those who refuse to participate in the count, you know,
Will be ashamed among Nigerians.

41   They will become ugly, wicked, and ignorant,
Helping thus to cheat the North.

42   Well, census *malams,* I warn you,
For God's sake, for the Messenger, the Apostle, the
      exemplary one,

43   Don't get irritated, you must have lots of patience,
And when counting, don't be slapdash.

44   Go softly, go carefully, without causing apprehension
And without harassing people with questions.

45   If someone asks you a silly question,
Answer them straight, don't get annoyed, you hear?

46   Do your jobs honestly, according to the rules,
In the town, the countryside, and in the Qur'anic schools.

47   *Ahaiye iyenana iyaye yi yurai yurai,*
Teacher, the thing that I do, don't question it.

48   I leave it to the Lord God—may He be exalted and glorified.
He knows everything before it enters your hearts.

49   Well, head counter, we're really expecting
     To see all the work done right.

50   Lest afterward people start to grumble
     And come to a disagreement.

51   Well, let's not reach a state of "Had we but known . . ."
     Words describing a sorry state!

52   "Had I but known" is a past regret,
     If you hear it, you know someone has suffered.

53   East and west, middle and north,
     We see you've prepared everything for us.

54   Lest we sell one thousand and fail to buy
     And a point is reached where everything is gone.

55   Thanks be to God, I am thankful
     For the desires of the Almighty—may He be exalted—the one king.

56   It is finished, with praise to God, the song is done,
     The song of the census of our unified country.

57   If you want an explanation, to save your questions,
     It is 'Yar Shehu who composed this, you hear?

58   If one asks for her address, look, it's not difficult,
     In the Old City, at Kofar Mata, just ask the way.

59   I thank God and the apostle, our example,
     God, His Companions, the followers, and the saints.

60   It has sixty verses, not five, you hear?
     I close in the name of He who need not boast.

        Thanks be to God.

SONG FOR THE WAR ON IGNORANCE
BY HAUWA GWARAM, 1974

1 In the name of God, grant me the wisdom
   To compose this song on the war on ignorance.

2 I intend to sing about those who lack wisdom,
   I take refuge in God, may He protect me from the ignorant.

3 I am a Qur'anic student who enlightens people,
   Come with me and learn about the war on ignorance.

4 You know about taking up the rope of knowledge and about
      ignoring it;
   Everyone who leaves wisdom [aside] endures bad fortune.

5 In times of ignorance, people wouldn't admit to
   Sickness, because of ignorance.

6 They ground together potash herbs and wild bark,
   To spread all over their bodies, in their ignorance.

7 If you said to them, "Here's the dispensary," so they'd stop
   For medicine to be given them, for ignorance,

8 They'd say that European pills are poison,
   They'd refuse the medicine and burn up with fever, in their
      ignorance.

9 You know all our affairs here are founded on good reason,
   Everyone you see is making war on ignorance.

10 The traders and royalty everywhere, you know,
   Even the European is fighting ignorance.

11 They say my sister searches for the secret,
   The reason for my making war on ignorance.

12 Sit down and listen well to the answer I'll give you;
   Indignation—that's why we fight ignorance.

13 Look at Nomau and the trouble he's had, wandering about,
   Bringing misfortune on himself because of ignorance.

14 He wanted to visit his parents' town,
   But he didn't know how to send a note, not having fought
      ignorance.

15 So the letter-writer came and wrote him a telegram for ten
      cents,

Now he knows Nomau's private affairs, because he fought
    ignorance.

16   Then Nomau went to the scales where they weighed his
        things,
    But he couldn't read the scales, because of ignorance.

17   Someone weighed his load at five dollars' worth and charged
        him seven,
    He paid them what they asked, because of ignorance.

18   He went to the railroad station with a watch on his arm,
    But the train left him behind because of ignorance.

19   He went to the women's toilet and was urinating there,
    They drove him out, for having no self-respect.

20   He wanted to go to Jos, so he boarded the Kano train
        instead, and away he went!
    He brought it all on himself by not fighting ignorance.

21   He boarded the train, he got up to wander around,
    The gamblers called him, because of ignorance,

22   They collected what little money he had and kept it,
    Leaving him only his watch and umbrella, because of
        ignorance.

23   He got to the station in Kano, and there was no one to
        meet him,
    He hired a bicycle—you hear, he was ever more ignorant.

24   He took a road one shouldn't and was arrested,
    He brought it all on himself by not fighting ignorance.

25   He was searched there—not a cent in his pocket,
    All he had was his watch and umbrella, all because of
        ignorance.

26   God protect us from failing to seek the advice of teachers,
    Do you hear? Such is the failure to fight ignorance.

27   Oh Lord, lead us on the straight path,
    The path for those who war on ignorance.

28   Brother, come here and pay attention to me,
    Let me explain to you what those who are ignorant must do.

29   Either for your tax or for your farm,
    Help yourselves and make war on ignorance.

30   Your groundnut loads you take to the clerk for weighing,
      He will lie about them to you because of your ignorance.

31   If the scale shows seventy pounds,
      He'll tell you forty—more ignorance!

32   For God's sake, in indignation for those who act thus,
      Help yourselves and make war on ignorance.

33   Our chief Umaru Yola I will speak of too—
      He's really helping those who fight ignorance.

34   When it was time to do the first census,
      We could not do it well for the war on ignorance.

35   Then our chief advised our leaders
      To call in the teachers in this war on ignorance.

36   So we were all enlisted, men and women,
      And we counted everyone, for we were not ignorant.

37   East and west, north and south too,
      We counted everyone, for we were not ignorant.

38   People of the north, men and women, let us rise up
      To embrace the war on laziness and ignorance.

39   Oh Lord, we beg You to help us on
      The road we should follow for the war on ignorance.

40   The man is an idiot, let him stop hiding in the crowd,
      Let everyone live without ignorance.

41   You will be popular and respected
      If you persevere in the war on ignorance.

42   Become a friend of good men, [and]
      Everyone will see and know that you fight ignorance.

43   Accept orders from your leaders
      And act on them, make war on ignorance.

44   To respond to an order is a good thing,
      But you will not grasp it unless you make war on ignorance.

45   Adults and children, we are called to class
      So we can understand everything and live without ignorance.

46   Children should go to primary classes and seek education,
      Adults should go to classes too, for the war on ignorance.

47   Local authorities! Government! Be zealous,
      And back us in our war on ignorance.

48   Enjoin the district heads and village heads, so that we pay
          attention to them
      And to the ward heads, in the war on ignorance.

49   If you spy a man who is planting goodness,
      You can be sure that in his heart he is not ignorant.

50   Stop and listen, ignorance is filth,
      The poison it has and that of a snake are no different.

51   People of the city, country, and administrative district, you
          know,
      All of us must strive together in the war on ignorance.

52   You know the damage involved in associating with the
          ignorant,
      It means getting oneself into bad treatment.

53   Whatever advice you give [an ignorant] man, he'll reject it,
      For he is already replete with ignorance.

54   People like this, we pull them out,
      And talk to them again about the war on ignorance.

55   Cease your malicious lame and baseless excuses,
      And follow my advice to go and fight ignorance.

56   Well, fellow, disagree with those who call you a beast,
      Saying that you and a donkey are no different in your
          ignorance.

57   The progress of the people and the country will cease,
      If there are those who take advantage of ignorance.

58   Now, I say, organizers, let us make an effort
      And admonish the teachers in the war on ignorance.

59   Let our country grow to fullness, let the people prosper,
      Because everyone has become without ignorance.

60   Traders, rulers, none of them, if you notice,
      Associates with the ignorant.

61   You, how can you sit or walk without shame?
      Hasten to where they fight ignorance!

62   You will be a wise man and of good character,
      Provided you make efforts in the war on ignorance.

63   Your character will be repaired, everyone will like you—
      Provided you make efforts in the war on ignorance.

64   People, look at the developments of the world today,
      Every thinking person, let him fight the war on ignorance.

65   Carry on with communal labor and mutual aid
      And also enroll in the class in the war on ignorance.

66   Repair the market stalls so you'll have shade,
      And fulfill your wishes so you fight ignorance.

67   Keep repairing the roads for the heavy traffic,
      When you finish with classes for the war on ignorance.

68   God be praised, we thank God,
      I've finished the song on the war on ignorance.

69   It is finished, with praise to God here I shall stop,
      Hauwa Gwaram I am, a fighter of ignorance.

                    Thanks be to God.

SONG ON UNIVERSAL PRIMARY EDUCATION
BY HAUWA GWARAM, 1977

1   In the name of God, I intend to compose,
     Advice on universal primary education.

2   Always to begin with we call on You the Lord God,
     To help us with universal primary education.

3   You are the One who enjoins us to seek knowledge,
     You are the cause of universal primary education.

4   Whatever we seek in this world,
     Nothing surpasses universal primary education.

5   I will implore kings and scholars
     To secure the trust, giving universal primary education.

6   Village heads, district heads, and you traders,
     Secure the trust to offer universal primary education.

7   You health instructors who go around town,
     Help us in the cause of universal primary education.

8   For God's sake, policemen and soldiers of the town,
     Help us to get universal primary education.

9   Market sellers and even pagans, come,
     Even the herders [need] universal primary education.

10   Also you farmers, help
     Your children to seek universal primary education.

11   You itinerant sellers in the town,
     Come here, where we offer universal primary education.

12   I am a Qur'anic student, at the feet of scholars,
     I too want universal primary education.

13   Our leaders have insisted on our behalf,
     They've urged us to give universal primary education.

14   Formerly adult education teachers
     Were the ones to give universal primary education.

15   Well, if we wander around everywhere now,
     Everyone will have a primary education.

16   We cried out at the emir's palace, at the leaders' places,
     "Help us to get a universal primary education!"

17   Prior to this [time], few women were teachers,
Well, now we will try to make some improvements for
    primary education.

18   God give us the power to achieve our hearts' desires,
And see teachers who give universal primary education.

19   You who teach our youths, teachers,
Strive for universal primary education.

20   For God's sake, be polite and humble, teachers,
And refrain from making people serve you.

21   Small children, come and heed this warning,
Those who drink, stop drinking if you want to succeed.

22   Lest you be called dogs and rats,
Give up your buying of drink during the day.

23   Here is a plan, divided in two sections,
City and village should have universal primary education.

24   Wherever you find an open space, start building,
So our children can have a free education.

25   You teachers, women and men, here is a warning,
Secure the trust of universal primary education.

26   Arabic and Roman script you must teach,
Cease being lazy, make a contribution.

27   The tipplers, the drinkers, throw them out!
All of you, take up the way of universal primary education.

28   The prostitutes around you are leading you astray,
The transvestites are keeping you from universal primary
    education.

29   Well, the federal government is watching you,
To see if you are preventing us from getting primary
    education.

30   The clothes you wear to go to class
Should be decent and proper for primary education.

31   The tight-tucked shirts and slim pants are not for you;
High heels, leave them, and you'll be contributing [to
    education].

32   You are not forbidden to use *idon taja*,
Cleanliness is lawful, to avoid filth.

33   Bathing and laundering, clipping fingernails and
      Brushing teeth. By doing all of this you will contribute.

34   If you are off to class, have a good meal
      Of porridge and milk. Give us universal primary education!

35   Also, don't smoke cigarettes or weed, not even a little,
      Much less hard drugs—give us universal primary education.

36   Stop beating children, take care of them all,
      Abuse is not part of universal primary education.

37   Children are your trust, teachers,
      If you abuse them you do wrong.

38   If you remember the care you've been given—
      All our teachers of old helped us, as you know.

39   They showered us with knowledge, without reservation,
      They were without selfishness, without wickedness.

40   It was Abdu Sha Nono who began to teach me,
      In Gwaram near Kano, there I began to learn.

41   I was taught how to do ablutions and to respect the body,
      May God forgive our superiors.

42   I will stop here, though I've left a little,
      Of the song I arranged on free education.

43   Thanks be to God, here I will stop,
      [I am] Hauwa Gwaram, of the free education movement.

           Thanks be to God.

SONG FOR THE PUBLIC UDOJI GRANT
BY HAUWA GWARAM, 1973

1   Let us begin in the name of God; I shall compose a song,
    On the public funds, the Udoji grant.

2   Men and women, give me your attention,
    I am explaining about the Udoji grant.

3   If you receive your money, don't waste it,
    Take good care of your Udoji grant.

4   If you sell your things to get a grant,
    Take it to the bank, this Udoji.

5   Where are your leaders? You will receive your grant
    At your retirement because we receive Udoji.

6   God is Great,
    He is responsible for our receiving Udoji.

7   I am warning young men and boys,
    If you do what is right [you'll get] Udoji.

8   For God's sake and for the Prophet's, pay attention
    To accounts at banks for your gratuity.

9   You buy motorcycles, which is what you want now,
    And women, you take them, because of Udoji.

10 The value of education or work is that
    You can repair your things.

11 Thieves and women are seated here,
    And young swindlers, they waste their gratuities.

12 There are traditional doctors and those who do spirit-trance,
    And magicians who have Udoji.

13 Women and teachers, listen to me,
    If I warn you against Udoji.

14 Bed and mattress, table and brass pots,
    I would not confuse you about Udoji.

15 There are senseless ones in these modern times,
    They want to cheat us because of Udoji.

16 There are many men who trick us,
    They would drive us into a pit because of Udoji.

17   I will stop here the explanation of Udoji,
      I finish this song on what's involved with Udoji.

18   It is finished, with praise to God, here I shall stop,
      The song, the wife is just like those who are miserly.

19   Hauwa Gwaram I am, I added to this song,
      Take care of your things because of Udoji.

           Thanks be to God.

SONG FOR ABDU BAKO'S ZOO
BY HAUWA GWARAM, 1973

1   Beginning in the name of God,
The Merciful, God,
God grant me eloquence,
Wise selectivity and sufficient material,
    Let's go visit the zoo.

2   God grant me understanding,
Alertness and insight,
Grant me sufficient knowledge,
Let me taste honey, not bitter fruit,
    Let's go visit the zoo.

3   God grant me insight,
So that I can describe the scene,
Let's get the entrance fee,
One naira, thirty kobo,
    Let's go visit the zoo.

4   We should praise those who are worthy,
Whether at home or abroad,
We understand intelligent work,
And the government understands it,
    Let's go visit the zoo.

5   Government, you have worked for us,
And so have your soldiers,
You are courageous,
You are fearless,
    Let's go visit the zoo.

6   God, the one to be feared,
Man, the one to be feared,
With cunning one steels oneself,
To tie up the wild beast,
    Let's go visit the zoo.

7   Politeness and obedience,
May get you a free pass,
You should refuse argument,
Here's one on whom God bestowed gifts,
    Let's go visit the zoo.

8   Alhaji Abdu Bako,
Fearless fellow, without peer,

The undaunted one who endures,
Far and wide you have given orders,
  Let's go visit the zoo.

9 Today here's a surprise,
Wild animals in cages,
And even water for them in tanks,
Come, let's go see the lion,
  Let's go visit the zoo.

10 We saw three kinds of monkeys,
A duiker, gazelle, and parrot,
Elephants, here's a mongoose,
A donkey, and your rabbits,
  Let's go visit the zoo.

11 Here's the antelope, here's the buffalo,
The wart hog, the rhinoceros,
Wild cats, leopards,
Kangaroo, and my vulture,
  Let's go visit the zoo.

12 I saw a crocodile in his pool,
Here's a tortoise, here's a python,
Here's a guinea pig, my leopards,
Here's a porcupine and a pelican,
  Let's go visit the zoo.

13 I saw a jackal, dog-of-the-bush,
Here's a hawk and a stork,
Here's a griffon, here's a kite,
Here's a red-eyed dove and a hornbill,
  Let's go visit the zoo.

14 A sandhopper, a hornbill,
Even water monitors and a guinea fowl,
Here's a grey heron and a blue-winged dove,
Crows and ducks,
  Let's go visit the zoo.

15 Here's the ostrich, here's the hartebeest,
Here's the hyena, here's the roan antelope,
Here's the ibis, here's the marabou stork,
The cattle egret and crownbird,
  Let's go visit the zoo.

16 Pigeon and owl,
Here are fish in the water,

Here are mangoes on the trees,
There's Maltex here and beer,
Let's go visit the zoo.

17 We're forgetting the crow,
Here are the white birds, "fulafunka,"
Here's the Gambian oribi near you,
Here are water spigots for their water,
Let's go visit the zoo.

18 East and west, be patient,
South and north, show self-control,
Come to Kano to see the lion
And the energetic squirrel,
Let's go visit the zoo.

19 We make every effort, we pray,
We continue to invoke God
That He might take us to His kingdom,
We kneel to Him and follow,
Let's go visit the zoo.

20 Consider our many people,
Let's beg the Everlasting One,
Let's take care with our lives,
May God protect us,
Let's go visit the zoo.

21 May God lengthen your time,
Governor Alhaji Bako,
May God consider your intentions,
May He grant you your fair share,
Let's go visit the zoo.

22 You see, whatever you plant,
That's what grows in your garden,
You won't plant sugarcane,
And reap your tomato-fruit,
Let's go visit the zoo.

23 Here is our admonition,
Women, let's improve our lot,
Let's be obedient to our men,
Even if they deceive us,
Let's go visit the zoo.

24 Now you may wander about
Among animals and birds,

In the open field and in their hiding places,
May God give us understanding,
    Let's go visit the zoo.

25   If you come to see the zoo,
Inquire, so we'll know you've come,
Let's go via Gandu to see the zoo,
Via Kofar Agundi one can come,
    Let's go visit the zoo.

26   The government is kind,
In its benevolence,
It helps the white oryx
Until it has no other needs,
    Let's go visit the zoo.

27   The government built Bagauda and Tiga Dam,
It made the city parks,
The hotel and cinema, you know,
Here are recreational buildings,
    Let's go visit the zoo.

28   It continues to fix the roads
For cars and motorcycles,
For bicycles, so that people can
Have the freedom of the roads,
    Let's go visit the zoo.

29   In the east there are cars,
In Jos, Maiduguri, Bauchi,
In Sokoto and Zaria we've made progress,
People can go to Maradi and Kunci,
    Let's go visit the zoo.

30   May God grant us [sufficient] reason,
To accept His example,
We've received a great reward,
Let us receive it openly,
    Let's go visit the zoo.

31   People, forgive me
If one of you is angry,
Because I have not mentioned each of you,
Telling of your good character,
    Let's go visit the zoo.

32   Thanks be to God,
Here I shall shorten the advice,

Here is verse thirty [*sic*],
And we'll add four more [*sic*],
      Let's go visit the zoo.

33   On Thursday I wrote this,
The tenth of May I finished,
In seventy-three I wrote this poem,
Whoever heard it liked it,
      Let's go visit the zoo.

34   Well, if you ask who it was,
Who composed this song, it was me,
Hauwa Gwaram I am,
She who explained to you—it's me,
      Let's go visit the zoo.

35   A Qur'anic student, I have sung,
And if you'll pay her we'll extend
Her poetic performance to Kaduna,
Because the spider's excellence lies in its web,
      Let's go visit the zoo.

Thanks be to God.

SONG FOR A VISIT TO THE BIRNIN KUDU HOSPITAL

BY HAUWA GWARAM, 1964

1   Thanks be to God, let us thank the Lord God,
      I shall begin this song on the health care workers.

2   On Monday the seventh in the second month,
      We went to visit the health care workers.

3   The hospital in Birnin Kudu honored
      Many important dignitaries and health care workers.

4   First we went to their supervisor's office,
      Our doctor, the one in charge.

5   Then to the place where one gives birth hygienically,
      We went to the women's rooms for health care.

6   We even saw the x-ray room,
      Where one goes if wounded or to check your health.

7   We went to the kitchen—I was delighted with it,
      And the laundry where they wash clothes beyond counting.

8   We went to the laboratory where, if you pass blood,
      They look at it to help you get better.

9   We went to the mortuary, the emergency room,
      We went to the dispensary, where one goes to be healthy.

10   We even saw the rooms for washing boils and the eyes,
      We went to the rooms to see how they heal.

11   We went to see the injection area,
      Then to the chart rooms where they record sickness.

12   We saw the place for boiling water,
      To destroy germs, to keep the patients healthy.

13   I'll list the names of the hospital workers,
      The men and women who work for health.

14   I know there are sixty,
      In the hospital at Birnin Kudu, the place for health.

15   I'll name the women and men—there are sixty,
      And a few more I saw, health workers.

16   There is one doctor in charge,
      If you go to seek the way to health.

17   It is our doctor in charge near the medicine,
      Who issues a card to each patient.

18   Here are Umaru and the storekeeper Himfat,
      Jimmai and Mari, they are health workers.

19   Dandija the caretaker, Lazarus and Amadu,
      Jampil, Joseph, they all do health work.

20   Adamu Kuntigi, Inusa and Alhassan,
      Garba the strong one, the health worker.

21   Here are Hauwa Sokoto, Goggo and Iliyasu, all
      Men and women health workers.

22   Garba the strong one, Adeka of Zangatu,
      Adeka—all of them strive for health.

23   Muhammadu and Sa'idu and Ma'u they are there,
      Ibrahima the strong one, all are health workers.

24   Sa'ada gives injections, he is a helper,
      And 'Yar Baba is the dispenser for health.

25   We saw Malam Kaile who gives injections,
      He also strives for health care.

                    Thanks be to God.

SONG FOR THE OPENING OF THE
SECOND FRIDAY MOSQUE IN KANO
BY HAUWA GWARAM, 1969

1   Oh Lord God, may He be praised, Predestinator and Just
      One,
      Help those who built the mosque.

2   Wealthy traders and the poor and our emirs,
      They all helped build the mosque.

3   This is the second Friday mosque in Kano,
      It will benefit the ardent mosque-goers.

4   On the twentieth day of sixty-nine in December,
      The Emir of Kano, Ado, opened the mosque.

5   Many people from everywhere and those from Kano
      Came to attend the opening of the mosque.

6   The military rulers of the districts of Kano came
      To attend the opening of the mosque.

7   From the north-central state they came to visit us,
      They came for the festivities of the opening of the mosque.

8   Alhaji Dalhatu, Kano's Imam, you know,
      Said the prayers for the opening of the mosque.

9   It was he who said the prayers, and Shehu Abdulkadiri, you
      know,
      Read from the Qur'an for the mosque.

10   Kano's Madaki Alhaji Shehu Ahmadu it was
      Who gave the account in Hausa in the mosque.

11   Tijjani Usuman translated the Arabic,
      The Emir of Kano also gave a sermon in Arabic.

12   Alhaji Nasiru Kabara translated to Hausa,
      And the Emir of Kano cut the ribbon for the mosque.

13   The state governors and soldiers filed out
      The south gate of the mosque.

14   As for me, I beg God, the All-Knowing,
      May He have mercy on those who built this mosque.

15   Alhaji Abdullahi Bayero you know,
      Made preparations to build this mosque.

16   May God brush the dust from his forehead,
For the sake of the Prophets, the Companions, and the mosque.

17   Kano's Emir Ado took up his father's energetic efforts,
He inherited his inclination toward having a mosque.

18   What all people want for Kano
Is five mosques in the city.

19   Let us have one here in the Hausa neighborhood,
To spare their crowding of people in the mosque.

20   And come to the Wudilawa section to find one there too,
For people to be enlightened in the mosque.

21   As in the Yola ward area, one will find a mosque,
Help us to build a mosque.

22   And so in Jalli too, let us get one,
In Kankarofi let us build a mosque.

23   What Alhaji Abdullahi built,
Alhaji Ado will plaster—the mosque.

24   I am certain if you work at it, soon we'll have five
With the help of the zealous ones who build mosques.

25   God forgive me my hidden sins
And have mercy on Alhaji Abdu, for the sake of the mosque.

26   People, help the Emir of Kano
To start the building of this mosque.

27   What I want from you all
Is to help fulfill the promise to strive for mosques.

28   It is finished with praise to God, here I shall stop, I have finished,
Hauwa Gwaram I am, I have composed a song for the mosque.

                Thanks be to God.

SONG FOR SELF-SUFFICIENCY
BY HAUWA GWARAM, 1976

1   In the eleventh month, on its sixth day,
         In seventy-six, we went on our visit.

2   We went to the farm in the Samaru area of Zaria,
         I went with Rufkatu, the woman who runs our farm.

3   Many women from the surrounding villages had come
         From out there in Basawa to learn self-sufficiency on the
             farm.

4   For us, from Kudan Shika and even from Danja and Hunkuyi
         And Dambo, they are all working to learn self-sufficiency.

5   I even saw women who could do carpentry work,
         They made our tables and chairs.

6   Some wore the local white weave cloth,
         Some wore *adire* or *kanfala* cloth—let's be self-sufficient.

7   Some worked making local white weave cloth,
         Some did construction so we could make use of our land.

8   One of them made the cook-everything stew and she added
             spinach to it,
         Another made traditional millet porridge for our sustenance.

9   Some of them wove large produce bags and spread them out,
         Others made *adire* or *kanfala* cloth—let's be self-sufficient.

10   I also saw hot peppers and tomatoes,
         Lettuce and cabbage planted—we are making use of our land.

11   Bananas, carrots, papaya and fig trees had sprouted,
         Along with red sorrel and onions on our farm.

12   Guavas, horseradishes, and even grapes,
         Here are small hot peppers—we're making use of our land.

13   Some are sewing and weaving robes,
         Hats, and antimacassars, so we can make good use of our land.

14   Some teach hygiene and health care—
         Child care, too—let us make good use of our land.

15   One of the women made bean porridge, fried and cooked,
         Others of us were learning to read.

16   Some planted yam, while some hoed sugar cane,
And sweet potato and cocoyam in our garden.

17   Even women with white skins like Europeans,
They wrapped up all kinds of things from our land.

18   The most interesting thing to me, you'll hear,
Was that there was not a man among us

19   Except for the journalists and the photographers,
To spread the news of us throughout the land.

20   I also saw chickens on one farm,
Small chicks and eggs in great numbers—our local sort.

21   Three thousand women, apart from the teachers,
Were being taught to make use of the land.

22   By God, they pooled their resources with no hypocrisy,
There were none who were deceitful in our group.

23   See the women here from ethnic groups everywhere—
There is no discrimination in our association.

24   I say, I assert, I believe
That our leaders are behind us.

25   By God, women, the officials too have helped,
They have helped women with our farms.

26   I say, I assert, I believe,
I've watched [these] women of keen ambition.

27   They received gifts of buckets and basins,
Sickle and hoe, to make use of the land.

28   Milk and beans and even modern fertilizer
And seeds to plant, they gave all this to our women.

29   Here are the farming teachers of the Samaru area,
They showed diligence, making use of their land.

30   By God, they taught all the students
Crafts, farming, and self-sufficiency.

31   May God grant us fulfillment of our desires,
Women of Kano, we see their diligence is like ours.

32   May God grant us fulfillment of our desires,
Women of Kano, they have persevered in our farming.

33   I shall wind things up here, lest you accuse me of dragging out
The song for the women who make use of our land.

34   I am Hauwa Gwaram, I've worked the land and I'm tired,
I made a garden to make good use of the land.

35   A worker for self-sufficiency I am,
I am pledged to make good use of our land.

         Thanks be to God.

Poems on Occupations and Self-Improvement

SONG OF SELF-IMPROVEMENT
AND COMMUNITY WORK
BY HAUWA GWARAM, 1971

1   In the name of God, I intend to compose a song
    On self-help through community work.

2   God—may He be exalted—help me to be alert
    As I compose my song on community work.

3   People, men and women, we must heed the government,
    The generosity of the Local Authority has provided for
        community work.

4   Here is the Area Council in the city of Kano,
    In town and country it has done community work.

5   The representative and his sanitation supervisor
    Of the L. G. A. [Local Government Authority] of Kano have
        also done community work.

6   I will speak of four city representatives,
    Who have helped themselves through community work.

7   Formerly when a person died he was carried on a bier,
    Now we have cars, through community work.

8   I will count the names of city districts on the south side,
    They helped themselves through community work.

9   Alfindiki and Daneji and Dorayi,
    They helped themselves through community work.

10 In Sagagi, up to Durumin Iya and Dogarai,
    They helped themselves through community work.

11 There are Gidan Sarki, and Durumin Zungura,
    They too are striving to finish community work.

12   Kurna and Gwangwazo and Kurmawa, all of them,
      Help themselves through community work.

13   Kabara and Indabawa and Marmara, they are determined
      To help themselves through community work.

14   Then here in Kurawa they have helped each other,
      Children and adults are doing community work.

15   In Tudun Wazirci, Sheshe, Soron 'Dinki,
      They help themselves through community work.

16   Here in Kankarofi, up to Rimin Kira, all of them
      Help themselves through community work.

17   In Wudilawa, Yakasai, and Yakasai gather together,
      And Unguwar Gini, community workers.

18   At Zage and Kofar Mata, in Zango—hear me—
      They help themselves through community work.

19   A hole-digger, a rake, a head-pan, brush, and
      A dump for the mess, all are tools of community work.

20   We've acquired many cars, all duly allocated,
      To collecting garbage from community work.

21   Dancing and jumping without trouble,
      With drumming and ululations to help community work.

22   The mosquitoes, bedbugs, flies, and lice annoy,
      But none are left, thanks to community work.

23   Washing teeth and cutting nails, all of them,
      Bathing and washing clothes are part of community work.

24   Well, the city areas to the west shall be named now,
      I will count them, those that do community work.

25   In Ayagi, Akwa, Bakin Ruwa, up to Dausayi,
      They help themselves through community work.

26   Well, in 'Dandago, Diso and Galadanci, come join us,
      You help yourselves through community work.

27   In Jingau and Manladan and Gyaranya, join us,
      Garangamawa, set yourselves to community work.

28   In Hausawa, Kabuga, Kaigama, and Mandawari,
      Come to Ciranci, let's carry on with community work.

29   In Magashi, Magoga, and Mararraba, too,
      Add Dogon Nama for community work.

30   In Mai Aduwa, Mandawari, 'Yarkasuwa,
      Lokon Maƙera, there are community workers.

31   Here are Rijiya Huɗu, Sanka, Sudawa, join us,
      Yalwa and Sabon Sara, with community work.

32   Let's not leave out these places,
      They are helping themselves through community work.

33   And now I'll return to the eastern wards,
      They've displayed diligence, those community workers.

34   Agadasawa, Cedi, and Bakin Zuwo,
      In Alkantara, they've set about to do community work.

35   Here are Cediyar Fero and Ciromawa, come join us,
      And help yourselves through community work.

36   Daganda, Darma, and Dambazau, they made efforts,
      In Dukawa, they've progressed in community work.

37   Here are Cediyar Fero and Jujin 'Yanlambu,
      Gabari and Koƙi, they continue with community work.

38   Kududdufawa, Kwalwa, and Kurna you will hear,
      They helped themselves through community work.

39   Durumin Arbabi and Zaitawa, come
      In the Kofar Wambai area, set yourselves to community work.

40   Zangon Barebari, 'Yan Muruci, Sharfadi,
      They help themselves through community work.

41   Kwarim Mabuga, Yola, up to Mazan Kwari,
      They helped themselves through community work.

42   Mallam Garari, Masukwani da 'Yandoya, come join them,
      They help themselves through community work.

43   Tudun Nufawa, 'Yan Awaki, and Tudun Wada,
      Mallam Garari, they have community work, come.

44   Satatima, Lallaki, Sharifai you hear,
      In Takalmawa there are community workers.

45   And here is Makafin Kofar Wambai,
      They've filled all the potholes during community work.

46 I want you to go round all the alleyways
    In the town, and there you'll see the community workers.

47 They've fixed the roads and added some streets,
    They've filled the potholes, those community workers.

48 Everyone who has worked repairing the roads everywhere,
    May God reward you for community work.

49 And now I will return to the northern area, going round,
    I've seen the self-help, the community work.

50 At Kofar Mazugal, Gwammaja, and Sarari, come join us,
    In Arzai and Makafi, continue with community work.

51 And at Kantudu, Adakawa, Daurawa, come join us,
    At Garke and Madabo, let us continue with community work.

52 'Yan Tandu, Limanci, and Juma, come join us,
    See folks in Kabuwaya, they continue on with community
        work.

53 Well, Gangamau and Makwalla and Masakar Kuda,
    Help themselves through community work.

54 Durumin Daje, Dukurawa, Aikawa, come
    And help yourselves through community work.

55 'Yar Cediyar also, 'Yan Gurasa and Dandali,
    And Tudun Maƙera—you should do community work.

56 At Kofar Dawanau, listen well that you may hear,
    Help yourselves through community work.

57 Shatsari, Dukurawa, and Shirawa, all of you come
    And help yourselves through community work.

58 Well, here are Karofin Dala and Kofar Ruwa,
    Here is Rijiya Biyu, all community workers.

59 Then Kabawa—listen that you may hear—
    In Karofin, Kangiwa, there's community work.

60 Well, every ward of Kano altogether,
    In the town—they've increased community work.

61 Well, here is our cause, women, we are making efforts,
    We've striven mightily and we continue with community
        work.

62 Here is Kabawa, help us here,
    Karofin, Kangiwa, and community work.

63 Well, I'm off to the Old Library,
    To the teachers' place, women of community work.

64 As for us, we have no desire to quarrel or gossip,
    But use our energy for community work,

65 We teach occupations to women so they can all do some work,
    Literacy too, through community work.

66 Women of Hadeja, Gumel, Kazaure, they are uniting,
    In Dambatta, and Gwarzo, we are continuing community
        work.

67 From Birnin Kudu, Rano, the heads of those districts
    Have provided us with women as community workers.

68 Weaving and sewing and different kinds of cooking,
    Arabic and Roman script we learn in community work.

69 Child care and infant care we teach
    And indigo dying on *kampala* cloth, in community work.

70 I will make the outside circuit, I will wander around a bit,
    For self-help in community work.

71 Sabon Gari, Brigade, Fagge, and Tudun Wada,
    Up to Dakata, they've increased community work.

72 People of Gandu Ta Kuntawa and Hausawa, join us,
    Those from Kumbotso and from Ungogo do community
        work.

73 From Gyadi-Gyadi, Tarauni, Horo, come,
    People from these three districts, set about doing community
        work.

74 From Kurnan Asabe and Rijiyan Lemo, join us,
    And Jajiri too, to set about doing community work.

75 People, excuse me, here I will stop,
    There remain many towns unmentioned that do community
        work.

76 I am Hauwa Gwaram, I am a self-helper,
    I am an organizer for community work.

                Thanks be to God.

SONG FOR THE ASSOCIATION OF WOMEN OF THE NORTH

BY HAUWA GWARAM, 1967

1   In the name of God, I will compose a song,
     About the solidarity of women in the north.

2   I invoke God's aid, may he increase my insight,
     That I may again compose a song for the women of the north.

3   People of Kano, we ask your support,
     May you help us, women northerners.

4   Many people are asking me
     The reason for an association in the north.

5   I want to enlighten everyone,
     So that they will know about the association of the north.

6   We are helping them with their occupational skills,
     So that they needn't wander about worthless in the north.

7   We have come together to help each other,
     Together with the women of the north.

8   Authorities of Kano, we ask that you
     Show us the way for the women of the north.

9   We pool our money for the welfare of
     The association of women of the north.

10   We pool our possessions because of friendship
     Among the women of the association of the north.

11   There are those with money and those who teach
     In the association of women of the north.

12   There are market sellers in the association,
     And common people in the association of northerners.

13   There are those who teach reading,
     In Hausa and English in the northern association.

14   We teach weaving shirts and hats,
     And sewing by machine in the northern association.

15   We teach child care and hygiene,
     We teach cooking to northerners.

16   We teach the art of conversation and headscarf tying,
      We teach proper behavior to the northerners.

17   There are those who want to join the association,
      Who are afraid of the women of the north.

18   If you come to us, join without fear,
      Come to the association of the north.

19   It will cost you thirty kobo to join
      And sixpence for a card for northerners.

20   From the association no one is excluded,
      Come to the association of the women of the north.

21   There are the affluent and those from the government
      In the association of northern women.

22   There are teachers in the association
      And ordinary folks in the association.

23   There is no discrimination between us
      In the association of the women of the north.

24   We pool our money to help ourselves
      And for our freedom, women of the north.

25   We make purchases and take them to the orphans
      In the association of women of the north.

26   We make purchases and take them to the orphans,
      We give them to the destitute, women of the north.

27   We buy a television by ourselves and take it to the soldiers
      At the Kano hospital—that's the help of the northerners.

28   We buy bicycles with association money
      And take them to the orphans of the women of the north.

29   We buy towels and plastic bags and blankets,
      We buy milk for the orphans of the north.

30   Well, now we have our own land,
      We will begin building, women of the north.

31   The Kano magistrate, the governor, the district officer,
      And the emir, please help the children of the north.

32   Governor of Kano, Alhaji Audu Bako,
      Has helped us, the association of the north.

33   He gave us four bales of cloth, it's true,
      To give to the destitute from the women of the north.

34   When we divided the cloth into nine piles,
      We took it to the countryside to help the northerners.

35   Our leader is Hajiya Ladi Bako,
      With her and other ethnic groups of women of the north,

36   We went to the Mil Tara hospital and gave them things,
      To Shahuci, the place for destitute northerners.

37   To Kumbotso, Bichi, and Ungogo and to
      Yadakunya—we went to the place of the northerners.

38   We went to Wudil, even to Dawakin Tofa,
      We gave to the destitute from the women of the north.

39   May God give us good fortune,
      May He give us the things we want in the north.

40   The association of Kano, with the self-help that was done,
      Gave us eight hundred naira for the women of the north.

41   The community department of the L. G. A. [Local
          Government Authority] of Kano,
      Gave us three hundred naira for the women of the north.

42   There are four or five I cannot name,
      Who have helped us, the women of the north.

43   Well, people, every one of you,
      Come to the association of the women of the north.

44   Let us praise the northerners,
      Let us exalt the members of the association of the north.

45   It is ended, with praise to God, here I'll cut short
      The song of the women's association of the north.

46   If anyone asks you who wrote this song
      About the women in the association of the north,

47   It is I, Hauwa Gwaram, who composed this song
      On women in the association of the north.

          Thanks be to God.

SONG FOR THE COURSE AT THE CHILDREN'S HOSPITAL AND FOR PUBLIC INVOLVEMENT
BY HAUWA GWARAM, 1969

1   In the name of God I will compose a song
     Of praise for these women and their knowledge.

2   Kano women, urban and rural,
     Help yourselves, come and learn.

3   I've come from Dutse Gaduwar,
     From the Sabon Gari clinic, to teach education.

4   You pregnant ones, greetings to you,
     Where are the ones with babies on backs?—Come and learn.

5   We are giving lectures for you,
     So you can help yourselves to learn.

6   We are giving lectures for you,
     Clean up your places, be smart.

7   I'll begin my explanation to you pregnant ones,
     Help yourselves to learn.

8   Be sure to attend to your bedrooms and cover
     The food you are going to eat—that's educated.

9   Where are those with babies on backs? Come and listen
       to me.
     Improve yourselves through learning.

10 A six-month-old baby, you should understand,
     You have the responsibility of feeding wisely.

11 Give him milk and porridge and eggs,
     If you have the means—that is educated.

12 And liver and marrow and tomatoes,
     Spinach and onions—this is wise advice.

13 If you give the boy water to drink,
     Filter and boil it and let it cool—that is wise.

14 Get a flask, if possible, and pour in
     The drinking water—show a child educated ways.

15 Each morning when we rise,
     Let us sweep our homes—that's educated.

16 The cloth the boy sleeps on—
   Hang it out to air, if you are wise.

17 Get warm water, don't miss a day,
   Wash the boy with it, that is wise.

18 Bring [the children] regularly to our place
   For us to check them—that's educated.

19 There is medicine that we should
   Administer ourselves, we who know how.

20 At our clinics in Sabon Gari,
   In Dala, and Marmara—let's be wise.

21 Our leaders, all of them,
   I greet them on behalf of the search for wisdom.

22 I am warning the people of this country,
   Help yourselves, come and learn.

23 There are schools for young and old
   In the city and country for getting education.

24 There are instructors for people,
   They are helping people to get an education.

25 They've employed us in craft work and hygiene,
   To earn our food, because of education.

26 Let's clean our water pots and hang up buckets,
   Let's air our clothes because that is wise.

27 Let's go where the water flows and dig holes
   To do our washing, because that is wise.

28 Let's dig a hole for collecting sweepings,
   Let's bury bottles—that's educated.

29 Let's get forked branches and set them up
   To dry our cooking pots, because that is wise.

30 Let's go to the toilet in the pit latrines of our homes,
   Let's sweep and wash them because that is wise.

31 As for the fingernails on our hands,
   Let's clip and wash them because that is wise.

32 We have enemies in our bodies
   Who want to cheat us, despite our wisdom.

33   The louse and biting insects,
      Flies and mosquitoes—get educated.

34   Men, here is advice I want to give you about
      Repairing your homes—to do so is wise.

35   Women and your children who are there with you,
      Bring them along when you come to be educated.

36   We are teaching weaving shirts and hats,
      And crocheted antimacassars in the pursuit of wisdom.

37   We are teaching sewing on the machine so you may know
          how
      And sewing by hand, in the pursuit of education.

38   There are teachers of reading,
      They are teaching cooking too, of a learned kind.

39   If you bring the women to our place
      And your children in the pursuit of wisdom.

40   We don't need money from you,
      We are helping them for the sake of education.

41   We want each one to learn how to write,
      To understand a letter, through education.

42   To understand measures and weights,
      To read a watch, one must have education.

43   To recognize money, to know the pound sterling and shilling
      So we can count our change [in the market] and be educated.

44   It is finished, with praise to God, here I shall cut short
      The song on women—come and learn.

45   If anyone asks who composed this song
      On women wanting to learn,

46   It is Hauwa Gwaram, I am a Qur'anic student,
      Who is teaching women—come and be educated.

                    Thanks be to God.

SONG FOR THE OPENING OF THE COURSE
AT THE OLD LIBRARY IN SABON GARI
BY HAUWA GWARAM, 1974

1   In the name of God I will compose a song
For women to come to the library to learn an occupation.

2   The community department of the L. G. A. [Local
Government Authority] of Kano
Wants to help women with occupations.

3   On the tenth of January we want
To open a course for women to learn an occupation.

4   In nineteen hundred and seventy four
We want to teach women an occupation.

5   There is a short explanation here in this song;
Listen to this about occupations.

6   We are not looking for money from you
And we will give you materials for your work.

7   I'll give you yards of cloth, a sewing machine, and wool
And a hand towel for use in your work.

8   I, Hauwa Gwaram, I appeal to you;
Come and help yourselves to find an occupation.

9   You independent women, come and find a trade,
Young women, come to the library to learn an occupation.

10   You divorcees, come here, stop hanging back,
Come to the Old Library for an occupation.

11   From Kumbotso, Fanshekara, and Ungogo,
From Gidan Alade, come to Kano for an occupation.

12   From Gyadi-Gyadi, Tarauni, Hotoro,
All three wards, come and learn an occupation.

13   Brigade, Fagge, Gaba, and Dakata,
Tudun Wada and Sabon Gari, here are professions.

14   May God end hatred between us and evil,
May he set our minds on professions.

15   As for me, I will teach you skills
In the Old Library—professions.

16   I teach the weaving of shirts and hats
      And crochet work—come to the library for professions.

17   I teach child care, I teach hygiene
      In the Old Library—professions.

18   Where are those with small children? Come with me
      In the Old Library for professions.

19   If you have a six-month-old baby to tie to your back,
      Its feeding is your responsibility, your work.

20   Give him milk and porridge and eggs
      If you have the means—because that's your work.

21   And liver and marrow and tomatoes
      And spinach; I'm explaining your work.

22   A child's drinking water, whenever you give it to him,
      Should be boiled then cooled—this is part of your work.

23   Every morning when you rise
      Sweep your house—it's part of your work.

24   The cloth the boy sleeps on should be
      Hung out to air—this is part of your work.

25   When you rise, if you mean to wash him,
      Use warm water—this is part of your work.

26   There is cleaning to do everywhere;
      Bring us your children because of our work.

27   In Sabon Gari, Maramara, and even in Dala,
      In Nasarawa they weigh their children—it's part of their work.

28   I want to warn the women of this town,
      Don't wander about, but attend to your work.

29   If you must go out
      Come back quickly and return to your work.

30   Consider what has happened recently
      Let it be a warning against neglecting your work.

31   Men by the roadside were summoned,
      Beaten, and driven away for ignoring their work.

32   You know those who do this are not very smart;
      Cheaters and thieves, refusing to work!

33   Avoid card-playing, draughts, and gambling,
      Cheating or stealing; cling to your work!

34   Avoid slyness and disdain for Muslims,
      Stop being untrustworthy; stick to your work.

35   For God's sake, for the Prophet and his Companions,
      Follow the times and do proper work.

36   A skill is something that everyone should have;
      Muhammad the Prophet had his own profession.

37   I ask whether there is one among you
      Who can say it's not good, one should quit one's profession.

38   Thanks be to God, I give thanks to God
      Who has given me insight to attend to professions.

39   It is finished in the name of God, here I shall stop
      Explaining to women about their professions.

40   If anyone asks who composed this song,
      For women to come to the library for professions,

41   Hauwa Gwaram I am, a Qur'anic student,
      Of Alhaji Ahmadu, who has a profession.

                Thanks be to God.

Poems of Condolence and Praise

SONG OF CONDOLENCE FOR TAFAWA BALEWA AND THE SARDAUNA OF SOKOTO
BY HAUWA GWARAM, 1963

1   Thanks be to God, we thank our Father,
May God relieve the chaos of Nigeria.

2   Oh brothers, I will tell you the truth,
If you'll listen carefully, here in Nigeria.

3   Oh brothers, I will compose a song of condolence,
If you will listen carefully, here in Nigeria.

4   The origin of this trouble
Was at the time of chaos in Nigeria.

5   It happened in the offices of emirs and judges
And of judges here in Nigeria.

6   It spread from Gwandu to Zaria,
It came to Kano, peace vanished.

7   By God, ever since the time of the revolt,
They plotted war throughout Nigeria.

8   They dug us a pit and we fell in headfirst,
They plotted war throughout Nigeria.

9   They dug us a pit and we fell in headfirst,
We betrayed ourselves, we gave up throughout Nigeria.

10   We lost both trap and bird,
How will we get a leader for Nigeria?

11   Let me beg God, praise Him the exalted One,
May He help them to find someone to lead Nigeria.

12   Three influential people have passed away from us,
They were the stairs to the well-being of Nigeria.

13   May God have mercy on the Sardauna, on Abubakar,
          And on Mamman Sanusi in Nigeria.

14   For they were believers, descendents of the Prophet, God's
          servants,
          Now they are gone and we have no peace in Nigeria.

15   Hassan and Lieutenant General Yakubu are the leaders,
          With them rests responsibility for all of Nigeria.

16   They took up their quivers, bows, pickaxes, and broadaxes,
          They got freedom to save Nigeria.

17   They made promises to the country of Nigeria,
          That they would lead the country of Nigeria.

18   They took up quivers, bows, pickaxes, and broadaxes,
          They found the way to pull out Nigeria.

19   If it were said that women should serve as soldiers,
          I too would help the leaders of Nigeria.

20   One must praise experts everywhere,
          May God have mercy on the Sardauna here in Nigeria.

21   Because he wanted us all to prosper in peace,
          Inside and out, beyond reckoning.

22   He wanted us all to be at peace
          And to follow our religion here in Nigeria.

23   Beginning with God on high, one can seize one's own,
          If you hurry, Nigeria can improve itself.

24   I shall not forget the day he went to Kacako,
          He united all of us, pagans and Muslims, all together.

25   Gwaram, Sumaila, and Dutse, including Birnin Kudu,
          He preached to us on the true traditions.

26   Now I will speak of his preaching to us,
          Let everyone open his ears and hear them all together.

27   He said we should strive to know our Father
          And obey His commands for Nigeria.

28   We should know the five daily prayer times
          And continue to observe them, we should stop rejecting
          Nigeria.

29 He said we should pay attention to the rights of our brothers
And to our teachers, to truly respect them.

30 He said that when the month of Ramadan begins,
That is the month of fasting, and we should observe it
properly.

31 The laws about marriage should be observed, not broken,
Let us protect [our] affairs, all of them beyond reckoning.

32 What is due our parents is theirs, you know,
Truly we must obey them and truly respect them.

33 He said what they need we should provide,
If we refuse, we shall suffer in Nigeria.

34 And disrespect toward our brothers, we must cease altogether,
Lying and egotism, let us truly leave them.

35 So sister, taking a bribe is forbidden,
Arrogance too is totally forbidden.

36 I turn now to speak of Tafawa Abubakar,
He was the key helper in Nigeria.

37 May God have mercy on him, Abubakar, man of truth,
He helped the people of Nigeria.

38 His stay in Lagos, his and the emir's,
Meant no discrimination against Nigerians.

39 He was a man who didn't like quarreling,
And he was not arrogant here in Nigeria.

40 By God, you know we suffered a terrible loss,
We can only be patient, that is certainly the truth.

41 Now I shall turn to speak of the commander in chief Yakubu,
He and Major Hassan are the lights of the world.

42 Everyone is praying for them,
May God help them to get freedom for the country of Nigeria.

43 I thank our soldiers, all of them,
[May they] drive out Ojukwu, that supreme bastard, from
the world.

44 They took promises to Makurdi and Enugu,
Repeatedly thus they [tried to] unify Nigeria.

45   Greetings to you, soldiers, men of valiant efforts,
      Seize him, bring him back to Nigeria.

46   Well, now I shall praise our leader here in Kano,
      The Emir of Kano, helper of the people of Nigeria.

47   Emir of Kano, Alhaji Ado Bayero,
      He is a tower of strength here in Nigeria.

48   He has no need for tricks, he is not deceptive,
      He does not know the gossipmongers of Nigeria.

49   He has the character of Abdullahi,
      He is not a party to evil in Nigeria.

50   If you would know the truth, sit down with him,
      If you are a hypocrite, then leave Nigeria.

51   He loves not the one who brings him gossip,
      He has no need to hear abuse from the people of Nigeria.

52   May God leave to us emir after emir,
      May God give each long reign in Nigeria.

53   Alhaji Abdu Bako is the governor of Kano,
      He has stretched out his arm to rescue Nigeria.

54   All teachers in the country of Nigeria
      Always pray for you without limit.

55   As for me, I praise you and beg,
      That I may get a place with you in Nigeria.

56   A place to make a home is what I ask,
      I will protect it from quarrels, Nigeria.

57   It is finished, with praise to God, here I shall stop,
      Hauwa Gwaram I am, if anyone wants to ask.

          Thanks be to God.

SONG OF PRAISE FOR THE GOVERNOR
OF KANO, ABDU BAKO
BY HAUWA GWARAM, 1966

1   In the name of God I intend to compose a song,
A song of welcome for Abdu Bako Dutse.

2   Alhaji Abdu Bako is the governor of Kano,
Everyone is glad you have come, Dutse.

3   Alhaji Malam Ja'e, chief of district heads,
Tijjani Danka, it was Sarkin Dutse.

4   Fifty-eight village heads you will hear,
I will arrange their names now in Dutse.

5   First among them is Limawa, he's the Sarkin Kaci,
Galamawa, Yalwa, they are under Sarkin Dutse.

6   Kannaye, 'Yargaba, and Wangara Jarimai,
Caicai, Isori, Taboba are there near Dutse.

7   Camo, Kyaran, and Dangwaje, then Abaya,
Darau, and Wurma, they are under Sarkin Dutse.

8   Well, I see Faisau and Gudduba, they've come,
Sabon Gari and the Mazazzaga people near Dutse.

9   We here are those from Ciroma and from Haddori Maje,
Add to those Tsirma, they are under Mai Kano Dutse.

10   Turko, Fuju, Dungu, Kwada, and Katika,
For Karfa people too, he makes his efforts near Dutse.

11   Well, see Tunannan, Kyawa, Andaza, and Fake,
Duhuwa, Katanga, and Madobi are here at Dutse.

12   Well, Kargo Kumi and Kwai Magari,
You and Kwadiya Malamawa at Dutse.

13   Runu and Jadi, add Jigawar Tsada, all,
Dantawuya, and Warwade in Dutse.

14   Jidawa, here's Biju, Kaca, Dundubus,
Duru, Garko, and Abalagu at Dutse.

15   Here are the places beyond the town where he's making
efforts,
To help the district heads near Dutse.

16 Of twenty district heads and six more,
    He is number one among you, Sarkin Dutse.

17 I shall end here, forgive me, people,
    I've finished the song for our district head of Dutse.

18 Alhaji Abdu Bako is the governor of Kano,
    We are glad he has come to visit Dutse.

19 It is finished with praise to God, here is the place for me to
        stop,
    Hauwa Gwaram has added to this song for Dutse.

        Thanks be to God.

SONG FOR ALHAJI SIR AHMADU BELLO, SARDAUNA OF SOKOTO

BY HAJIYA 'YAR SHEHU, 1960

1   May God help our president and the premier
To prevail over enemies, all of them.

2   Oh Lord God, I beg of you, Lord of Truth,
You are generous and merciful, you alone are capable.

3   Oh Lord God in respect of the Prophet, who is an example,
His family, friends, and the saints.

4   Help me to speak the truth,
For the sake of Muhammad, the Messenger, and the prophets.

5   Well, I'll compose a song on our president and on the premier,
The Sardauna, descendent of Shehu, pillar of the north.

6   Oh Lord help our leader, the premier,
Descendent of Fatima Zahara, for the sake of the prophets.

7   God, You created the premier,
You intended him to protect the north.

8   You inherited from your ancestor, Shehu, Premier,
He too, Usumanu, protected the north.

9   And northerners, let us help the premier,
The Sardauna, descendent of Shehu, God is supreme.

10   People of the north, by God, let us give thanks
To our Father, the Lord, the King of Truth.

11   When he gave us Ahmadu, our president and our premier,
Northerners no longer were in trouble.

12   Those who were expecting the north to sink,
Were causing commotion everywhere in the north.

13   Because they do not love northerners,
They were looking for ways to destroy the north.

14   Only our president, the premier of Nigeria,
Persevered night and day.

15   It was he who put on armor and chain mail and stood firm
With shield and spear to defend the north.

16   It was he who took up the sword of Shehu, hero of yesteryear,
      The great-grandson of Mohammadu Atiku, the premier.

17   He is our Bawa Jangwarzo, our Shehu, the premier,
      He is our Kaura Hasau, our father, the premier.

18   He is 'Dan Waire, our Sir Ahmadu, the premier,
      The descendent of Mohammadu Bello, God is one.

19   And I will persist in cataloguing the qualities of the premier,
      Praying to God to increase his health.

20   Oh God, I beg you at dusk and dawn,
      To lengthen his life, our leader, the premier.

21   May God protect the leader of the north,
      May God guard him from Nigeria's evil men.

22   He is both mother and father of the north in one,
      All northerners rely on him, the premier.

23   He endured abuse and envy and stood firm,
      He showed that God made you all together.

24   Only the ignorant and shameless evil ones in the world,
      Envy you, premier.

25   We true northerners in truth
      By God will never reject our father, the premier.

26   Lost donkeys don't ask the way,
      They are the ones who find fault with you, Shehu the Premier.

27   Oh God, leave us our president, the premier,
      Sir Ahmadu, Sardauna, the world's greatest.

28   See his majestic presence and his good humor,
      Oh God, leave us our president, and the premier.

29   He is Shehu the reformer of Nigeria,
      All Muslims in the world praise him.

30   It is you who are the important helper for the world
      Of Islam, there's no doubt you are capable.

31   East and west, south, you know, like the north,
      It is you who are the guide, Shehu Premier.

32   He made the circuit, he surveyed the world,
      That the north may get its share in the world.

33   All true northerners in truth,
      Know that he traveled for the sake of the north.

34   He didn't sit still, much less let the north be oppressed,
      Because he does not want the north to suffer.

35   He went to Makka and Madinah, both,
      Always traveling to protect the north.

36   He went to London, America, and Arabia,
      He went to Pakistan, France, and India.

37   He went to Kuwait, to Australia, I heard,
      Even to Egypt and to Jerusalem, to all these places he went.

38   To Dar es Salaam and to Rome, you know, in all these places
         he stopped,
      He went to Moscow, father of the north, the premier.

39   To Baghdad and Iraq, you know, he went round,
      To Germany and Russia, our father, the premier.

40   I cannot list all [the places] in the world [he visited],
      Because they are too many for me to name.

41   Bull elephant, patient father, father of Nigeria,
      You are serving us for the sake of the north.

42   But some seek to get the north in trouble,
      They are plotting to cheat the north.

43   They say their intention is to go to get something for soup,
      [But] from southerners, northerners get only trouble.

44   Let's consider our father, the premier of the north,
      We are sure he'll not leave us in trouble.

45   Our Alhaji, the premier of Nigeria,
      The great-grandson of Muhammadu Bello, he pondered,

46   He remembered his ancestor Shehu, hero of yesteryear,
      Usuman he, too was our father of Nigeria.

47   He ended cheating in the north altogether,
      And canceled out evil completely.

48   Oh Lord, I beg you, king of truth,
      To help our Alhaji, the premier.

49   Oh Lord, I beg you at dusk and dawn,
      To protect him from all evil, the premier.

50   God, it is you who created the premier,
Spare him misfortune in this world.

51   On the day of judgment you are capable,
Be kind to Ahmadu, for the sake of the prophets and saints.

52   Oh Lord, put him in the place where there is no trouble,
In paradise, where there is no trouble.

53   God, show him the prophet and prophets,
And Shehu Usman, Bello, and the saints.

54   Oh Lord, you clothed all his descendents,
And even his parents, all of them.

55   May God help all Muslims in the world,
Protect us from all misfortune.

56   Mother and father, I count them as one,
May God protect all theirs from misfortune.

57   It is finished, with praise to God, the song is done,
May God give us Shehu, leader of the Tijjaniya.

58   Beyond this explanation, let me tell you, Hajiya,
'Yar Shehu it was who composed this remembrance.

59   Of the ethnic groups, let me say she's a Fulani woman
From Dambatta, our town, without a doubt.

Thanks be to God.

SONG OF CONDOLENCE FOR
MURTALA MUHAMMAD
BY HAUWA GWARAM, 1976

1   Oh God, forgive secret sins,
    I extend my condolences for one who loves you.

2   We knew your servant Murtala Muhammad,
    It is You who take away all your servants.

3   Wisdom and courage flow from your love,
    And no one has power over water or air [but You].

4   By God, every upright person who is alert,
    Knows that no one who is a hypocrite loves You.

5   On the thirteenth of February,
    Mamman Murtala your servant was assassinated.

6   In seventy-six, on a Friday morning,
    We arose to find we'd lost Murtala, who loves You.

7   On this day a pitiful thing happened in the world,
    Everyone you see ceased activity.

8   Everyone loved Murtala Muhammad
    For his good character, within and without.

9   Oh God, watch over his wives and children,
    Protect them from evil, everyone who is your servant.

10 Jealous betrayers and shameless ones,
    Will not be found when people have grown [more] like You.

11 God have mercy and forgive him,
    For the sake of all the saints, this officer, one of your followers.

12 Muslims and Christians, all of you,
    Let us endure patiently this bereavement.

13 As for the remaining Muslims that have been gathered—
    Have mercy on them in your greatness and glory.

14 God have mercy on Ibrahim Taiwo first,
    He died in the faith—cloak him in holiness.

15 Oh God, as for all his brothers—
    Save them from evil, give them success.

16   I greet you, oh Emir of Kano,
And the emir's mother and the governor and his wife.

17   I greet the district heads and the village heads,
Including the teachers and all your workers.

18   People, we are mourning our loss of Murtala,
We first knew of water pumps during your government

19   Well, you see the tax during the Murtala government,
Father and son, was reduced for you.

20   To four naira and fifty kobo,
If you paid more, you were showing your ignorance.

21   The Fulani were relieved of their cattle tax,
And they too mourn your loss.

22   All the work you did, were I to investigate it all,
Every one of us would long for you.

23   May God forgive me all my sins,
Hauwa Gwaram I am, I have sung praise for you.

Thanks be to God.

SONG IN PRAISE OF THE SOLDIERS
BY HAJIYA 'YAR SHEHU, 1967

"This song, Binta, I composed it in 1967, at the time of the war, when someone not from the government of Nigeria let it be known that Ojukwu was no longer in Nigeria. We did this song as news, and President Yakubu Gowan was looking for singers, but on the topic of the soldiers. So that's how it was that I came to sit down and compose praise for the soldiers."

1   Let us begin in the name of God, our Lord God of all,
    You are our generous, merciful one, all powerful.

2   Whatever one wants done in the world,
    In the name of God is one's best way of planning altogether.

3   Well, I will sing of the soldiers, people of Nigeria,
    God grant me the wisdom and perception to do so.

4   Before I come to the soldiers of Nigeria,
    Well, I will touch on some others here in Nigeria.

5   They are the southerners, the gluttonous ones of the world,
    It is said their intention is to rule us altogether.

6   From the beginning, the west and all of the north,
    It was our money that was used to help them all together.

7   For all their time they still have no town
    Or clothes or food in their land, they had nothing.

8   As for us, see our groundnuts and cotton and cattle
    Clothing and food in our land, without question.

9   In the same way the western region had no conflict,
    They had cocoa and kola nuts, they lived in peace.

10 We ate with them and drank with them, they give no
        thanks,
    And we built their districts for them altogether.

11 Until they began boasting and showing off,
    Saying they were responsible for the wealth of Nigeria.

12 Our wealth was all gathered together for them
    And they exploited the petrol, they ridiculed us.

13 It is said they intended to subvert all of Nigeria,
    And they would collect all its wealth and put it all together.

14   Then at once they began to plot
      They began to undo the order in Nigeria.

15   On the twenty-fifth of Ramadan,
      The fifteenth of January, without question.

16   In the year of the Prophet nineteen hundred and sixty,
      And six, on the twentieth, in the cold of the morning,

17   They killed all our leaders, no one was left.
      They seized power and control of the whole country.

18   They said to us they would unite Nigeria
      And there would be no federation or states, not one.

19   They made us their servants, lacking a leader
      But always with a lot of trouble, enmity, and argument.

20   And even including their photo, to look for trouble,
      Of Chukuma Nzeogwu, they kept showing us.

21   One day, God seized Nigeria,
      Because what God has ordained no one can question.

22   At once he took our Nigeria, all together,
      He put Nigeria in just hands with honesty.

23   He was Commander Major Yakubu, you hear,
      A careful man with insight about the world.

24   Major-General Commander Major Yakubu can manage
      To run the government that will be Nigeria.

25   He summoned the leaders of the states of Nigeria
      They are the governors of our country, all together.

26   For the sake of sharing, reconciliation, and well-being,
      Because he does not want Nigeria to disintegrate.

27   Then a useless fellow, wicked one of the world
      The worthless fool, useless, foul-mouthed one

28   He was General Ojukwu, worthless one of the world
      May God make Nigerian soldiers deal with him.

29   He refused to respond, created chaos
      They say he has no love for Nigeria.

30   And that he rose up to provoke; that is, he quarreled
      And seized all the government supplies.

31   People tried to coax him, the bastard, the fighter,
      To settle down peacefully without arguing.

32   But he just jumped in with his boastfulness, making trouble.
      One day, suddenly he reaped his reward.

33   Until he was skipping over, impoverishing himself.
      His madness they say made him leave Nigeria.

34   They say he had no desire to be part of Nigeria
      That for him Biafra was his only country altogether.

35   He forgot about promises to help the condition of Nigeria
      To keep it a nation and a federation.

36   Our leader Gowon was a real man
      Who prefers peace over fighting.

37   He was patient, like a lizard, not boastful,
      Supreme commander, with worldly wisdom.

38   He summoned all brave men of Nigeria,
      They were soldiers, men who did not dodge their duty,

39   In order to catch Ojukwu, the worthless one in the world,
      Who betrays trust, the leader of the outcasts.

40   May God forgive all the sins of the world,
      And be generous in granting paradise to all who die.

41   When I recall the many men of Nigeria,
      Even as my eyes fill with tears.

42   May God forgive Maimalari, the men of yesterday
      And then Kuru Mamman, man of strong wishes.

43   And even Ademologu, all, no one is left,
      As well as Pam, they have killed them all.

44   Well, we were lucky, they have left us one outstanding person,
      Mamman Shuwa, by God, he was beyond question.

45   As for you, you are the rock, the person pounding you was
            in trouble,
      If one cooks, one will not drink soup.

46   No one will eat your shrew-mouse jerky, not one strip,
      Nor even buy it, because it stinks.

47   You are an old stone, you nag to cause trouble,
      Energetic Gowon is a pillar of Nigeria.

48   Who was Ojukwu to pull you around? One kick, he was gone,
      Even Congo, you are the one who led Nigeria.

49 Mamman Shuwa, here is the leader of Nigeria,
   He gave you all our Nigeria altogether.

50 He entrusted all the soldiers of Nigeria to you,
   You secured the trust, don't ever agree to injustices.

51 For here is a sign, see Benin, you hear,
   They agreed to promises, they followed their hearts.

52 And they were ashamed, for in both paradise and the world,
   There was no one among them who would have victory,
    much less laughter.

53 May God protect the soldiers of Nigeria,
   They are men of dignity, not concerned with wealth.

54 Who was Ojukwu? An unfortunate tribalist,
   The protector before you of Nigeria's soldiers.

55 The day you met with the Nigerian soldiers,
   By God, that was the day you told them the truth.

56 You started a war to defeat all of Nigeria,
   The lying dog-hyena, quarreling.

57 You remember our soldiers of Nigeria
   Who fought the war in the water and the sky.

58 Attacked in the water, dense thickets, and dark shadows,
   On the high ground of rocks and hills

59 See, there are weapons here in abundance in Nigeria
   See the young men, the diligent ones in the world.

60 Here are tanks and artillery guns all together
   Here are submarines and a bomb that could finish the world.

61 The submarine goes inside water as a heavy load
   If a vehicle climbs on it, it just sinks down.

62 The bomb is sent up into the sky
   To be dropped on the enemies of Nigeria.

63 Greetings to you, our soldiers, Nigerians,
   You always are diligent in defense of Nigeria.

64 May God help you, soldiers of Nigeria,
   Put them on top of the enemies of the country

65 By God, Ojukwu, bastard quarreler,
   You have devastated our well-being here in Nigeria.

66   You freedom fighters, get up all together
      To catch Ojukwu, worthless one in the world.

67   Even the important countries of the world
      Know of the diligent soldiers of Nigeria.

68   They went to Germany, France, you may inquire,
      They went to Burma and even to India

69   As well as in our place here in Nigeria,
      One they call Ojukwu he provoked you with argument.

70   May God help the soldiers of Nigeria.
      They fulfill their promises altogether.

71   And our leader in Nigeria all together,
      May God help him to govern us and keep us well.

72   Thus, Hassan Usuman, pillar of the north
      See lieutenant-colonel of the men of the world.

73   You have authority over all the north,
      Even the state governors, all of them.

74   You are the deputy in charge of advice for Nigeria,
      Patriots of a nation do not involve the selves in scandalous
         activities.

75   And there in the western state is Brigadier
      Adebayao, he beat the mouth of scandalous people.

76   May God protect our Nigerians, all together,
      And even the governors, all of them.

77   This is the end, thanks be to God, here I will stop,
      May God help all Nigerians.

78   For this explanation, let me tell you, Hajiya
      By the nickname 'Yar Shehu it is, who was the questioner.

            Thanks be to God.

PRAISE SONG FOR ALHAJI ADO BAYERO, EMIR OF KANO

BY HAJIYA MAIZARGADI, 1980

1   Thanks be to God, Oh Lord God,
    Our support, God be praised, the master of Makka and
      Medina,
    Master of the city of Kano, master of Zaria,
    Servant, whatever you need, ask it of God, our support, who
      fulfills our desires,
5   Who, if He gives to you today, will also give to you tomor
      row, glory to God without end.
    Thanks be to God, Lord God, our support,
    The Predestinator, the Consentor, the Omniscient, the
      Life-Giver, our support.
    Glory to God, master of Makka and Medina,
    Master of the city of Kano, master of Zaria,
10 Sleep well, defender of the faithful
    Emir of Kano, Alhaji Ado Bayero, sleep well, son of Abdu.
    The shadow of Dabo blocks the sun,
    Alhaji who is here, who is well,
    From today until the end of the world, thanks be to God for
      the generosity He has shown.
15 Bull Elephant, descendent of Dabo,
    Our righteous one, who is here well,
    Greetings to the master of thousands, master of Abdu's horse,
      Bull Elephant, descendent of Dabo,
    Our righteous one, who is here well,
    If you invoke God, the generous one, there is no desire He
      will not fulfill for you, both today and tomorrow,
20 Glory to God, He will hear you and provide for you
    In the good fortune of the Bull Elephant,
    Head of the town, Dabo, I sing for Malama Binta,
    Guest of the people of Niger,
    Guest of the city of Kano, guest of Zaria, may God protect
      you in your travels,
25 May you go and return safely,
    If you go on a plane, good wishes at both ends of your trip,
    When you go, go well,
    There is life and separation, Malama Binta,
    There is life and separation, one sleeps and arises, one day he
      will be finished,

30   May God give us long life,

If you go home, greet your mother and father for us, if they
    are there,

I say you have our affection, Binta, I give thanks, I am
    grateful, I am grateful for the goodness of the Emir of Kano,

The goodness of Fulani Abba,

The son of the Emir of Katsina, grandson of Dikko, friend of
    the colonials, and even the soldiers,

35   May God give us rest,

May God have mercy on Fulani Umma,

God have mercy on the Emir of Katsina, of the house of dates,

May God grant us rest,

I say may God help the current Emir of Katsina,

40   Alhaji Usman Shehu Nagogo.

I say the grandparent of Bashir and Binta paid me, and it
    wasn't a loan,

May God have mercy on Lilla and excuse her,

May God give us rest,

Father of Hassan and Hussein, if he is at home, I thank him
    properly.

45   I give thanks, I increase the blessings on the Emir of Kano,
    Alhaji Ado,

Everywhere I go, it is with his goodness, son of Abdu,
    slandering Dodo

I give thanks for his wealth, the [giver of] ladies' shirts,

I give thanks Balaraba Tukuba, I give thanks, I thank you,

Balaraba Fulani Saude,

50   Daughter of the Sardauna,

Daughter of the slayer of men, grandchild of the slayer of men,

May God give him long life with her in the house, that's fine,

Fulani Saude, the day that we went to bring her back,

The day that we went to Sokoto,

55   [We took] a hundred and two horses,

I say, neither motorcycles nor cars,

I say this, no one got up when we went to get Saude

We went and returned safely,

I am in a car, I say, see the daughter of the slayer of men,

60   Granddaughter of the slayer of men

[We] will bring her to the home of the Emir of Kano, Alhaji
    Ado Bayero, the remedy of the government,

Grandson of Alu Mai Sango,

He too in the time of his grandfather had many horses,

His grandfather pierced him with a spear,

65   May God forgive him,
       Son of Maje Nasarawa, grandson of Maje Nasarawa,
       Greetings to the grandson of Alu Mai Sango,
       From today until the end of the world, thanks be to God,
          Bull Elephant,
       He inherited the house of Famda,
70   He inherited the house of Takai,
       He inherited the house in Dorayi, in Gogel,
       Emir, head of the city of Kano,
       Since you inherited your very own house you will have a
          good end, father,
       The quick one gives houses and horses,
75   May God give him lots of rest,
       I thank the father of Hadiza, I give thanks to the father of
          Ade-Ade.
       I thank him, I increase my thanks,
       Father of Salamatu, father of Usumanu Ahman,
       You paid me and it wasn't a loan,
80   I thank him, I increase my thanks, Bull Elephant, descendent
          of Dabo,
       Our excellent father,
       You gave me a gift and it was not a loan,
       May God help the head wife of Kano, the mother of the town,
       May God bless Rakiya the tall one, the head wife of Kano,
85   Greetings to the supporter of Fulani Dudu, Bull Elephant,
          descendent of Dabo,
       May God make your life end happily,
       And give me permission to return to Ningi,
       I went to see the grandfather of my children,
       Grandson of Usuman Shehu, the emir of the town of Ningi,
90   Good wishes to Alhaji Malam Inusa,
       The emir of the town of Ningi, head of Bura and Warji,
       If he is in the home of Jallabai,
       Here is the son of Muhammadu, and Muhammadu, to
          whom I give thanks, I thank them,
       Greetings to the rug-spreader who piles and pushes,
95   He paid me and it wasn't a loan,
       May God have mercy on Adamu Maje of Birnin Kudu,
       May God have mercy on the Ciroma of Ningi, Mohammadu,
          and forgive him,
       May God have mercy on the rug-spreader,
       May God have mercy on the protector and forgive him,
100   May God give us rest,

I thank him for Hauwa,
I give him thanks, I thank him, I thank him for Maimuna,
    he paid me,
He paid me and it wasn't a loan,
Grandchild of Maimuna, grandchild of Hauwa, son of
    Hauwa,
105   Protector of Rakiya, he paid me a lot and it wasn't a loan,
Thanks be to his daughter, who paid me, it wasn't a loan,
If he is in the Jallabai house,
The husband of the daughter of the Emir of Kano, Fulani of
    the palace,
The husband of Hajiya Hauwa, she is not Maimuna, tall
    husband of Amina,
110   He paid me and it wasn't a loan,
I thank the one who gave me a robe,
I give thanks, I thank the emir, the protector of the people of
    Ningi,
I give thanks to the grandson of Yahaya,
If he is at home, I am giving thanks, I add to my thanks, I
    thank him,
115   Emir of the people of Ningi,
God have mercy on the Ciroma of Ningi, Mohamman, son
    of Rabi, he paid me,
Protector of the daughter of Kano, he paid me, protector, I
    thank him,
I am giving thanks [to the] children of Mohammadu and to
    Mohammadu I give thanks,
Protector Yusufu, descendent of Dabo, he paid me,
120   Protector Nuhu, I give thanks to him,
To go around with Karim I got up,
I will return with drums and my own bag [of money]
When I go, take a vacation and rest until I return, I'll go and
    return safely.
I give thanks, emir who knows the people of Ningi,
125   If I get up to return to Sabon Gari,
I will go to the place of the king of the night,
Everyone says the rock is heavy
Truly the small one who carries a big load is stronger than a
    construction worker,
For all the riches I have, I give thanks,
130   If I return to read, to see Ibrayo and the stable boy, son of
    Galadima who was removed,

131–152 [unclear on tape]
153 I give thanks Malama Binta, you paid me and it wasn't a loan,
      May God guide you safely and return you safely,
155 Go and return safely,
      Thanks be to God, she has given a gift from God,
      Beloved friend,
      Beloved Habibi, you paid me,
      You will give me what I long for,
160 May God make things go well for you,
      Thanks be to God, she gave me a gift from God,
      Guest of those of the head wife's compound, I give thanks to
        Binta,
      Head of the head wife's compound, she is glad you went to
        see her, she is happy,
164 Good friend of the praise singer Maizargadi.

PRAISE SONG FOR THE EMIR OF KANO
AND THE EMIR OF NINGI
BY HAUWA MAI DUALA, 1979

1   Well, God, who divides falsehood from truth, the true king,
           master of today and tomorrow,
       I am the servant of Inusa, leader of the Ningi people,
       Of Garba, the emir, the relative of Alhajiya Hauwa,
       Beloved friend,
5   Beloved spirit of the world; he who despises smallness,
       Has never stepped on a scorpion. You heirs, hear me,
       Crack the shell if you would know the color of the nut,
       Man of the deceased,
       Your woman, your kinswoman Hauwa Dutse, you didn't
           abandon her,
10   Malam Inusa, present master of the Ningi folk,
       Stop and let me begin, hail to the important one,
       Mother of the emir, mother of all the town,
       Mother of the emir, mother of all the town,
       Alhajiya, mother, she showed me the way to do things
15   The giver of robes,
       The giver of robes,
       Excuse me! The remedy for "I'm not giving you oil" is "Give
           me a mortar that I may pound baobab leaves."
       Alhajiya, mother, she showed me the way to do things,
       Excellent one of Kano,
20   Thanks be to God, Fulani Dudu,
       Fulani Dudu,
       Fulani showed me the way to do things,
       God, the divider of falsehood from truth,
       The true king, the master of today and tomorrow,
25   The king, controller of men's movements,
       The king of men's inheritance,
       Adamu Ado Bayero, Ado, descendent of Muhammadu,
       Leader of the army of Kano, who acts without delay,
       Emir Ahman has come,
30   Who infuriates his enemies,
       Go brothers and fight for the sake of God—you must endure,
       It is Audu who has inherited his house today,
       Wax that resembles honey—when you see it, you have no
           doubt,
       Greetings to Adamu of Ningi,

35 The current Emir of Kano, the current Emir of Kano,
Descendent of Umma Kulthum,
Descendent of Maliya,
Thanks be to God, I saw the emir, the leader of the people
  of Katsina,
I saw the emir, the leader of the people of Katsina,
40 Descendent of the house of Dikko, friend of the colonials,
Emir of Kano, you showed us how to go about things,
Spear-throwing that mocks brave men,
Spear-throwing that mocks brave men,
The new baby girl in Kano, 'Yar Mamman,
45 The new baby girl in Kano, 'Yar Mamman,
Hey, in a small boat it was he who brought me
Umma, who has house servants,
Descendent of the commander of the faithful,
Today, not tomorrow, you play for him,
50 Adamu, friend of the colonials,
The water is yours, the fish are yours,
The people of Wudil are yours
Cloth that imposes its will,
The sleeping mat of your head gunman is the hunt,
55 Because he is no stay-at-home,
One of Damburam Abubakar,
One of Damburam Abubakar of the drum,
One of Barde, Kano leader,
Beloved friend of the spirits of the world,
60 One of Fulani Dudu,
He showed us how to go about things,
Son of the Fulani, Umma, sweet juice of the palm-nut,
  fair-skinned one,
Emir of Kano, from today,
You see the guard,
65 May God ease their pain,
Greetings to you, Emir of Ningi, under whom it is pleasant
  to live,
Where have you left it for me, daughter of the commander
  of the faithful?
Where have you left it for me, daughter of the Emir of
  Katsina?
I saw you, I was glad,
70 Thanks be to God, the body is now strong,
And you, the current Emir of Kano,

On your behalf I spoke of your complaints to your father,
    you hear.
I saw you, I was happy,
You gave me ten robes, ten from you,
75   Mighty Aminu, mighty Aminu.
Our mighty Aminu,
You can go as far as Jidda,
God have mercy on the son of your house,
May God give you peace in death,
80   Mighty Usumanu,
Ahman travels the world over, there has been much trouble
    in the world, and it has not been a nice place,
God the important one,
May God forgive him, I beg,
Umma of the white compound,
85   'Dan Galadima of Kano, someone prevent her from fighting
    with 'Yar Mamma,
King, warrior of the room,
Binta. Friend of the daughter of the commander of the
    faithful,
Here, you are becoming a daughter of the Emir of Kano,
In the city, this daughter lives,
90   Nine women will give you a gift,
One made it rain in the town,
One made you festival clothes,
Three supervise you here,
One must give you pleasantness,
95   Good friend of Fulani,
Good friend of Fulani Abba,
Of Binta I cry out,
Daughter of the Mai Gari of Katsina,
Usumanu,
100   Nagogo,
[For] Usumanu Nagogo Abba she did drumming, give me
    now,
Well, it is necessary wherever you look, to take care,
God have mercy on Dikko, friend of the colonials,
God have mercy on Dikko, friend of the colonials,
105   Beloved friend, beloved Habibi,
God have mercy on Fulani and forgive her,
God grant us an easy death,
God ease her life,

Death, master of dividing us, listen, don't you see the sadness
    involved in dying, Divider?
110   Not because of the business of dying,
Who is the One above all others?
Stop and do everything right,
The time has changed,
I thank Alhajiya Juji,
115   Because she saw . . . she brought Baturiya, because of
    Maizargadi Juji,
I saw Baturiya with my own eyes,
Malama Binta,
Malama Binta,
Everyone knows you,
120   He followed the children and escaped. I saw you, I reduced
    my calabash drumming,
May God stop . . . so that you can perform properly. . . .
    When it is time for work, Binta,
Binta she is worrying, with those questions,
You are the owner of bed, mattress, and blanket,
Owner of a pillow,
125   Ayya, women, all children of women,
At the palace by day, at the palace by night,
Binta did drumming at the palace,
Maizargadi, I agree with you,
Here is a friend of God,
130   At the palace by day and night,
Keep Binta safe for me,
I share friendship with you,
Keep Binta well for me,
I share friendship with you,
135   Because of Maizargadi Juji,
I see the palace with my own eyes, friend of the daughter of
    Dikko, friend of the colonials,
Nagogo . . . Juji return ready to sing,
Today the dirt of the latrine,
Oh God, I told him to attend to the begging,
140   At the palace by day, at the palace by night,
Greetings . . . Baturiya. Important one,
I am Mother Hauwa, because I told you they are nice,
But in Bauchi they [have] mothers, in Ningi,
In Ningi they have mothers, I am a daughter of Kabila, I
    have returned,

145   I have worked at it . . . the praise singer of Emir Garba Tafawa,
Master of the airplanes and of the trains,
Yakubu, son of Yakubu, I greet you, Garba Tafawa,
Traveling around the world, seeing the world,
Your council is the world . . .

150   Usumanu Shagari,
Today he has given the government authority, he knows his
      limits,
You see the expert does not play,
. . . mistress of the upper level,
Mai Gari of Kano,

155   Important One, eat with orphans, drink with orphans,
Emir of Kano of earlier times, of the current,
Ado, be patient with us, as one should be,
Because of Maizargadi,
Both day and night I see Binta in the palace.

160   I am Hauwa, praise singer for Inusa, head of the Ningi folk,
      and for Fulani Hauwa,
Because he created all things,
God, who divides falsehood from truth, the true king, the
      master of today and tomorrow,
Alhajiya Juji show me the way to the palace in the day, to the
      palace in the night,
Let me go and stay until Tuesday,

165   So that I may see you, and feel fine,
If I see that you refuse to be poor . . .

Poems as Historical Chronicles

SONG FOR KANO STATE
BY HAUWA GWARAM

1   In the name of God, I begin a song,
     I will praise the government of Kano.

2   Because the government of Kano has made an explanation,
     We are expressing glad tidings for the city of Kano.

3   You know for many years,
     People have wanted a state of Kano.

4   Alhaji Ado, Emir of Kano,
     We thank you for getting us Kano.

5   You know for many years,
     People were hoping to establish a state of Kano.

6   Alhaji Ado, Emir of Kano,
     We thank you for getting us Kano.

7   You've received the blessed virtue of your ancestor,
     Sulaiman Dabo, of the city of Kano,

8   The Madaki of Kano and the Waziri of Kano,
     Representatives, we are grateful to you for Kano.

9   Magajin Gari, may peace be with you,
     I am happy with you for the state of Kano.

10   Let's go to the offices of the various teachers,
     And congratulate them for establishing Kano.

11   And to Alhaji Abdu Bako, the governor of Kano,
     We congratulate you on Kano.

12   And I shall greet your ten commissioners,
     Only when I've returned to this account of Kano.

13   Where is Mai Tamasule? I come to you,
          I congratulate you on Kano.

14   And Inuwar Dutse, I congratulate you,
          May God bless you in the city of Kano.

15   Where is Baba Ɗan Baffa? I come to you,
          On the occasion of the establishment of a state here, around
            the city of Kano.

16   And Muhtar and Sarkin Bai, I come to you,
          May God help the city of Kano.

17   Where is Sani Gezawa? I congratulate you,
          May God help the city of Kano.

18   And for Inuwa Dutse, I congratulate you,
          May God bless you in the city of Kano,

19   Magajin Gari of Kazaure, Madaki of Hadeja,
          I congratulate you on establishing Kano.

20   First I will explain Kano:
          There is a place where one can repair cars in the city of Kano.

21   We have print shops and places to print papers
          In Arabic and Roman script in the city of Kano.

22   There are schools, small and large,
          There's a library in the city of Kano.

23   There are factories and information,
          There are Shari'a courts in Kano.

24   There are hospitals, small and large,
          We have groundnut pyramids in Kano.

25   We have cloth-weavers and blanket-weavers,
          We have Singer sewing shops in the city of Kano.

26   We have blacksmith shops for bowls and plates,
          We have a Necco manufacturer in the city of Kano.

27   We have Parkinson and Coca Cola,
          And powder and oil and perfume in Kano.

28   We have a Chacalas factory and one for plastic,
          We have a place for groundnut oil in Kano.

29   There are markets unlimited,
          There are veterinaries in the city of Kano.

30 There are Kingsway, Challaram's, even Chacas,
    There's a Bata Shoe Store here in the city of Kano.

31 And engineers and contractors,
    Contract workers in the city of Kano.

32 We have hawkers on every road,
    We have banks in the city of Kano.

33 There's television and cinema, you understand,
    There are places to visit in the city of Kano.

34 We have farmers and iron forgers,
    There are hunters in the city of Kano.

35 We have dyers and shoemakers,
    And tailors in the city of Kano.

36 There are bricklayers and laborers,
    There are those who wash and iron in Kano.

37 We have leadership, we have readership,
    We have occupations in the city of Kano.

38 You know, whoever comes here, we have one to surpass you
    In wisdom and power in the city of Kano.

39 We have a powerhouse in Fanshekara,
    For lights and drinking water in the city of Kano.

40 We have butchers, and a place to butcher meat,
    And engines for cooking it in the city of Kano.

41 We have an airport, there is a railway,
    We have stations for public cars in Kano.

42 And hoes pulled by cows, cows for work,
    There are workers in the city of Kano.

43 Anyone who wishes can find an occupation,
    We'll have a place for it in the city of Kano.

44 We have courtesy, we have good relations,
    Friendship and mutual respect in the city of Kano.

45 Kano judges, including our district heads,
    And village chiefs and ward heads in Kano.

46 All over Nigeria they have status,
    But nowhere like ours in the city of Kano.

47   Let's begin with Gwandu, they have noble generosity there,
       But not like we have here in Kano.

48   Katsina and Bauchi and Zazzau, you know,
       They have groundnuts, but not like here in Kano.

49   [If] we go to Adamawa, Nufe, as far as Katagum,
       You know there's none like us in the city of Kano.

50   People of Gombe and Daura, you know,
       They've occupations, too, but not like in the city of Kano.

51   People of Kwantagora, they have expertise,
       But it's nothing like here in Kano.

52   [In] Ilorin, Igala, Ibira, Okene,
       They have money, but not like in Kano.

53   Abuja, tin for Birom, consider them,
       But their industries are not like those of Kano.

54   Benue, Jukun, in Wukari—they have fish,
       There's nothing to compare with here in Kano.

55   Whatever you have in your areas,
       We have a thousandfold in the city of Kano.

56   Women and men, listen to this statement,
       A statement of praise for the government of Kano.

57   You know for many years, for a long time,
       We were hoping to establish a state of Kano.

58   I thank God, who gave me this insight,
       To compose this song on the city of Kano.

59   Thanks be to God, I've finished the song,
       Of explanation of the city of Kano.

60   If you ask who wrote this song,
       Hauwa Gwaram it is, in the city of Kano.

61   It is finished, with praise to God, here I shall leave it,
       The song of praise for the government of Kano.

                    Thanks be to God.

SONG FOR THE FULANI EMIRS
FROM ƊAN AMU, REVISED BY HAUWA GWARAM, WITH HAJIYA TA SIDI

"I, Hauwa Gwaram, composed this poem on the Fulani Emirs. But
Alhaji Ɗan Amu, the Imam of Kano, first composed it in Arabic. I
went to the home of Sidiya, wife of Kano Emir Alhaji Inuwa, and we
read it together, then I did some research on it until we came up with
this version. She said she had got it from the 'Uwar Soro's quarters in
the palace, in the apartment called Farin Gida. That's how it happened that she had it, and I asked her to give it to me. I went to
Alhaji Ɗan Amu's place and asked for permission to revise it. And
then I wrote it in the Roman script and was able to do this because I
had gone to school. As for the parts concerning the Kano Emirs Sanusi,
Inuwa, and Ado, I wrote about their times. Their reigns were not
included in the original because the song was written earlier, during
Emir Abdullahi's time." [Revised circa 1976, recorded August 12,
1979.]

1   I thank God, I intend to compose an ode,
      A composition on the emirs of the city of Kano.

2   I shall compose the names of the Fulani emirs,
      So that everyone may hear them one by one in Kano.

3   Sulaiman was the first of our emirs,
      After him, Alwali brought progress to Kano.

4   In that time, Shehu had power,
      May God forgive the Emir of Kano.

5   In that time, Shehu had power,
      Sulaiman became the Emir of Kano.

6   Know that for thirteen years he ruled,
      He was the king of the city of Kano.

7   After him, then Dabo, son of Muhammadu,
      Brave warrior, he gave life to the government of Kano.

8   For wisdom and work there was [no one like] Dabo,
      [A man] of God, the most high, in the city of Kano.

9   You know, for twenty-six years he ruled,
      He was the king of the city of Kano.

10   After him, Usman took over,
      God gave him the rule of Kano.

11   He was of good character, he was good,
        He was always thinking of the city of Kano.

12   He was of good character, he was good,
        He was merciful to the people of Kano.

13   He ruled for nine years, and a few months,
        He, Usman, in the city of Kano.

14   After him came Abdu Maje Karofi,
        Brave warrior, saint, in the city of Kano.

15   He knew the laws, he established them,
        Good ones and wise, in the city of Kano.

16   You know, for twenty-seven years he ruled,
        He was emir of the city of Kano.

17   After him, they put in Muhammadu Bello,
        He was his full brother, in the city of Kano.

18   You know, for eleven years he ruled,
        He was emir of the city of Kano.

19   There were alms and gifts from Bello,
        He was merciful to the people of Kano.

20   There were alms and gifts, that's how Bello was,
        He gave thanks with them in the city of Kano.

21   After him, then his son, Mamman Tukur,
        To him God gave the kingship of Kano.

22   He finished just one year, no more,
        In his government in the city of Kano.

23   After him they put Alu, son of Maje,
        Karofi, who ruled over Kano.

24   You know, for nine years he ran his government,
        He was the king of the city of Kano.

25   After him, the lion, great emir,
        Maje Nasarawa, the Emir of Kano.

26   Brave warrior, who held everyone [in control],
        God have mercy on the Emir of Kano.

27   Brave warrior, who united everyone,
        May God have mercy on him, in the city of Kano.

28   Generous and beyond compare,
     You know, there was none like him in the city of Kano.

29   Generous and beyond compare,
     Of all the kings of the city of Kano.

30   Everyone knows for sixteen years he ruled,
     He was righteous, this Emir of Kano.

31   Our Abbas, son of Abdu, of the great emirs,
     Who have passed on, holders of the government of Kano.

32   After him, then Usumanu received the office,
     For seven years he ruled the city of Kano.

33   The son of Abdu was eloquent,
     He contributed to the government of the city of Kano.

34   In this time he introduced Mai Tambari,
     Commander of the faithful in the city of Kano.

35   After him, then our own took office,
     Bayero, of the great emirs of Kano.

36   A respected man of good character,
     A man of good temperament, the Emir of Kano.

37   A man of insight, a complete man,
     A man of beauty, the Emir of Kano.

38   A man of eloquence, a man of influence,
     A man of learning and hardworking, in Kano.

39   He was dignified, and inspired respect,
     Everyone loved him, the Emir of Kano.

40   He had intelligence and was thankful for it,
     Religious and modest, the Emir of Kano.

41   If there's a meeting, ask the emirs,
     Not us, the people of Kano,

42   "Who is the man who surpasses all his colleagues?"
     Certainly you'll be told—the Emir of Kano.

43   "Which man is a *malam,* an upright person?"
     Surely they'll tell you, the Emir of Kano.

44   "Which of all men is an honest worshipper?"
     Surely they'll tell you, the Emir of Kano.

45   "Who is pure and not avaricious?"
       Surely they'll tell you, the Emir of Kano.

46   "Where is the one who intends good for all?"
       Truly they'll tell you, the Emir of Kano.

47   "Where is the generous one without fear?"
       Everyone will tell you, the Emir of Kano.

48   "Where is the one who takes up men's burdens?"
       Among generous men, the Emir of Kano.

49   You know he will give much wealth,
       Protecting his dignity, the Emir of Kano.

50   East, west, to the south and all the north,
       A respected man, the Emir of Kano.

51   Purity like his I've never seen,
       Right or left, in the city of Kano.

52   He was given the name of his grandfather,
       And we loved him, Abdu, the Emir of Kano.

53   Religion and honor he loved,
       Write down his character, the Emir of Kano.

54   If someone said he preferred his own religion,
       He would contradict the opinion of the Emir of Kano.

55   In his time Abdu caused many things
       To be done in the city of Kano.

56   He was the first to go to Makka
       Of all Emirs of Kano.

57   There's a mosque that he built,
       There's a mosque in the city of Kano.

58   In his time many Arabs came
       From Khartoum, here, to the city of Kano.

59   Water pumps and lights were installed in his time,
       At that time you brought them here to the city of Kano.

60   An office, new street layout, post office, radio,
       Printing press and middle school in the city of Kano.

61   Hospital and airfield,
       They were all brought to the city of Kano.

62 Hospital and airfield,
   There are schools of health too in Kano.

63 There are hospital schools to be sure,
   There is an occupational school in Kano.

64 There are trading companies, even textile factories,
   Lorry parks in the city of Kano.

65 There are council chambers everywhere,
   There are libraries in the city of Kano.

66 And many other things, here I'll be brief,
   May God have mercy on the Emir of Kano.

67 We have many places here in this country,
   Between Bornu and the city of Kano.

68 Never had one been known to visit them,
   Of all the emirs of the city of Kano.

69 Our emir himself went to them,
   He visited them all, this Emir of Kano.

70 For he knew that power is God's,
   Not his, not theirs, the emirs of Kano.

71 For twenty-seven years he ruled,
   He was the leader of the city of Kano.

72 After him, then his son, Mamman Sanusi,
   Took over the government of the city of Kano.

73 Courage and generosity was his,
   A servant to God, the Emir of Kano.

74 Surely Muhammadu was fearless,
   Certainly one must respect the Emir of Kano.

75 On a Thursday his reign was ended,
   God's will was fulfilled in Kano.

76 He had served for nine years,
   He returned to Katagum, leaving Kano.

77 After him, they put in Muhammadu Inuwa,
   For six months he was the leader of Kano.

78 He was of good character, he was a good man,
   Everyone loved him in the city of Kano.

79   He was of good character, he cancelled the debts
      Of everyone in the city of Kano.

80   For obedience, I've seen no one like him,
      You know there was no haughtiness in the Emir of Kano.

81   Abbas was his father, God have mercy on him,
      May God have mercy on the Emir of Kano.

82   After him they gave it to Abdu's son, Ado
      Bayero, of the revered emirs of Kano.

83   [In the Muslim year] one thousand three hundred eighty
      Three, he took over the government of Kano.

84   The character of his father was there with him,
      The people love the Emir of Kano.

85   He resembles his father,
      With a face like his father's, the Emir of Kano.

86   With patience undiminished,
      Like Abdu Bayero, the Emir of Kano.

87   In his speech, if he's giving a talk,
      He resembles his father, the Emir of Kano.

88   His gaze, if he raises it, will look
      Like Audu Bayero's, the Emir of Kano.

89   He is intelligent and insightful,
      He is spotlessly pure, the Emir of Kano.

90   He is learned in Arabic script and thought;
      He speaks English, this Emir of Kano.

91   By God, if he mounts a horse or puts on a turban,
      He resembles his father, the Emir of Kano.

92   Whether walking or sitting on his throne,
      He's just like his father, the Emir of Kano.

93   With goodness like Abbas's he has
      The dignity of a Bayero, the Emir of Kano.

94   God have mercy on all the emirs
      Who have passed on, holders of the government of Kano.

95   May love and respect for you increase,
      Peace to you, peace to you, Emir of Kano.

96   God protect you in these wicked times,
      And this year protect the government of the Emir of Kano.

97   I invoke blessings on the Prophet,
      I thank God for creating Kano.

98   God forgive all the emirs,
      Who have passed through the government of Kano.

99   Muhammadu 'Dan Amu composed this song,
      With the sons of teachers of the council of Kano.

100   Hauwa Gwaram I am, I've changed it a bit,
      With Hajiya Ta Sidi, on the Emirs of Kano.

          Thanks be to God.

SONG OF EXPLANATION ABOUT BIAFRA
BY HAJIYA 'YAR SHEHU

1   Oh God, I beseech You,
For the sake of your Prophet, Muhammad
King of all creation,
He has reached your abode.
    His noble nature has no end.

2   Oh God, I ask that You help me,
Give me the perception to explain,
Because I am not knowledgeable,
For only God knows,
    I will explain so there's no mistake.

3   I will explain about our country,
It is our Nigeria,
For our families, our grandparents,
In all West Africa, there is no one like us,
    Our wealth is so great it has no end.

4   In the west and the north, which is ours,
On victory, they came to our country
We do everything ourselves,
Clothing and our kings,
    Even food, in our country without a care.

5   Here in the north in our state,
There is blacksmithing and tanned hides,
There are sheep and our cattle,
There is beniseed and our cotton,
    There are pyramids of groundnuts.

6   In the west they have theirs,
There is cocoa in their state,
There are kola nuts there,
Even palm oil in their state,
    No enmity or conspiracies.

7   At that time the south had no resources,
No town, no reason
No one who was rich
No one with honor,
    No food or clothing, no one cared.

8   You see wickedness of victory,
     They joined us with soldiers of misfortune,
     See their character, like hyenas,
     See their stark naked tribalism
              See their back-stabbing attitude and promotion of
                   enmity.

9   See their character like wild animals,
     They ruined our economy,
     We pulled them out of great anguish
     And they took pride in their arrogance,
              They did not appreciate the money spent on them.

10   They thought they had gains,
     That's why they promoted enmity,
     Both the good ones and the scoundrels,
     They killed important people and took over
              Not even close to peaceful coexistence.

11   You and your state's soldiers,
     Even Ironsi, your leader,
     You were conspiring against us in a worse situation
     You killed our people, not yours,
              Because of hypocrisy, and conspiracy.

12   You wed without dowry,
     They say your intention was to take over the leadership.
     Because our state has manual labor
     By God, you are being senseless, friend,
              The leadership is not succeeding.

13   You Ibo, you are ashamed,
     You see the work here and behind,
     Which you did out of rivalry,
     Since here you see a sign
              For God's sake, warning will not end.

14   Except for worthlessness and craziness,
     You thought only of yourself
     Everything that a person plants
     Will sprout, without a doubt.
              What grows will be reaped.

15   You have killed important people of our country,
     From west to our north

You have combined all our various boundaries
So you could take our work
        And even our homes and farms, through your
            underhandedness.

16   See your father, the dog Ironsi,
        Then you all act rebelliously,
        Without a fine of even a dime,
        You killed ours without lenience
            If he advised you, no one disagreed with him.

17   See his worthless advisor
        Even Azikwe, a betrayal of trust
        A person would refuse you good and no one would question
        Until he fanned the flames and set the fire,
            Because of greediness for power, he continued to
              cheat.

18   If he conspired, then he inspired fear,
        He spread anger everywhere,
        For his own purposes he used people,
        From time to time we came to Owerri
            To run out wickedness and conspire against
              swindling.

19   Based on tribalism and return,
        Then Ironsi set about to catch people,
        Those who were left, the title-holders,
        Northerners were given authority,
            Then he ordered them killed, without a care.

20   Then, by God, he was fair,
        Because he is the one who punishes
        And he knew they betrayed the people,
        Then he put Ironsi in gradually,
            He died and his leadership did not last.

21   By God, the king, the title-holder,
        He owns all creation,
        By God, he forbade an act of cheating
        He punished all creation,
            If they took things or committed crimes he would
              not stop or leave them.

22   Forging on, they took to the road
        That avoids the right sign

By God, the king, he was beyond reach,
He who ends and gives life,
      He killed their government, it didn't last.

23   By God, he knows the do-gooder
Who is not lazy,
He, who would bring dignity to a nation,
Who will guard everything permissible
      Without oppression or conspiracy at all.

24   By God, he made choices from us,
He chose our Yakubu,
To protect our country,
Nigeria,
      From the hands of conspirators.

25   General Commander,
Our Yakubu Gowon has
The good sense of past important ones, there,
He called the important ones together
      To unite the nation and promote peaceful
         coexistence.

26   They killed ours without punishing the culprits
Then Ojukwu without decency,
With the character of a black-hooded cobra,
He insisted there should be a sentence,
      That they should pay war indemnity to those
         swindlers.

27   You hear uselessness and craziness
You should think of yourself,
You who killed his thoughts
You killed your father's animal
      That is why you should not discuss the payment of
         war indemnity.

28   He said that they would retaliate.
Who offended you so that it calls for retaliation?
It is cheating, and we were the ultimate victims
For running away and getting up in arms.
      We leave you to God, without fail.

29   God does not allow acts of wickedness
And does not like enmity
That's why laws are created [so that]

Who cheats would be apprehended.
    Give a verdict without showing enmity.

30 You were called to come for reconciliation,
    But you turned away in enmity.
    One keeps on persuading you
    To settle the rifts, [but you refuse],
        You say you don't know Nigeria.

31 Was it he, Ojukwu, who incited you
    Because you lacked good sense?
    He separated you from your government,
    He prepared you for your destruction,
        Because he spoiled our Nigeria.

32 He called on you to give up yourselves,
    Even your children and all of your properties,
    To buy into trouble among you.
    Those few fighter jets
        Have not helped you in battle.

33 Guns without limit,
    And bombs that crush to ashes,
    He has soldiers, even mercenaries,
    And prepared all kinds of crazy things
        That are senseless, he doesn't know what belongs
            in the world.

34 Then he said to you, see the planes
    The lies and capital of the bastard Ojukwu,
    A master braggart and liar,
    Then he told you to rise up.
        To receive your country, Nigeria.

35 Then he kept on jumping and boasting,
    See, he is getting more benefits,
    Nonsense, stupid and useless,
    Then he put wickedness into their state
        Because of his evil he did not deliberate on his
            actions.

36 Then he put a name to wickedness,
    They call it "Biafra," it was not well planned
    Then he got up to continue boasting
    They say neighbors inspire cravings
        They will help you conspirators.

37   You hear, the bastard, the liar,
      Eventually they made him ashamed,
      They told him he lied,
      It was not their idea to refuse obedience,
              They had no idea about a place called Biafra.

38   For fear of his action he came up with a new plan
      He manipulated things and filed a complaint,
      Saying that the Muslims started it all
      You hear this boldfaced lie
              Invented to find someone to blame.

39   Our leader is with God,
      He is the one who witnessed him, God.
      He does not differentiate between prayer
      Nor much less following God in Islam
              Or Christianity, He will not care.

40   Then he took his complaint to America,
      Up to London, as far as Africa,
      Up to Rome, and Israel, he sent it.
      That Muslims are enjoying business,
              And that they will take over the country.

41   Some of them followed their path because of this,
      They took up their bundle of lies,
      They hid their crimes,
      They ruined our trust of them
              For lack of shame about this conspiracy.

42   Then he got up, shouting,
      He kept on making an uproar and shouting
      He was calling the Ibos, those arrogant ones,
      They were straining ceaselessly,
              They say they will seize all of Africa.

43   Then the general commander
      He called out to bring about settlement
      To prevent spilling blood for this
      To prevent our country from becoming a desert.
              Then Ojukwu said he would not stop.

44   Then Ojukwu incited rebellion
      Then he sent his guerillas
      To the borders so they could guard its borders
      To drive out everything, including the livestock,
              Until not even people were left.

45 The general commander
  Immediately gave his orders
  To the soldiers, telling them to stop at the border
  And that no one should disobey this order
    Because they had no permission to make a raid.

46 Then on the sixth day, without doubt,
  Of July, this is the truth,
  Biafra attacked.
  The government was there at its limit,
    The soldiers of our great Nigeria.

47 They bothered them here at the border
  They were a government without orders
  They sent an attack signal to the commandant
  At once he gave them orders,
    They did not touch civilians.

48 The country's leader gave you, Yakubu
  Advice to keep away from Ojukwu,
  Because he knew he would destroy you,
  Your welfare and wealth,
    Do not turn around in response to the call.

49 Then he hired jet pilots
  They took that bomb that turns things to ash.
  You see Lagos, he sent it there,
  As for Kaduna, and Kano, it hit
    But missed its intended target.

50 Supreme commander
  At once he gave orders
  To go to Enugu and come back
  With the infidel Ojukwu, he and
    The important leaders of the plot.

51 This day, I think it was at prayer time,
  For men who lack weakness
  Soldiers, your lives are with God,
  If there's a chance, it's with God,
    They did this to stop the conspiracy.

52 They all interact in the bush,
  See hyenas and snakes,
  When there was rain they didn't feel it
  They slept only in the bush
    Reliable men, they never tired of rebellion.

53   They made up praise epithets for Yakubu,
      The army troops, the protectors.
      The Biafrans, the boasters
      They headed toward you, roaring.
              They took off running without turning back.

54   At once you scattered the crowd
      The losers were suddenly afraid,
      You gathered up their guns
      You brought more prisoners of war,
              You see their bastard did not even care.

55   The battalion of freedom and trust,
      You are in government without chaos
      You fought with men in daytime
      You hit and beat each other
              You killed them and theirs without surcease.

56   At once they surrendered
      They left Ogoja in retreat,
      They left for you even their things,
      Guns beyond number
              They left it all to you without turning back.

57   You followed them as far as Obolo,
      Then Obodu at breakfast
      You chased out even civilians
      They borrowed just like a vulture
              They found no place to stop.

58   You drove men out of Nsukka
      The Biafrans cried out
      Well! Weapons without limit
      No chance for them to take them along,
              Only themselves, they went without stopping.

59   No chance to take up spears
      Only to piss and shit in fear,
      You have become the government without reverse
      You have protected every area
              You continue to beat them without surcease.

60   Praise to the Lord God,
      There is no God but the one God,
      You did dispose of men in a trash heap
      Until even the vultures celebrate
              They eat meat with no one interrupting them.

61   They left to you all of Nsukka,
This day, no doubt,
Every Ibo has cried,
As they make assumptions about Nsukka,
      That in all Africa none will be able to conquer it.

62   Because here was their center,
Headquarters of the bastard head of their state,
Here is the home of Zik [Azikwe], their leader,
And their people's university,
      Losers, unfortunates, swindlers.

63   You left Nsukka behind
Then Nzeogwu went out to meet the road
Instead of hiding
Then he was obstinate, stubborn
      Because of shamelessness for those hostile
        conspirators.

64   At once Chukuma took off
To Ironsi's in a minute
You see him with a piece of a letter
His heart refused reward
      For the things that he had done with enmity.

65   You see the bastard and the loser
Here in Kaduna they did their treachery
Both mother and father are hyenas
Here he learns of victory
      But because he is a tribalist he is careless.

66   You brought Chukuma, you showed him
You buried him here in Kaduna,
Where he did damage and lived
No more chance to break the trust,
      No more torture or swindling.

67   You seized Boni in a hurry,
Here Biafra was your goal,
The petrol there was locked up from the start,
And once you began to roar,
      They left it to you, never looking back.

68   I will stop my account here,
For there is much more to say
More than for accounting,
I wrote it to show
      That the unworthy never tire of running away.

69   Then Ojukwu changed the road again
    There in Benin State, there he turned
    He gave away money and his possessions,
    At once Ochume turned,
            Then he renounced Nigeria.

70   Then Ochume said to Banjo
    See Biafra, that ambushed us
    At once someone said to the major
    From today it's Benin State, not Ijaw
            Only Ocheme Owonwo, the enemies.

71   The lieutenant general commander
    He called Mamman to go with
    The battalion of freedom fighters in order to
    Deal with the rebels and
            Ocehme and Owonwo, the enemies.

72   Murtala, you dazzled everyone
    Pillar of support to the Kano folk
    You diluted the poison of the southerners,
    Your army dispersed them all.
            They left Benin without looking back.

73   You followed the tracks of the miserable ones,
    The destitute, without foresight
    But with surfeit of bragging and boasting,
    Even until they reached Asaba in the chase,
            They had no place to shelter.

74   They left Benin nonstop,
    They went to the father of southerners,
    Then he got up, he was shouting,
    Until he turned Banjo and the rest into corpses,
            They died without enjoying a penny.

75   You see, greed entices you
    It separates you from your government
    It prevents you from becoming a community.
    See the contempt you bring on yourself
            See the money, worthless, you won't have a penny.

76   You followed your heart's desires,
    You brought oppression to your state.
    The wealth of all your government
    You handed over to Ojukwu.
            For this, you have not rested well.

77   Murtala beat you up
      You escaped with sweat on your forehead.
      No food to eat or satisfaction,
      No jealousy among losers.
              You did not worry that your region would suffer
              loss.

78   Murtala Mamman, God's servant
      Supreme lieutenant commander
      All the region of Benin State owes you.
      You divided them from the oppression of
              Ojukwu Owonwu, which is endless.

79   The battalion of freedom fighters belongs to you,
      Men of no doubts.
      Where you go, they will follow,
      Even into fire, where they'll follow
              In order to lift up our Nigeria.

80   You left Benin without malice.
      You got up to Enugu,
      To catch Ojukwu, the evil one,
      Along with his advisors, the bastards.
              Plotters and swindlers.

81   There you met with Shuwa in the bush,
      Even Danjuma and the soldiers,
      Lieutenants on strike,
      You are colonels, the brave ones
              You are the strength, you enders of hatred.

82   Three big ones are trustworthy,
      Here are rocks that burnt.
      Even in the Congo you have made a name
      You are inseparable,
              Worthy men, you won't tire of running.

              Thanks be to God.

"Well, people, as for this song, it ends here. The reason for its ending thus is that there is a page that has been lost; I can't find it. And as it is, I cannot reproduce it. For this reason, this mistake that I made, I apologize to God and you and all others."

GLOSSARY

All terms are Hausa unless otherwise noted.

aiki: work

ajami: Hausa language in Arabic script

algaita: double-reed shawm

ban dariya: limericks

basmala (Ar.): opening invocation: *Bismillahi ar-Rahmani ar-Rahim* (In the name of God, the Merciful, the Compassionate)

boko (Eng. borrowing): book

bori: spirit possession

cikin gida: harem, women's quarters

dagi, durƙusan taguwa: insignia, knot of the north

gaɗa: girls' singing and clapping

garaya: guitar-like musical instrument made from an elliptical gourd

girma: large in size or importance

hadith (Ar.): report, narrative, sayings of or about the Prophet Muhammad

hawan sallah: ceremonial parade on horseback following the Ramadan month of fasting

jaji: woman appointed to lead groups of women to Nana Asma'u for educational sessions

jihad: struggle to promote acceptance of the word of God

kakaki: long metal horn blown for chiefs, emirs

kiɗan ƙwarya: drumming on overturned calabashes

kiɗan mara: music made by clapping together calabash fragments

kiɗan ruwa: drumming on overturned calabashes floating on water in larger calabashes

kiɗan sakaina. See *kiɗan mara*

kirari: praise epithet

kishiya: co-wife

kobo (Eng. borrowing): coin, monetary unit equivalent to penny; orig. from the English term "copper"

ƙore (pl. *ƙwarya*): calabash

kukuma: one stringed lute

kulle: wife seclusion

ƙwarya (pl. *ƙorai*). See *ƙore*

malam sing. m., *malama* sing. f. (pl. *malamai*): teacher, learned person, scholar

maroƙa: beggar singers

mawaƙa: masters of song

maza: men

naira: paper currency, monetary unit equivalent to dollar

qasida (Ar.): ode, praise poem

ramzi: chronogram

reno: child care

sana'a: occupation

sannu: greeting (lit., "hello")

shantu: long gourd trumpet used by women

sunna (Ar.): Islamic rites and customs; the example of the life of the Prophet Muhammad

takhmis (Ar.): the adding of two lines to existing hemistichs to turn couplets into pentastichs

tashen sallah: drumming to solicit gifts during the last four days of Ramadan fasting

turmi: mortar for corn

waƙa (pl. *waƙoƙi*): poetry, song

yabo: praise

'yan taru: women disciples of Nana Asma'u

yara: children

zakat: charity, generosity

zambo: satire

zumunci: relationship by blood or marriage

NOTES

1. "EVERY WOMAN SINGS"

1. Personal communication, Kano, Nigeria, March 1979.

2. This is not to imply that all Hausa women write poetry or sing; many engage in textile crafts, make snacks to sell, and engage in myriad other expressions of creative talent (Schildkrout 1979, 1982).

3. The fieldwork periods run from January 1979 to July 1980 (doctoral dissertation fieldwork) and January 1982 to July 1983 (postdoctoral fieldwork).

4. For this and all subsequent definitions of Hausa language terms, refer to Abraham's *Dictionary of the Hausa Language.*

5. All of these things are activities that I as a single woman had to do during my residence there.

6. To begin with, the research of most male Western scholars has not dealt with Hausa women's roles. Exceptions to this include the work of Allan Christelow and Alan Frishman, both of whom speak Hausa and have lived in Kano. Works such as Renee Pittin's studies of alternative careers (1979, 1983, 1984) and the research of most of the authors in Coles and Mack's volume on Hausa women (1991) argue against the stereotypes of subordinated Hausa Muslim women.

7. This was performed by Binta Katsina, recorded in March 1980 at the conference of Hausa students, Bayero University, Kano. I collected, transcribed, and translated this and all works cited throughout this book unless otherwise noted.

8. Some extemporaneous poets do record for radio and television stations: Binta Katsina, Maimuna Choge, and Hajiya Faji are prime examples.

9. Many studies perpetuate the image of illiterate, unproductive Hausa Muslim women by measuring them against Western standards of public productivity instead of investigating from within the culture, through Hausa language and values.

10. See my article in *The Maghreb Review* 29, no. 1 (February 2004) for a discussion of the importance of orality in Muslims' education.

11. A Hausa woman demonstrated this to me in the Kano palace in 1980. See also MacKay 1955.

12. One of the most prolific authors on this topic is Ibrahim Yaro Yahaya, whose many volumes of children's songs in Hausa are available in Hausaland.

13. The legacy of the traditional pre-Islamic spirit-possession cult known as *bori* is evident in calabash drumming and dancing.

14. This is also shown in a 1986 National Geographic Explorer series program entitled "Under a Crescent Moon." This praise singer has died.

15. See my article in Adenaike and Vansina (1996) for an account of my field experience in Kano.

PROFILE ONE

1. "*Na rubuta wannan, amma ni ba zabiya ba ce,*" personal communication, January 22, 1980.

2. Comments that follow are from interviews I conducted with Hauwa Gwaram during fieldwork in Kano, Nigeria, 1979–1980. Translations are mine.

2. "THE SONG IS POETRY'S DOMAIN"

1. When I saw this design on someone's bag at the train station in New Haven, Connecticut, I greeted that person in Hausa, and they responded in kind. My parents—who are not Hausa-speakers—saw the design on a man's robe in Heathrow Airport, said "*Sannu*" ("Hello") and were greeted with an enthusiastic response in Hausa.

2. Arab and Islamic influence has been important to Northern Nigeria at the highest socioeconomic levels since the tenth century, when trans-Saharan caravan trade brought the Arabic language and Islamic theology. Islamic influence has been pervasive at all levels of society only for the past two centuries, following the Sokoto jihad, which helped make Islam the religion of the masses.

3. At the secondary and university levels, students can attend Arabic schools that offer a full range of disciplines (history, mathematics, sciences).

4. Sidi Sayudi, a scholar in Sokoto, knew a great deal about meter in the abstract. Personal communication from Jean Boyd, April 2002.

5. Personal communication from A. Neil Skinner, Madison, Wisconsin, December 1980, and see comments of Hajiya 'Yar Shehu and Hauwa Gwaram in their profiles.

6. See Furniss (1996) and profiles of Hauwa Gwaram and Hajiya 'Yar Shehu in this book for more information on the Hikima Kulob, the Wisdom Club, a poetry circle in Kano in the 1960s.

7. Leaders of the Sokoto jihad intended to promote the acquisition of literacy among women as well as men as a means of pursuing spirituality. It has been argued that the jihad resulted in restrictions on women, including the imposition of veiling and seclusion in the home, but such restrictions resulted from subsequent leaders' misinterpretations of the *Shehu*'s sentiments on women's rights. Indeed, the *Shehu* specified that any man who impeded or denied the education of his wife was an irresponsible Muslim.

8. The process of reworking a poem to new effect was a common one in Arabic poetry and not at all suggestive of plagiarism, as it might be in the West.

9. Boyd and Mack's *The Collected Works of Nana Asma'u, bint Usman ɗan Fodiyo 1793–1864* was issued in a Nigerian publication by Sam Bookman Publishers (Ibadan) in 1999, two years after its publication by Michigan State University Press in 1997.

10. Jean Boyd explains the contrast between the official reports and actual practice by citing the following: In a letter dated September 9, 1929, E. R. Hussey, director of education stated, "It is suggested that an attempt should be made with girls' education at two selected centers of population such as Kano and Katsina." Commander John Carrow, who was resident officer in Sokoto during the 1930s, stated in an annual report, "Female education started in 1933 has already proved successful. . . . [R]apid progress. . . . Emirs and other Native Authority officials have been most helpful" (*Annual Report on the Sokoto Province*, 1933). Forty years later, he explained, "What I am trying to emphasize is the unplanned way in which female education started in Nigeria. There was no demand for this education. In fact it was against the whole of African opinion—Emirs, District Heads . . . and the people." Letter to Jean Trevor, February 27, 1973. This letter and the *Annual Report on the Sokoto Province* are in the Jean Trevor Papers, MS 79, Special Collections, Old Library, University of Exeter, Exeter, England.

11. In the home, the senior wife, along with other women residents, received instruction from these teachers on such practical topics as health care, hygiene, home repair, child care, and income generation. Jean Boyd reports that this program, in contrast to Nana Asma'u's program of educating women, was "very hit and miss."

12. Personal communication from Jean Boyd, April 2002.

13. The *qasida* originates in pre-Islamic Bedouin poetry and is sometimes described as "profane anti-text to the sacred text of the Qur'an" (Stetkevych 1993, xi).

14. The Sunni way of life recommends following the example (*sunnah*) of the Prophet Muhammad. Many studies of Shehu Usman ɗan Fodiyo explain his works and those of his family (see especially Hiskett 1973; Boyd 1989). But as Boyd notes, the British suppressed knowledge of the true nature of the jihad and did not allow the publication of Fodiyo-related literature in translation for the populace.

15. These histories were from Arabia; see *Labaru na Da da na Yanzu* (*News of the Past and the Present*) (Zaria: Translation Bureau, 1934).

16. Jean Boyd disagrees with this perspective, reasoning that it is an easy accusation until and unless earlier works can disprove it.

17. I took a stack of manuscripts to the Press, lobbied for it, wrote the introduction, and edited the volume.

18. *Bori* is the non-Islamic Hausa cult of spirit possession conducted as a curative rite. Its historical origins are unclear; scholars disagree as to whether it is a vestige of pre-Islamic cults or developed in response to the reformation of Islam established in the nineteenth century Sokoto jihad. *Bori* is characterized by nocturnal ceremonies of drumming and song, many of which are performed by women. During these sessions music aids in inducing trance in the afflicted individual (the adept), who is then felt to be possessed by the spirit from the *bori* pantheon best suited to drive out the offending spirit causing the individual's malady. Some women musicians perform for *bori* sessions as well as for public performance in more widely accepted social circles.

19. These are not analyzed here but are included in my tape collection housed in the Archives of Traditional Music at Indiana University (accession number 81-100-F/B). In several cases, they are the same songs that I recorded in public performances.

20. For instance, a "Radio and TV Programmes" column in the July 16, 1979, *New Nigerian* newspaper lists these programs for Kaduna Radio on that day: "1:30 Music while you work; 2:00 *Kawa zuwa kawa* [*Friend to Friend*]; 2:45 *Lafiyar uwar jiki* [*Health Is the Mother of the Body*].

21. Personal communication with a professor at Bayero University in Kano, May 19, 1980.

22. Women educated to the levels of university education tend to channel creative compositional energies toward writing novels and dramas.

23. Personal communication from Jean Boyd, whose collection has these songs (School of Oriental and African Studies [SOAS], University of London, PP Ms 36/G18).

24. Personal communication from Jean Boyd, April 2002.

25. With the exception of the case of *innas* who ruled in Gobir, as indicated earlier.

PROFILE TWO

1. In Kano in September 2002 I was told that she had died, but no one could find a family member or verify this.

2. Comments that follow are from interviews I conducted with Hajiya 'Yar Shehu during fieldwork in Kano, Nigeria, 1979–1980. Translations are mine.

3. This refers to the effort of the eastern region of Nigeria, which adopted the name Biafra, to secede from Nigeria, which resulted in civil war in the years 1967–1970.

3. PERFORMING ARTISTS

1. This name is spelled in Hausa without the "h," because a Hausa "c" is pronounced "ch." For convenience in this study, Hajiya Maimuna Coge's name is spelled "Choge" to facilitate proper English pronunciation.

2. Hauwa Gwaram moved to Kano when she was first married; she lived and worked there her entire adult life. Hajiya 'Yar Shehu also spent her adult life in Kano but also maintained a household in nearby Dambatta, her home town.

3. Her name means "daughter of drumming."

4. The University of Sokoto's Dr. Birniwa confirmed these names (personal communication, September 12, 2002) and noted that Dr. B. B. Usman has collected nearly twenty songs on farming by Hauwa Mukkunu.

5. Several scholars have discussed male royal musicians (Ames 1973; Besmer 1983). They are "in constant attendance at the palace, and announce the arrival of the distinguished visitors . . . by trumpet fanfares, drumming and [praise]shouting. They also salute the king . . . nightly during the annual feast of Ramadan" (Smith 1965, 31). These male musicians (in 1980, a few were women who were performing in the place of their fathers, who had trained them because there were no boys in the family to carry on the role) perform for the emir in public and private gatherings of other men, but only their female counterpart, the royal *zabiya,* is allowed to accompany the emir all the way into the harem, the heart of the palace, the women's quarters.

6. Also, a woman occasionally will inherit her father's position as a royal musician.

7. Jean Boyd reports that she saw new "millionaires" tossing out money and bestowing Mercedes cars on praise singers during the 1970s when oil profits flowed and revenue was misappropriated into private accounts.

8. The female praise singer is "known as *zabiya* [lit. guinea fowl] from the shrill ululating sound which it is her function to let out at odd moments, such as during the king's address to his assembled subjects after Sallah" (Smith 1957, 31). Her ululation is not delivered randomly but for the express purpose of emphasizing the action of the moment.

9. Other researchers have reported that certain women of the palace community in Kano have discounted the work of all *zabiyoyi* as "meaningless" (Muhammad 1977, 9–12), anxious not to be associated with entertainers, who are characteristically individuals of low status. Although these women do in fact enjoy performances by *zabiyoyi,* they are reluctant to admit to such interest. Among certain female artists, the social stigma attached to *maroka* and *zabiyoyi* makes them resist being included in these categories. I find this puzzling, since the harem women I knew well were very accepting of the royal court praise singer, a woman appointed to the position by the emir. One needs to ask the origin of social stigmas; do they depend on a gendered reading of who is valued in society?

10. Royal male musicians sometimes are "turbanned" as an indication of honorary status. Women are not turbanned. Whether this is because a woman is assumed not to be able to bear a turban or due to other reasons bears investigation.

11. Personal communication with women of the emir's palace during fieldwork in 1980.

12. In the process of procuring authenticated versions of nineteenth-century Nana Asma'u's works for our translation, Jean Boyd relied on the stamp of approval given by the formal reading of a knowledgeable scholar of Asma'u's works. If a correction needed to be made for the written version to match his memorized version, that scholar was qualified to make the change, and the final written version, with the scholar's corrections, was considered to be the authentic form of the work.

13. The previous *zabiya* of the royal court in Kano, Hajiya 'Yar Daudu, was regularly

accompanied on the one-stringed lute (*goge*) by a man who was called her husband. It is said that everyone calls such an accompanist a "husband," "but that is only wishful thinking, because that *should* be their relationship" (personal communication from Hausa women in Kano, Nigeria, March 1979). The implication is that this is the only respectable relationship between men and women seen in public together.

14. This was pointed out to me by staff members of television station KNTV in Kano, Nigeria, while I was reviewing videotapes during fieldwork in February 1980.

15. *Shantu* music traditionally has been women's leisurely evening entertainment while men have congregated at a home's entryway to converse, but both activities are being replaced by television viewing in the evenings. At one time it was primarily young brides who had time to play *shantu* music in the evenings, but now even they often spend time listening to the radio or watching television instead.

16. In relation to this kind of circumstance, and especially in connection to the next chapter, Jean Boyd notes that when a political figure brought women singers to a function in Sokoto, the men in the audience turned their backs in indignation, offended to be subjected to such displays.

17. Levin reports a similar arrangement in Tashkent (1996, 41).

18. Personal communication from Balbasatu Ibrahim, September 13, 2002.

19. Personal communication, Kano, February 16, 1980.

20. Levin reports a similar situation among singers in Tashkent (1996, 42).

21. For testimony on these perspectives, see profiles of Hauwa Gwaram and Hajiya 'Yar Shehu. Deborah Pellow raises an important question here as to whether these women channel their talents into other creative pursuits. I cannot answer that and hope that another study will do so.

22. Personal communication during fieldwork, November 22, 1979; a Hausa woman sang along with Dan Maraya Jos, a well-known entertainer who was performing on television.

23. A younger performer, Hajiya 'Yar Kada of Sokoto, explained in a television interview in 2002 that she developed her skills on her own, simply learning by singing and working with a chorus that supported her efforts. She was accompanied by seven women in a chorus, one of whom was her ten-year-old daughter.

24. Delivery seems to make the difference between the beggar and the prosperous singer. Beggars may declaim in the street but rarely are they given space at more official gatherings. They are not considered to be professional singers and are not usually skilled enough to sustain significant delivery.

25. Personal communication from Balbasatu Ibrahim, September 13, 2002.

26. David Ames (1973, 135) discusses this issue, as does Thomas Hale in his more recent *Griots and Griottes* (1998; chapter 6, "Would You Want Your Daughter to Marry One?"). The attitude was confirmed repeatedly in personal communications to me in Kano, Nigeria, in 1979 and 1980.

27. In the late 1970s, the Emir of Katsina had several *zabiyoyi*, the Emir of Kano only one.

28. Levin reports a Tashkent singer who performed similarly for radio stations (1996, 39).

29. Women in Hausa society regularly earn private income by selling food or handicrafts they have made; their children sell them on the street. Some also own land that they have others farm, or they collect rent on houses they own. Their dowries are also their own to use as investments or disposable wealth.

30. A Hausa woman in Kano, Nigeria, demonstrated this on March 18, 1980.

31. Personal communication in Kano, Nigeria, February 11, 1980.

32. Demonstrated by Hausa women performing in Kano, Nigeria, August 25, 1979, described in Ames and King (1971, 12).

33. An increased reliance on appliances such as blenders, mixers, and refrigerators contributes to the decline of music associated with tasks such as pounding grain and grinding vegetables. Food preparation and preservation are facilitated by these machines. Their increasing popularity has an inverse effect on the propensity for using traditional implements as musical instruments.

34. Speaking of contemporary Muslim Tashkent performers, Levin observed, "[I]t is typical of musicians . . . that they are never just musicians. They always do something else: they're musician-poets, or musician-philosophers, or musician-comedians" (1996, 37).

35. In 1981, Kano State's Governor Rimi drastically restricted the participation of village heads in paying homage to Kano's Emir Alhaji Ado Bayero. Rimi's action severely threatened the continued existence of this traditional dramatic ritual.

36. Personal communication from the head of KNTV broadcasting in Kano, Nigeria, February 25, 1980.

4. METAPHOR

1. Hajiya Maizargadi, praise singer for the Emir of Kano, used this expression in a discussion of her friend 'Yar Daudu's style (November 1979).

2. As I was revising this manuscript, the July/August 2002 *Saudi Aramco World* arrived with the cover story's title: "Water's Other Name Is Life"—water is central to life everywhere.

3. Schimmel refers to a Turkish medieval poet's mystical verse involving a paradox of Ultimate Truth hidden as inside a nutshell: "[T]he attempt to attain reality or truth is often likened to the hard work that is needed to break a nut before one can enjoy the sweet, wholesome kernel" (1994, 131–132).

4. This and the spirit of the paragraph are from Adonis's discussion in *An Introduction to Arabic Poetics* (1990) and his citations of al-Jurjani's ideas in *Dala'il al-I'jaz* (Misr: Maktabat al-Qahirah, 1969) and *Asar al-Balagha* (Cairo, 1959).

5. Obligatory prayers include more than simply oral recitation: they also include preparatory cleansing (ablutions of the extremities and orifices by rinsing with clean water), three physical stances (standing, bowing, prostration), and the recitation of specific chapters of the Qur'an as one moves from position to position. Some prayers are set, some are superogatory.

6. This is one of the best known of the *hadith qudsi,* a divine tradition that records God's own utterances, unlike the *hadith nabawi,* or prophetic tradition (Netton 1992, 90).

7. Not only is Eve not named, but the term "Adam" simply means "of the soil," because Adam was created from the clay of the earth.

8. A paraphrase of the two verses cited would be "God does not change the situation of a people until they change it in themselves"; quoted in Wadud 1992, 25.

9. The extent to which these implications are understood explicitly among the Hausa has not, to my knowledge, been investigated, but certainly one can argue for the implicit effect on those who are intimately familiar with the Qur'an.

10. Murata 1992, 197. See her discussion of Sufi Ibn Arabi's *Fusus al Hikam* (*Bezels of Wisdom*).

11. Qur'an, Chapter 2:256: "Let there be no compulsion in religion . . ."

12. See citations throughout the Qur'an, especially those noted in Chapters 2 and 4.

13. Schimmel (1994, 134) emphasizes that it must be religious knowledge (*ilm*) that is sought, not frivolous knowledge. More widely interpreted, this can mean any knowledge related to the natural world, which is the manifestation of God's being.

14. Adonis (1990, 38–39) discusses "The Metaphor of the Qur'an" ("Majaz al-Qur'an") by Abu 'Ubayda (728–825), "The Meanings of the Qur'an" ("Ma'ani al-Qur'an") by al-

Farra' (d. 822), and "The Problematic of the Qur'an" ("Mushkil al-Qur'an") by Ibn Qutaybas (828–889), among others.

15. Jean Boyd suggests that oral poetry reflects pre-Islamic influence which persists in Hausa culture, manifested mostly clearly in the *bori* cult activities that are embellished by drumming on water (*kidan kwarya*), a woman's performance style.

16. Schimmel (1994, 132) discusses the use of riddles in mystical teachings in Islam. See also the numerous publications on the mythical Sufi Mulla Nasruddin, the holy fool whose silliness is parallel to Zen Buddhist koans. Many of the Mulla Nasruddin stories are also found in Zen Buddhist teachings.

17. Here the transcription and translation are mine. Other *karin magana* are from Kirk-Greene 1966.

18. Personal communication from A. Neil Skinner, Madison, Wisconsin, September 1981.

19. Personal communication from A. Neil Skinner, Madison, Wisconsin, August 1981.

20. The term *'uwa* is also extended thus: *'uwar makera* ("mother of the smithy," i.e., the anvil), and *'uwar yaki* ("mother of the army, i.e., commander in chief"); personal communication from A. Neil Skinner, Madison, Wisconsin, September 1980. Jean Boyd reports that Sidi Sayudi calls *'uwar 'Yaki* the "old guard."

21. *Gari,* now glossed as "town," once had a wider connotation, perhaps that of "known environment" (personal communication from A. Neil Skinner, Madison, Wisconsin, September 1980), so the title *mai gari,* which is more literally "master, or overseer, of the town" would have held a great deal of esteem as the title for one in an important position. This is Nagogo, late Emir of Katsina.

22. *Babba* is a synonym of *girma,* indicating large size as well as importance.

23. Personal communication from A. Neil Skinner, Madison, Wisconsin, September 1980. Consider the use of *mai* in proper names: Maizargadi, Maimuna Choge, Mai Duala Ningi.

24. Jean Boyd contributed these examples.

5. THE SOCIAL FUNCTIONS OF
HAUSA WOMEN'S CREATIVITY

1. This is discussed in Schimmel 1994, 134. She notes that religious knowledge is what should be sought.

2. Jean Boyd notes that Malam Junaidu in Sokoto was trained by a woman scholar and that Jean Trevor had reported that in 1934 women scholars were common in the region.

3. During the nineteenth-century Sokoto jihad, the kings (traditionally known as *sarki*) of northern Nigerian urban centers were replaced with emirs, indicating allegiance to Islam over traditional Hausa practices. In Sokoto, the dynastic head is also the spiritual leader for the entire Northern Region; he is known by the title Sardauna, or Sultan, instead of emir. As a result of colonial rule, during Nigeria's early years of independence (after 1960) a premier was the designated political head of the entire Northern Region. In recent times, that office has been supplanted by regional governors who function as part of the national government administration. Among the Hausa in the north, emirs and the Sardauna in Sokoto continue to sit as traditional rulers, in cooperation with national government political officers.

4. *Allah tsare mu rashin fatawa ga malami / To kin ji aikin rashin yakida jahilci.*

5. Contemporary Muslim women increasingly rely on Qur'anic sources to justify their autonomy in education and personal human rights issues. See especially Mernissi 1991 and Ahmed 1992.

6. Personal communication from Jean Boyd, January 2003.

7. "Datelines Africa" column in *West Africa*, March 23, 1981, p. 652.

8. Prior to the nineteenth-century jihad, Kano's kings were known by the Hausa term *sarki*. Since the jihad, they have been called emirs, from the Arabic *amir*, which is overtly representative of Islam in the region. The separation of religious beliefs from politics is a recent development whose philosophical basis is not yet fully accepted in Northern Nigeria.

9. *To, wannan waka ita ce ta sarakunan Filani daga gare ni Hauwa Gwaram. Wato, ai na jinta Alhaji dan Amu liman Kano shi ne ya yi ta da Arabiya. Ni kuma na je wa gurun Sidiya matar Sarkin Kano Alhaji Inuwa. Muna yin karatu. Na bincika sai muka same ta. Ta ce a gurun 'uwan soro ta karba 'uwan soro ta faren gida. Shi ne . . . ni kuma na ce ta ba ni. Na je na tambayo izo mai gurun Alhaji dan Amu na rubuta ta da boko dalilin da na karanta ke nan. Ammma da Sarkin Kano Sanusi da Sarkin Kano Inuwa da Ado ni ce na fadi lokacinsu domin tun da lokacin da ba a yi su ba aka yi wannan waka. A zamanin Sarkin Kano Abdullahi. To, Bismillahi arrahmani arrahim . . .* (personal communication, Kano, Nigeria, 1979).

10. For example, instead of twenty-six years, she says that former Kano Emir Dabo ruled for twenty-three years, that Mamman Tukur ruled one year instead of two, that Abdullahi II ruled twenty-six years instead of twenty-seven, and that Sanusi ruled nine instead of ten.

11. These are the houses of Famda, Takai, Dorayi. I assume she is referring to the fact that the emir is understood to be the main landholder of the entire city of Kano and that he "rents" places out to families for large periods of time—100 years or so.

12. I am grateful to Jean Boyd for these details.

13. Nasr (1976, 10) discusses the inextricable relationship between function and beauty in the original meaning of the Persian term for "art" (*san'at*).

PROFILE FIVE

1. Levin notes that in Bukhara, the poetic form *ghazal* is strongly connected to Sufi activity, "reveal[ing] Sufi inspiration in the poetic imagery, in the very notion of . . . a personal glimpse of God," and that as *maddahs* sang Sufi-inspired verse, recited moralistic stories, and chanted *hadiths* and excerpts from the Qur'an, "women had their own performers: dancer-singers . . . [who] entertained female guests at [weddings] . . . [and] lamented the dead at funerary rites" (1996, 205, 102).

2. "The Prophet was not an ascetic . . . and by the law of the *sharia* there's no prohibition against music. There's a hadith about the fact that when the Prophet came from Mecca to Medina, the people of Medina met him with *surnais* [oboes], drums, and musical celebration. A girl said to the Prophet, 'If you go now to war and come back to Medina whole, I'll sing you a song with the drum.' And when he came back he said to the girl, 'I have returned; now sing me a song.' Another hadith says that when you chant the Qur'an you should let your voice be beautiful. There's an oral legend that's not in the hadiths that when God created man, he ordered the soul to go into the body, and at that very moment, the sound of music was heard, and going past this music, the soul went into the body" (Levin 1996, 108–109).

6. ORAL AND WRITTEN HAUSA POETRY

1. See Hassan 1992, 28, in which he cites Hiskett's (1984, 80) argument that the names of Hausa letters in the alphabet are sufficiently old to indicate that they are truly Hausa in origin and not dated to a later Fulani era of literacy such as the nineteenth century.

2. I am grateful to Kathy Sheehan Imholt for her observations on this perspective.

3. The sense that God is the Creator of the seven heavens and the earth (Chapter 2:255) is discussed at length in Schimmel 1994, 16.

4. Personal communication from A. Neil Skinner with regard to Mudi Sipikin's works, March 1981. The author's signature in final verses is a technique that dates to sixth century Persian ghazal poetry, with further refinement by fourteenth-century Persian poet Hafiz.

5. Anaphora and epistrophe, the repetition of a word or phrase at the beginning or end of successive lines, respectively, are common techniques in these extemporaneous works.

6. This occurs in lines 80, 89, 92, 103, 125, 139, 141, 169, and 171.

7. This occurs in lines 88, 102, 112, 124, 168, 181, and 192.

8. See lines 51, 82, 94, 98, 113, 136, 142, 162, 175, 178, 182, and 193.

9. This from discussions with A. Neil Skinner.

10. *Faranshi* is France, meaning a former French colonial holding, i.e., the Republic of Niger, just north of Nigeria.

11. They repeat lines 5, 9, 10, 11, 14, 21, 23, 28, 32, 35, 36, 37, 47, 53, 55, 74, 75, 80, 90, and 117.

12. See Schuh 1989 and 1994 and Furniss 1996 for more on tone and scansion.

BIBLIOGRAPHY

Abraham, R. C. 1962. *Dictionary of the Hausa Language.* London: University of London Press.

Adamu, Mahdi. 1978. *The Hausa Factor in West African History.* Zaria, Nigeria: Ahmadu Bello University Press.

Adonis. 1990. *An Introduction to Arab Poetics.* London: Saqi Books.

Ahmed, Leila. 1992. *Women and Gender in Islam: Historical Roots of a Modern Debate.* New Haven, Conn.: Yale University Press.

Ali, Abdullah Yusuf. 1988. *The Holy Qur'an: Text, Translation and Commentary.* Elmhurst, N.Y.: Tahrike Tarsile Qur'an, Inc.

Ames, David. 1973. "A Sociocultural View of Hausa Musical Activity." In Warren d'Azevedo, ed., *The Traditional Artist in African Society,* 128–161. Bloomington: Indiana University Press.

Ames, David, and Anthony V. King. 1971. *Glossary of Hausa Music and Its Social Context.* Evanston, Ill.: Northwestern University Press.

Andrews, Walter G. 1993. "The Ottoman Turkish Kaside." In Christopher Shackle and Stefan Sperl, eds., *Qasida Poetry in Islamic Asia and Africa,* vol. 1, *Classical Traditions and Modern Meanings,* 87–103. Leiden: Brill.

Besmer, Fremont. 1971. "Hausa Court Music in Kano." Ph.D. diss., Columbia University.

———. 1983. *Horses, Musicians, and Gods: The Hausa Cult of Possession-Trance.* South Hadley, Mass.: Bergin and Garvey.

Boyd, Jean. 1986. "The Fulani Women Poets." In Mahdi Adamu and A. H. M. Kirk-Greene, eds., *Pastoralists of the West African Savanna,* 127–142. Manchester: Manchester University Press for the International African Institute.

———. 1989. *The Caliph's Sister: Nana Asma'u, 1793–1864, Teacher, Poet, and Islamic Leader.* London: Frank Cass.

Boyd, Jean, and Graham Furniss. 1993. "Mobilise the People: The *Qasida* in Fulfulde and Hausa as Purposive Literature." In Christopher Shackle and Stefan Sperl, eds., *Qasida Poetry in Islamic Asia and Africa,* vol. 1, *Classical Traditions and Modern Meanings,* 191–253. Leiden: Brill.

Boyd, Jean, and Beverly Mack. 1997. *The Collected Works of Nana Asma'u, bint Shehu Usman dan Fodiyo 1793–1864.* East Lansing: Michigan State University Press.

Brenner, Louis. 2001. *Controlling Knowledge: Religion, Power, and Schooling in a West African Muslim Society.* Bloomington: Indiana University Press.

Christelow, Allan. 1991. "Women and Law in Early Twentieth-Century Kano." In Catherine Coles and Beverly Mack, eds., *Hausa Women in the Twentieth Century,* 130–144. Madison: University of Wisconsin Press.

———. 1997. "Louis Massignon and the Algerian Muslim Intellectuals: Colonial Domination and the Problem of Trust." Paper prepared for the conference "Louis Massignon: The Vocation of a Scholar," Paris, University of Notre Dame, October 3.

Cohen, Ted. 1980. "Metaphor and the Cultivation of Intimacy." In Sheldon Sacks, ed., *On Metaphor*, 1–10. Chicago: University of Chicago Press.

Coles, Catherine. 1990. "The Older Woman in Hausa Society: Power and Authority in Urban Nigeria." In Jay Sokolovsky, ed., *The Cultural Context of Aging: World-Wide Perspectives*, 57–81. New York: Bergin and Garvey.

Coles, Catherine, and Beverly Mack, eds. 1991. *Hausa Women in the Twentieth Century*. Madison: University of Wisconsin Press.

Cooper, Barbara. 1997. *Marriage in Maradi: Gender and Culture in a Hausa Society in Niger*. Portsmouth, N.H.: Heinemann.

Daba, Habib Ahmed. 1981. "The Case of ɗan Maraya Jos: A Hausa Poet." In U. N. Abalogu, G. Ashiwaju, and R. Amadi-Tshiwala, eds., *Oral Poetry in Nigeria*, 209–229. Lagos: Nigeria Magazine.

Denny, Frederick. 1985. *An Introduction to Islam*. New York: Macmillan.

East, Rupert. 1936. "A First Essay in Imaginative African Literature." *Africa* 9, no. 3: 350–357.

Fika, Adamu. 1978. *The Kano Civil War and British Over-Rule*. Ibadan: Oxford University Press.

Frishman, Alan. 1991. "Hausa Women in the Urban Economy of Kano." In Catherine Coles and Beverly B. Mack, eds., *Hausa Women in the Twentieth Century*, 192–203. Madison: University of Wisconsin Press.

Furniss, Graham. 1977. "Some Aspects of Modern Hausa Poetry: Themes, Style and Values with Special Reference to the 'Hikima' Poetry Circle in Kano." Ph.D. diss., University of London.

———. 1996. *Poetry, Prose and Popular Culture in Hausa*. Edinburgh: Edinburgh University Press.

Hale, Thomas. 1998. *Griots and Griottes: Masters of Words and Music*. Bloomington: Indiana University Press.

Hassan, Salah M. 1992. *Art and Islamic Literacy Among the Hausa of Northern Nigeria*. Lewiston, N.Y.: The Edwin Mellen Press.

Hill, Clifford Alden. 1972. "A Study of Ellipsis within 'Karin Magana': A Hausa Tradition of Oral Art." Ph.D. diss., University of Wisconsin–Madison.

Hiskett, Mervyn. 1973. *The Sword of Truth: The Life and Times of Usman dan Fodiyo*. New York: Oxford University Press.

———. 1975. *A History of Hausa Islamic Verse*. London: University of London, School of Oriental and African Studies Press.

———. 1977. *An Anthology of Hausa Political Verse*. London: Department of Africa, School of Oriental and African Studies.

———. 1984. *The Development of Islam in West Africa*. London: Longman.

Hofstad, David. 1971. "Changing a Colonial Image: Poet-singers and a Dynamic Newspaper Feed Northern Nigeria's Political Awareness." *Africa Report* (October): 28–31.

Hull, Richard. 1968. "The Development of Administration in the Katsina Emirate Northern Nigeria, 1887–1944." Ph.D. diss., Columbia University.

King, A. V. 1967. "A ɓoorii Liturgy from Katsina (Introduction and *Kiraarii* Texts)." *African Language Studies* 7: 105–125.

Kirk-Greene, A. H. M. 1966. *Hausa Ba Dabo Ba Ne*. Ibadan: Oxford University Press, 1966.

Kunene, Daniel. 1971. *Heroic Poetry of the Basotho*. Oxford: Clarendon Press.

Last, Murray. 1967. *The Sokoto Caliphate*. London: Longman.

———. 1983. "From Sultanate to Caliphate: Kano ca. 1450–1800." In Barkindo Bawuro, ed., *Studies in the History of Kano*, 67–92. Ibadan, Nigeria: Heinemann Educational Books.

Levin, Theodore. 1996. *The Hundred Thousand Fools of God: Musical Travels in Central Asia (and Queens, New York).* Bloomington: Indiana University Press.

Lord, Albert. 1960. *Singer of Tales.* New York: Athenaeum Press.

Lugard, Frederick. 1970. *Political Memoranda: Revision of Instructions to Political Officers on Subjects Chiefly Political and Administrative, 1913–1918.* 3rd ed. Edited by A. H. M. Kirk-Greene. London: Frank Cass.

Mack, Beverly. 1983a. "'*Waka Daya Ba Ta Kare Nika*' ('One Song Will Not Finish the Grinding'): Hausa Women's Oral Literature." In Hal Wylie, Eileen Julien, Russell J. Linnemann with Sue Houchins and Marie-Denise Shelton, eds., *Contemporary African Literature,* 15–46. Washington, D.C.: Three Continents Press.

———. 1988. "Hajiya Madaki: A Royal Hausa/Fulani Woman." In Patricia Romero, ed., *Life Histories of African Women,* 47–77. Atlantic Highlands, N.J.: Ashfield Press.

———. 1991. "Royal Wives in Kano." In Catherine Coles and Beverly Mack, eds., *Hausa Women in the Twentieth Century,* 109–129. Madison: University of Wisconsin Press.

———. 1996. "Women's Work in Kano." In Carolyn Keyes Adenaike and Jan Vansina, eds., *In Pursuit of History,* 29–41. Portsmouth, N.H.: Heinemann.

———. 2004. "Muslim Women's Educational Activities the Maghreb: Investigating and Redefining Scholarship." *The Maghreb Review* 29, no. 1 (February 2004).

Mack, Beverly, ed. 1983b. *'Alkalami a Hannun Mata'* [*A Pen in the Hands of Women*] [in Hausa], by Hauwa Gwaram and Hajiya 'Yar Shehu. Zaria, Nigeria: Northern Nigerian Publishing Co.

Mack, Beverly, and Jean Boyd. 2000. *One Woman's Jihad: Nana Asma'u, Scholar and Scribe.* Bloomington: Indiana University Press.

Mackay, Mercedes. 1955. "The Shantu Music of the Harems of Nigeria." *African Music* 1, no. 2: 56–57.

Mashi, Musa Barah. 1982. "*Gudunmawar Hajiya Barmani Choge mai Amada ga Adabin Hausa.*" B.A. final paper, Bayero University.

Mernissi, Fatima. 1991. *The Veil and the Male Elite: A Feminist Interpretation of Women's Rights in Islam.* Reading, Mass.: Addison-Wesley Publishing Co.

Merriam, Alan. 1964. *The Anthropology of Music.* Evanston, Ill.: Northwestern University Press.

Muhammad, Dalhatu. 1977. "Individual Talent in the Hausa Poetic Tradition: A Study of Akilu Aliyu and His Art." Ph.D. diss., University of London.

———. 1979. "Interaction Between the Oral and the Literate Traditions of Hausa Poetry." *Harsunan Nijeriya* 9: 85–90.

Murata, Sachiko. 1992. *The Tao of Islam: A Sourcebook on Gender Relationships in Islamic Thought.* Albany: State University of New York Press.

Nasr, Seyyid Hossein. 1976. *Sacred Art in Persian Culture.* Ipswich: Golgonooza Press.

Netton, Ian Richard. 1992. *Popular Dictionary of Islam.* Atlantic Highlands, N.J.: Humanities Press International.

Newman, Paul, and Roxanna Ma Newman. 1979. *Sabon Kamus na Hausa Zuwa Turanci* [*Modern Hausa-English Dictionary*]. Ibadan, Nigeria: Oxford University Press.

Nicolas, Guy. 1975. *Dynamique sociale et apprehension du monde au sein d'une societe hausa.* Paris: Institut d'ethnologie.

Nigerian Literacy Board. 1931. *Labaru na Da da na Yanzu* [*News of the Past and the Present*]. Zaria, Nigeria: Translation Bureau.

Paden, John. 1973. *Religion and Political Culture in Kano.* Berkeley: University of California Press.

Palmer, Herbert Richmond. 1967. *Sudanese Memoirs: Being Mainly Translations of a Number of Arabic Manuscripts Relating to the Central and Western Sudan.* Lagos, 1928; reprint, London: Frank Cass Press.

Pellow, Deborah. 2002. *Landlords and Lodgers: Socio-Spatial Organization in an Accra Community.* Westport, Conn.: Praeger.

Perham, Margery. 1956–1960. *Lugard.* Vol. 2: *The Years of Authority 1898–1945.* London: Collins.

———. 1983. *West African Passage.* London: Oxford University Press, 1983.

Pittin, Renee. 1979. "Marriage and Alternative Strategies: Career Patterns of Hausa Women in Katsina City." Ph.D. diss., University of London, School of Oriental and African Studies.

———. 1983. "Houses of Women: A Focus on Alternative Life-Styles in Katsina City." In Christine Oppong, ed., *Female and Male in West Africa,* 291–302. London: George Allen and Unwin.

———. 1984. "Documentation and Analysis of the Invisible Work of Invisible Women: A Nigerian Case-Study." *International Labour Review* 123, no. 4: 473–490.

———. 1996. "Negotiating Boundaries: A Perspective from Nigeria." In Deborah Pellow, ed., *Setting Boundaries: The Anthropology of Spatial and Social Organization,* 179–193. Westport, Conn.: Bergin and Garvey.

Renard, John. 1996. *Seven Doors to Islam: Spirituality and the Religious Life of Muslims.* Los Angeles: University of California Press.

Richards, I. A. 1976. *The Philosophy of Rhetoric.* New York: Oxford University Press.

Scheub, Harold. 1974–1975. "Oral Narrative Process and the Use of Models." *New Literary History* 6: 353–377.

———. 1977a. "Body and Image in Oral Narrative Performance." *New Literary History* 8, no. 3 (Spring): 345–367.

———. 1977b. "Performance of Oral Narrative." In William Bascom, ed., *Frontiers of Folklore,* 54–78. Boulder, Colo.: Westview Press.

Schildkrout, Enid. 1979. "Women's Work and Children's Work: Variations among Moslems in Kano." In Sandra Wallman, ed., *Social Anthropology of Work,* 69–85. London: Academic Press.

———. 1982. "Dependence and Autonomy: The Economic Activities of Secluded Hausa Women in Kano, Nigeria." In Edna Bay, ed., *Women and Work in Africa,* 55–81. Boulder, Colo.: Westview Press.

Schimmel, Annemarie. 1994. *Deciphering the Signs of God: A Phenomenological Approach to Islam.* Albany: State University of New York Press.

Schuh, Russell. 1989. "Toward a Metrical Analysis of Hausa Verse Prosody: *Mutadaarik.*" In Isabelle Haik and Laurice Tuller, eds., *Current Approaches to African Linguistics,* vol. 6. Providence, R.I.: Foris Publications.

———. 1994. "A Case Study of Text and Performance in Hausa Metrics." Paper presented at the 25th Annual Conference on African Linguistics, Rutgers University, March 24–27.

Skinner, Neil. 1980. *An Anthology of Hausa Literature.* Zaria: Northern Nigerian Publishing Co.

Smith, Mary. [1954.] 1981. *Baba of Karo: A Woman of the Muslim Hausa.* 2nd ed. New Haven, Conn.: Yale University Press.

Smith, M. G. 1957. "The Social Functions and Meaning of Hausa Praise-Singing." *Africa* 27, no. 1: 26–43.

———. 1959. "The Hausa System of Social Status." *Africa* 29, no. 3: 230–252.

———. 1965. "The Hausa of Northern Nigeria." In James L. Gibbs, Jr., ed., *Peoples of Africa,* 121–155. New York: Holt, Rinehart & Winston.

———. 1978. *The Affairs of Daura: History and Change in a Hausa State, 1800–1958.* Berkeley: University of California Press.

————. 1983. "The Kano Chronicle as History." In Barkindo Bawuro, ed., *Studies in the History of Kano,* 31–56. Ibadan, Nigeria: Heinemann Educational Books.

Stetkevych, Suzanne Pinckney. 1993. *The Mute Immortals Speak: Pre-Islamic Poetry and the Poetics of Ritual.* Ithaca, N.Y.: Cornell University Press.

————. 2002. *The Poetics of Islamic Legitimacy: Myth, Gender, and Ceremony in the Classic Arabic Ode.* Bloomington: Indiana University Press.

Stowasser, Barbara Freyer. 1994. *Women in the Qur'an, Traditions, and Interpretation.* New York: Oxford University Press.

Sule, Balarabe, and Priscilla Starratt. 1991. "Islamic Leadership Positions for Women in Contemporary Kano Society." In Catherine Coles and Beverly Mack, eds., *Hausa Women in the Twentieth Century,* 29–49. Madison: University of Wisconsin Press.

Umar, Muhammad Balarabe. 1984. "Symbolism in Oral Poetry: A Study of Symbolical Indices of Social Status in Hausa Court Songs." Thesis, Ahmadu Bello University.

Wadud, Amina. 1992. *Qur'an and Woman: Rereading the Sacred Text from a Woman's Perspective.* Kuala Lumpur: Fajar Bakti. 2nd ed. (New York: Oxford University Press, 1999).

Works, John A., Jr. 1976. *Pilgrims in a Strange Land.* New York: Columbia University Press.

Yahaya, Ibrahim Yaro. 1973. "*Kishi* Feeling among Hausa Co-Wives." *Kano Studies,* n.s. 1, no. 1: 83–89.

————. 1979. "Oral Art and Socialization Process: A Socio-Folkloric Perspective of Initiation from Childhood to Adult Hausa Community Life." Ph.D. diss., Ahmadu Bello University.

————. 1981. "The Hausa Poet." In U. N. Abalogu, Garba Ashiwaju, and Regina Amadi-Tshiwala, eds., *Oral Poetry in Nigeria,* 139–156. Lagos: Nigeria Magazine.

INDEX

Abbas, Muhammadu, 71, 95
Abubakar, Alhaji Sir, 94
Ado, Alhaji, 19
adult education, 7, 17, 28, 82, 85, 86. *See also* Asma'u, Nana; education for girls and women
Agency for Mass Education, 28
Aguiyi-Ironsi, General, 74, 93. *See also* "Song of Explanation about Biafra"
Ahmadu, Bello, 67, 69
Ahmadu, Usumanu, 71
algaita (reed instrument), 51
al-Ghazali, 61
al-Jawzi, Ibn, 25
al-Khansa, 123
Alkali, Zaynab, 10
Amada, Uwaliya ma, 40
Amu, Alhaji dan, 94, 124, 261
Arabi, Ibn, 60
Asma'u, Nana: extension teaching and, 19, 79; as a role model for contemporary poets, 25–26, 42, 86; scholarship of, 5, 10, 24–25; teaching of, 10, 24–27, 42, 79, 86
Association for Women of the North, 19
Atiku, Mohammadu, 93
Azikwe, Nnamdi, 77

Ba, Mariama, 10
Bako, Alhaji Audu, 66, 93
Balwa, Alhaji Sir Abubakr Tafawa, 67, 92
Bayero, Aljahi Abjullahi, 95, 119
Bayero, Aljahi Ado (Emir of Kano): opening of mosque, 113; praise epithets for, 93–94, 119; praise singing for, 54–56, 70–72, 96; restrictions on homage to, 286n35; right to inheritance of, 95. *See also* Maizargadi, Hajiya Ajuji; "Praise Song for Alhaji Ado Bayero, Emir of

Kano"; "Song for the Emir of Kano and the Emir of Ningi"; "Song of Condolence for Tafawa Balewa and the Sardauna of Sokoto"
Bayero, Hajiya Abba, 12
Bayero University, 84, 101, 110, 128. *See also* Hausa Conference
beggar singers, 31, 41–42, 45, 55, 285n24
Bello, Alhaji Ahmadu, 39, 82, 92–93
Biafran civil war, 15, 39, 66, 74, 81, 92, 97, 283n3
bori. See spirit-possession cult
British: Alhaji Muhammadu Dikko's friendships with, 72; and attitudes toward women, 28; and economic disadvantage of Northern Nigeria, 81; educational system of, 19, 27; and Westernization of Hausa culture, 14. *See also* colonialism; education for girls and women

calabash (*kidan kwarya; kore; kwarya*): accompaniment for women singers, 43, 100; and *bori* cult, 281n13, 287n15; played by women, 45, 50, *99*, 115, 125
census, 15, 68, 81, 90, 97. *See also* "Song on the Census"; "Song on the Census of the People of Nigeria"
charity, 62, 79, 95
children's songs, 32
Choge, Hajiya Maimuna Barmani: and allusions to proverbs, 65; an extemporaneous performer, 40; physicality of performance style, 18, 44, *99*, 124; Sufism of, 100; travel of, 101; use of invocation, 110; use of repetition, 114–117, 120–123, 125–127; use of satire, 84–85. *See also* "Song for the Hausa Conference"
chronograms in poetry, 112–113
cikin gida. See women's quarters

"Song to Prepare to Drive on the Right-Hand Side," 91, 169–173

songs of co-wife jealousy (*kishiya*), 32, 45

spirit-possession cult (*bori*): Binta Katsina and, 100–101; description of, 283n18; influences on contemporary Hausa music, 281n13, 287n15; and oral song, 31, 80, 97; references to God in music of, 110; and social status, 80; and women musicians, 32, 51

stereotypes: of Hausa women, 3, 15, 26, 281n9; of ignorant farmer, 82–84

Sufism, 100

Sunni, 29, 283n14

talking drums, 34. *See also* calabash

tambari (drum), 51

television, 32, 40, 48, 52–53, 78, 100, 281n8, 285n23

Translation Bureau. *See* Literature Bureau

travel: gender and restrictions on, 53, 78; and Muslim spiritual values, 62; women performers and, 40, 53, 78, 100–101. *See also* hajj; Makka; pilgrimage

turbanning ceremony, 55, 284n10

turmi (percussion), 51

ululation (*kuru-ruwa*), 42, 51, 55, 284n8

ungendering, 8, 46, 101, 128

universal primary education, 19, 28, 81–82, 88, 97. *See also* "Song of Warning"; "Song on Universal Primary Education"

war on drugs, 15. *See also* "Song of Warning to Those Who Take Drugs I"; "Song of Warning to Those Who Take Drugs II"

War on Ignorance, 81, 97

water drums, 44

wedding celebrations, 31, 47, 52, 101

Westernization: and changes in jobs available to Nigerians, 81–82; and education, 18, 23, 27, 88; and food preparation, 286n33; and Hausa women's poetry, 15, 24, 81, 86, 94; negative impact on Hausa culture, 81; and stereotypical views of Hausa women, 15

widowhood, 6, 49, 55

Wisdom Club, 18, 20, 38

Women in Nigeria (W.I.N.), 80

women scholars, 27. *See also* Asma'u, Nana

women's autonomy: Islam's fostering of, 4, 11–12, 287n5; poetry-writing as a means to, 5, 77, 101; praise-singing as a means to, 55; and stereotypes about seclusion, 3

women's charitable associations, 79

Women's Education Program, 28

women's occupations: business owners, 7, 38, 76; crafts, 86–87, 281n2, 285n29; farming, 86, 285n29; hospital work, 37; market vendors, 86, 281n2, 285n29; professionals, 9, 37, 86, 101, 119; translators, 38; white-collar workers, 86. *See also* itinerant teachers

women's quarters, 10, 31–32. *See also* harem; seclusion

wordplay (*kirari*), 73–74

work songs, 11, 32

World War II, 30

written poetry, reading of, 42–43

'Yan Izala movement, 94

'Yan Taru, 19

zabiyoyi. See royal praise singers

Zahara, Fatima, 93

zikiri singing, 100

Zungur, Sa'adu, 82

Beverly B. Mack is Associate Professor in the Department of African and African-American Studies at the University of Kansas. She is co-author (with Jean Boyd) of *One Woman's Jihad: Nana Asma'u, Scholar and Scribe* (Indiana University Press, 2000) and *The Collected Works of Nana Asma'u, 1793–1864.* She is co-author (with Catherine Coles) of *Hausa Women in the Twentieth Century.*